Nietzsche's Renewal of Ancient Ethics

Also available from Bloomsbury:

Joy and Laughter in Nietzsche's Philosophy,
edited by Paul E. Kirkland and Michael J. McNeal
Nietzsche and Friendship, by Willow Verkerk
'The Gift' in Nietzsche's Zarathustra, by Emilio Corriero
The Parallel Philosophies of Sartre and Nietzsche, by Nik Farrell Fox

Nietzsche's Renewal of Ancient Ethics

Friendship as Contest

Neil Durrant

BLOOMSBURY ACADEMIC
LONDON • NEW YORK • OXFORD • NEW DELHI • SYDNEY

BLOOMSBURY ACADEMIC
Bloomsbury Publishing Plc
50 Bedford Square, London, WC1B 3DP, UK
1385 Broadway, New York, NY 10018, USA
29 Earlsfort Terrace, Dublin 2, Ireland

BLOOMSBURY, BLOOMSBURY ACADEMIC and the Diana logo
are trademarks of Bloomsbury Publishing Plc

First published in Great Britain 2023
This paperback edition published 2024

Copyright © Neil Durrant, 2023

Neil Durrant has asserted his right under the Copyright, Designs and
Patents Act, 1988, to be identified as Author of this work.

For legal purposes the Acknowledgements on p. ix constitute
an extension of this copyright page.

Cover image: Hercules and Antaeus (© Zoonar GmbH / Alamy Stock Photo)

All rights reserved. No part of this publication may be reproduced or
transmitted in any form or by any means, electronic or mechanical,
including photocopying, recording, or any information storage or retrieval
system, without prior permission in writing from the publishers.

Bloomsbury Publishing Plc does not have any control over, or responsibility for,
any third-party websites referred to or in this book. All internet addresses given
in this book were correct at the time of going to press. The author and publisher
regret any inconvenience caused if addresses have changed or sites have
ceased to exist, but can accept no responsibility for any such changes.

A catalogue record for this book is available from the British Library.

A catalog record for this book is available from the Library of Congress.

ISBN: HB: 978-1-3502-9887-3
PB: 978-1-3502-9891-0
ePDF: 978-1-3502-9888-0
eBook: 978-1-3502-9889-7

Typeset by Integra Software Services Pvt. Ltd.

To find out more about our authors and books visit www.bloomsbury.com
and sign up for our newsletters.

To my great love, Carolyn, whose heroism in support of this project cannot be overestimated

Contents

Preface		viii
Acknowledgements		ix
Note on texts and translations		x
List of abbreviations		xiii
1	Introduction	1
2	Against Christian love	15
3	Against pitiful compassion	35
4	A naturalist alternative	53
5	Nietzsche's new Homerism	71
6	The individual as contest	93
7	Friendship as contest	125
8	Conclusion	153
Notes		159
Bibliography		184
Index		197

Preface

This book marks the end of a long and personal process of discovery. It is now nearly fifteen years since, through the reading of Nietzsche and other philosophers and authors, I came to leave my Christian faith and therefore, among other things, revoke my ordination as a priest within the Anglican Church of Australia. At that time, my intellectual interests centred on Christian metaphysics, the doctrine of the Trinity and the ethics of *agape* love. Reading Nietzsche opened my mind to new ways of seeing the world and opened my life to new ways of living and being. Studying for my PhD, and writing this book, bring that particular intellectual and personal journey to some sort of conclusion. I hope that this book infuses its readers with Nietzsche's adventurous and experimental spirit and is a spur to live in a playful and optimistic way, in the way of Nietzsche's heroes.

Acknowledgements

Special thanks to Dr Michael Ure and Dr Paul Muldoon, for enduring many contests in the development of my PhD thesis at Monash University, which is the basis for this book.

Thanks to Professor Martina Möllering for her unwavering guidance and support to develop my PhD into this publication.

This research was supported by an Australian Government Research Training Program (RTP) Scholarship.

Note on texts and translations

Developing his account of ethical social relationships was a monumental task for Nietzsche, a task made difficult for the contemporary interpreter by Nietzsche's writing style. His method was not to write systematic philosophy but rather to attack traditional morality in a non-linear fashion, approaching several topics from many angles at once, seeking as much to disturb as to persuade, to destabilize as to formulate, to provoke as to solve. His weapon of choice was the aphorism rather than extensive and focused formulations of systematic philosophy. The result is a complex constellation of sharp statements, acerbic witticisms and confrontational, contradictory and often humorous argumentation.

The combination of the immensity of his task and his use of the aphoristic style have important consequences for this book. As some critics have complained, it can be difficult to see more than a disconnected series of attacks in his writing because he does not systematically develop solutions to the problems he brings to our awareness.[1] The result is that it is difficult to bring coherence to his views given the sheer number of texts involved, their fragmentary nature and sometimes contradictory content.

This leads to several crucial decisions: which texts to select as representative of underlying themes, how to deal with the question of (in)consistency, the possibility of Nietzsche's intellectual development over time and the selection of appropriate English translations for those such as myself whose German language skills are deficient.[2]

Selecting which texts to analyse has at least two dimensions to it. The first is the relationship between his unpublished notes, essays and other writings; and the second is the question of the periodization of his published works. My approach to the first issue, along with several other scholars, is to focus on his published works, with minimal reference to his unpublished notes. This is because Nietzsche revisited his published works throughout his writing career as he refined his thought and its expression. This reworking of his publications gave him the opportunity to make choices about which elements from his notebooks to include in his published corpora. It seems likely to me that he excluded elements from his notebooks for publication because he thought them deficient rather than that he simply overlooked them. It seems to me that his published works present what he considered to be the best versions of his thought and the unpublished notes include at least some texts that he was dissatisfied with.

His early unpublished essays, one of which is important for this volume, present a slightly different case in that they represent a set of material that he did not or could not get published but which were nevertheless prepared for publication in the course of his academic duties. There is, in my view, a significant difference between a fragment captured in a notebook while walking in the Italian Alps and an essay of several thousand words that has been worked and reworked for an academic audience. It is to this latter category that the essay *Homer's Contest* belongs, an important text that I rely on extensively.

With respect to his published works, these are frequently categorized as falling into his early (pre-1876), middle (1876–82) and late periods (1882–9). This periodization of the development of his thought is not sufficiently nuanced for the purposes of this book. In order to find the most coherent and least contradictory presentation of his ethical themes, I draw from texts published in the period 1881–7, particularly *Daybreak* (1881), *The Gay Science* (1882, 1887) and *Thus Spoke Zarathustra* (1883–5), with some passing references to *Beyond Good and Evil* (1887) and *On the Genealogy of Morality* (1887).[3] I emphasize *Daybreak*, *The Gay Science* and *Thus Spoke Zarathustra* because these texts seem to me to represent the best of his attempt to bring his ethical project to maturity.[4] By the time Nietzsche wrote *On the Genealogy of Morality* in mid- to late 1887 his thought has changed in ways that, at least in my opinion, make them less useful for understanding his ethical project.[5] In his later works we see a less considered radicalism before his mental collapse in Turin in January 1889.

With regards to establishing authoritative original texts and English-speaking translations, the task has been significantly simplified in recent times. In the English-speaking world, an acceleration in the study of his philosophy can be traced to work done in the 1960s and 1970s by Walter Kaufmann (1921–80) in North America and R. J. Hollingdale (1930–2001) in the United Kingdom. These scholars both together and separately produced major translations and interpretations of Nietzsche's work in English for the first time.[6] Notwithstanding the importance of these works, Nietzsche studies in English are presently enjoying the release of what will no doubt become the authoritative translation of his complete works, published through Cambridge University Press in the series Cambridge Texts in the History of Philosophy.[7] It is on these translations that I rely throughout this thesis, with the one exception of *On the Genealogy of Morals* where I use Smith's translation.[8]

All italics in quotations from Nietzsche's texts are original.

Studies in the original German texts have been significantly supported by the critical edition of the complete works of Nietzsche edited by Colli and Montinari, *Kritische Gesamtausgabe Werke und Briefe* (*KGWB*), and the development of the *Digitale Kritische Gesamtausgabe Werke und Briefe* (*eKGWB*) at http://nietzschesource.org. Where I refer to the German text, I have used the *eKGWB*.

Where I make reference to the Greek text of the New Testament, I refer to *The Greek New Testament*, published by the United Bible Societies.[9] Where I refer to English translations, I use the New International Version.

I certify that I have made all reasonable efforts to secure copyright permissions for third-party content included and have not knowingly added copyright content to my work without the owner's permission.

In accordance with the copyright provisions for the use of the New International Version (NIV) translation of biblical texts:

Scripture taken from the HOLY BIBLE, NEW INTERNATIONAL VERSION®. Copyright © 1973, 1978, 1984 by the International Bible Society. Used by permission of Zondervan. All rights reserved.

List of abbreviations

I follow the standard conventions for abbreviations as indicated below. I have generally referred to the final editions of texts where late inclusions or prefaces have been added. Where this is significant, I will draw attention to it.

AC	The Anti-Christ
BGE	Beyond Good and Evil
BT	The Birth of Tragedy
D	Daybreak
DWV	The Dionysian World View
EH	Ecce Homo
GM	On the Genealogy of Morals
GS	The Gay Science
HAH	Human, All Too Human
HC	Homer's Contest
TI	Twilight of the Idols
TSZ	Thus Spoke Zarathustra
UM	Untimely Meditations

1

Introduction

Friedrich Nietzsche (1844–1900), writing in the final quarter of the nineteenth century, remains a controversial and stimulating figure in philosophy. The continuing interest in Nietzsche covers many aspects of his philosophy, including metaphysics, ethics and epistemology. There is a large body of literature that recognizes and discusses the variety of precedents for, and influences on, Nietzsche's thought.[1] These range from classical influences such as Homer,[2] Heraclitus,[3] Democritus,[4] Pyrrho,[5] Plato,[6] Aristotle,[7] as well as Stoicism, Epicureanism and Skepticism,[8] all the way to more contemporaneous influences such Kant,[9] Schopenhauer,[10] Lange,[11] Burckhardt, Darwin and Spencer.[12]

From this wide array of topics, this book focuses on the influence of Homeric ideals on Nietzsche's ethics. More specifically, we can see in Nietzsche's work his own development of one important theme. This theme has been well documented by Adkins's monumental study published in 1970, namely, the tension in classical ethics between altruism and cooperation on the one hand, and competition and contest on the other.[13] If in between a strictly altruistic and a strictly competitive approach to ethics there lies a wide spectrum of approaches, there is a growing appreciation in the literature on Nietzsche that his interest in Homeric ideals pushes his thought towards a contest-oriented approach. This has developed into a school of interpretation where Nietzsche's ethics is described as 'agonistic', referring to the ancient Greek *agon* or contest.[14]

In this book I offer a new approach to Nietzsche's agonistic ethics in which the ideal of friendship takes centre stage. I claim that Nietzsche develops a concept of friendship that transcends ideas of altruism and cooperation that are commonly associated with ethical social relationships and is diametrically opposed to the importance sometimes attached to love (exemplified by Christianity) and compassion (exemplified by Schopenhauer). The challenge of Nietzsche's agonistic approach to ethics is to find a way to understand how the idea of contest shapes intimate social relationships.[15] In this book I argue that friendship – or more properly, higher friendship – is a significant part of Nietzsche's answer to this challenge.

Nietzsche's ideal of higher friendship, I claim, can be understood as a relationship in which individuals are free to respond to one another in any way that they consider appropriate to the specifics of each person's character and circumstance. In this ideal, interaction between friends is based on an emergent and continually developing understanding of one another's inner lives, and it is freed from the constraints of what Nietzsche calls 'customary morality'.[16] Because these responses are so specifically fine-tuned to the needs of each person based on their personal circumstances and the internal configuration of their own thoughts and emotions, and they are not limited by the behaviours required by society and what it considers to be morally acceptable, friends can respond to one other not only with love and compassion *but also with any other stance that might contribute to each person's life task*. In other words, and perhaps counter-intuitively, the more intimate a friendship is, the more agonistic it can become. Within this framework, intimacy is not contradicted by enmity, opposition, difficulty and the like. Rather, there is a sense in Nietzsche's work that real intimacy requires contest, and that ethical contest takes place in the context of true personal intimacy.

The result is a concept for a type of intimate social relationship – which Nietzsche calls higher friendship – that can be understood as a more fruitful form of intimate relationship than many others, including love relationships, because higher friendship is able to incorporate almost everything about the persons involved, a vast array of human experiences including aversive and oppositional ones, within an overarching framework. This framework is the framework of Homeric contest: it is intrinsic in the structure of this contest, at least as Nietzsche understood it, that otherwise aggressive or destructive impulses are transformed into productive and fruitful agonistic engagements.[17] Higher friendship, I will show, is potentially even more intimate than those forms of relationship licensed by customary morality because it is specially tailored to the characteristics of those involved, it is free to respond to each individual in any way that suits, and as such it opens up understandings of one another that are otherwise invisible because of the proscriptions of social convention.

Thus, the power of Nietzsche's concept of higher friendship, I argue, lies in its ability to incorporate something approaching the totality of an individual's emotional and behavioural experiences, even those that are typically thought to undermine or destroy intimate personal relationships. Nietzsche achieves this by developing his understanding of higher friendship along Homeric lines, so that friends can become adversaries within the structure of their relationship, with the result that as adversaries both are able to flourish. That is, as I aim to show in this book, Nietzsche saw in the Greek concept of *agon* the possibility to free people from arbitrary, religious or metaphysical moralistic constraints and to simultaneously provide an alternative mechanism for moderating their behaviour so that the result of the contest is not destructive, but beneficial, to the contestants.[18] In this book I develop this idea of friendship, and show that it can be understood through Nietzsche's concept of great love, a love that contrasts with romantic or compassionate in love precisely in its capacity to incorporate contest, and with it, aversive emotions and adverse behaviours.

This is where I begin the study: in Chapter 2 I contrast Nietzsche's idea of great love with the Christian ideal of self-sacrificial love. I argue that the contemporary emphasis on the importance of love for social relationships has Judaeo-Christian roots and that Nietzsche's agonistic interpretation of social relationships provides a distinctive and credible alternative. Specifically, Nietzsche responds to the idea in the Lutheran tradition that true Christian love requires the lover to sacrifice themselves for the beloved.

Following Nietzsche's own biography, I move from the subject of Christian love in Chapter 2 to the topic of Schopenhauer and compassion in Chapter 3. I outline Nietzsche's rejection of compassion, and in particular, his engagement with Schopenhauer's philosophy and its emphasis on compassion as a singular moral virtue. In the combination of these two things – Nietzsche's rejection of both love and compassion as foundations for ethics – lies one of the core provocations of Nietzsche's philosophy. The singular importance of love and compassion for contemporary ethics reveals itself everywhere in popular media, music and literature. Nietzsche's alternative – higher friendship that incorporates, enmity, opposition and even hatred – can be confronting. On the one hand, this may be due to the preternatural resilience of the ideas of love and compassion as important touchstones in Western ethics. There may be readers of this book who are unwilling to challenge the value of love and compassion in ethical social relationships, and these readers are likely to be dissatisfied with my account of Nietzsche's ethics. For those readers open to critically evaluating love and compassion, Nietzsche's proposal for an ethics of higher friendship may be at least intriguing, if not appealing. However, even for these more adventurous readers, difficult questions are likely to emerge about how we can positively describe ethical intimate relationships in which aversive emotions (e.g. hatred and enmity) and adversarial behaviours (e.g. opposition) are endorsed and even encouraged.

These issues are recognized throughout the literature.[19] Some scholars consider them intractable and have concluded that Nietzsche does not offer an ethics at all, but rather a philosophy of solipsism, narcissism[20] or 'might is right' *Realpolitik*.[21] Other scholars, myself amongst them, have begun to demonstrate an underlying set of ethical principles within Nietzsche's work that may not be immediately apparent. Because of the difficulty of this subterranean task, even within this group of scholars there remains significant diversity of opinion as to the description and application of Nietzsche's ethics. There are those that think he offers a version of idealism or perfectionism (e.g. following Kant);[22] others focus on power and virtuosity as his core ethical themes;[23] others (following the French philosopher Michel Foucault[24]) consider Nietzsche as a type of virtue ethicist, influenced by ancient Greek ideas of self-cultivation found in the Stoics and the Epicureans;[25] and others adopt the Homeric-agonistic stance I have described above.[26]

These schools of thought are not necessarily incommensurate or contradictory, and often scholars will include combinations of these elements in their interpretation. Given the variety of Nietzsche's thought, his aphoristic and diffuse style, and the general difficulty of a project that rejects commonplace values such as love and compassion, it is not surprising that scholars have emphasized different elements of his work. In this book I focus on the Homeric-agonistic interpretation of Nietzsche's ethics because in my view the Homeric concept of *agon* offers not only a coherent framework for integrating some of these confronting themes in Nietzsche's panoply of ethical ideas, but it also a way to bring some of these schools of thought together. In particular, these Homeric themes in Nietzsche's work can be used to synthesize otherwise divergent strands of interpretation that tend to focus separately on different aspects of his overarching philosophical project. The spirit of this present inquiry is to outline for Nietzsche's readers a new approach that brings together some of these themes: the Homeric ideal of contest can, as we will see, be useful for understanding not only his ethics, but also his naturalist-materialist tendencies and his psychology.

In Chapter 4 I start to examine Nietzsche's renovation and reapplication of Homeric contest by looking to the then-emergent world of biological science. I outline some of the core themes of this development, arguing that Nietzsche moves away from metaphysics and idealism towards more scientifically oriented explanations of observed phenomena. This is a highly contested area, commonly referred to as Nietzsche's 'naturalism'. Many scholars have commented on this aspect of Nietzsche's philosophy and how this might influence our interpretation of his ethics. The field is divided – there are those that think Nietzsche remained interested in metaphysics[27] and idealist approaches to ethics,[28] and those that, like myself, take the view that Nietzsche's naturalism incorporates a drive towards an anti-metaphysical pragmatism.[29] This is not to say that Nietzsche presents a consistent or thorough naturalist or materialist philosophy. Rather, it seems to me that the trajectory of his philosophical project when considered as a whole involves an attempt to incorporate physical and natural sciences into a materialist explanation of human experience, even experiences that do not lend themselves to this kind of interpretation particularly well.[30] For the purposes of this book, I refer to his naturalism as this general trajectory in his thought, acknowledging the complexity of the topic and some inconsistency in his various statements in this area.

Amongst those that agree that Nietzsche attempts a naturalistic and anti-metaphysical explanation of the human experience, there is substantial disagreement about the shape of Nietzsche's naturalism and what this means for his ethics.[31] My claim in this book is that Nietzsche's naturalism can be understood on the basis of an analogy between the mechanisms of evolutionary biology as a natural science and the Homeric ethos of contest as a social phenomenon. By applying concepts from evolutionary biology to the classical notion of the contest, he was able to transform the concept of contest so that it could be applied to social relationships and to ethics in general. This is, at least in part, because he saw in these ideas an answer for what were for him the more problematic elements of Christian and Schopenhauerian metaphysics.

Further, I argue that Nietzsche is far more subtle in his application of this scientific paradigm to human social relationships than is often understood. I suggest that he charts a narrow course between reductionism on the one hand (as in, for example social Darwinism) and a kind of special pleading for humanity's unique place in nature's Pantheon on the other. I argue that, in building his distinctive agonistic ethics, he borrows ideas from this scientific endeavour in order to elaborate his application of contest to human social relationships. The two most important of these are abundance (in the production of species) and difference (through genetic variation as species develop over time).

In Chapter 4 I claim that Nietzsche draws from various strands of nineteenth-century evolutionary biology the idea that the natural world is characterized by overflow and abundance. In *GS* §349, for example, he writes:

> As a natural scientist, however, one should get out of one's human corner; and in nature, it is not distress which *rules*, but rather abundance, squandering – even to the point of absurdity.

The idea of squandering to the point of absurdity is here presented as a feature of a natural scientist's observations in a text that is largely concerned with Darwinism. This idea, often described with aqueous metaphors, is also found in texts that describe the great individual and their social relationships. In *GS* §55, for example, he writes:

> the passion that overcomes the noble one is a singularity, and he fails to realize this: the use of a rare and singular standard and almost a madness; ... a self-sufficiency that overflows and communicates to men and things.[32]

There are many complexities, false starts and blind alleys in Nietzsche's exploration and application of naturalism to his ethics of higher friendship. What I aim to show in this book is that the concept of abundance provides an integrating idea between his naturalism, his psychology and his ethics. As part of nature, human beings participate in the superabundance of the natural world, both internally as individuals and as social beings.

The same is true of the concept of difference and differentiation.[33] I claim that Nietzsche's concept of difference and its importance for his ethics is, at least in part, also derived from his interest in evolutionary biology. I argue that Nietzsche saw a parallel between the idea of random genetic variations that generate differences among individuals over long periods of time for the strengthening of the species and the idea of moral and intellectual difference as a means for strengthening individuals and societies.

In Chapter 5 I begin to show how the concept of agonistic contest can bring together these elements of his thought – his naturalism, his psychology, and his ethics. Nietzsche's interest in Homer was evident early in his academic career. His unpublished essay *Homer's Contest* (1872)[34] lays the foundations for his adoption of contest into his ethics.[35] There he argues that contest formed the basis of ancient Greek (Hellenic) culture, rescuing it from 'savagery' and promoting the ongoing discovery of ever-new forms of human excellence.[36] Whether it be through competitive games, rhetorical sparring or the battlefield, contest is understood by Nietzsche to have provided the conditions under which both individuals and society strengthened themselves in the Hellenic cultural context:

> without envy, jealousy and competitive ambition, the Hellenic state, like Hellenic man, deteriorates. It becomes evil and cruel, it becomes vengeful and godless, in short, it becomes 'pre-Homeric' – it then only takes a panicky fright to make it fall and smash it. Sparta and Athens surrender to the Persians as Themistocles and Alcibiades did; they betray the Hellenic after they have given up on the finest Hellenic principle: contest ... [37]

In this essay the *agon* is presented as a social institution that provides both the creative energy for maintaining and improving civic life and the moderation of that energy so that its worst possibilities were restrained.[38] Christa Davis Acampora neatly summarizes:

> Agonistic contest, Nietzsche speculates, is a productive force that regulates without subjugating the interests of individuals, coordinating them without reducing them to the interests of the community, and providing radical openness for the circulation of power that avoids ossification into tyranny ... Nietzsche envisions the best possible situation as one in which these interests are reciprocal and in tension: the community desires the production of greatness cast in terms it establishes; the most potent competitors achieve the affirmation of the community that provides the conditions for the possibility of their victories, but they also aspire to become standard bearers and thereby bring about the reformation of judgement generally.[39]

Herman Siemens is another scholar who has focused on the importance of contest for Nietzsche's thought and philosophical practice. He writes:

> What Nietzsche values in the agon, then, is the way it fosters particularity and creative spontaneity among a plurality of individuals. In this regard, he sees the agonal polis as a kind of breeding ground or hothouse for human excellence, or rather, human excellences, a regime of power that offers the best conditions for experiments in human excellence.[40]

In Chapter 5 I outline and build on the work of these scholars to present Nietzsche's ethics as an adaptation of the idea of contest that incorporates insights from evolutionary biology. The result is a new form of Homeric ethos – Nietzsche's new Homerism – that transforms the Homeric idea of contest. I propose that Nietzsche does this in two ways. Firstly, he shifts away from the typical description of contest in terms of externalized, public performance (e.g. warfare, competitive games, and rhetorical jousts) towards an examination of the psychological constitution of the individual as a contest of internal drives. Secondly, he expands the scope of contest by drawing from it a general proposition about the value of adversity for individual flourishing, so that contest is no longer limited to a set of socially prescribed functions. Rather, for Nietzsche, the value of adversity for individual flourishing is a general idea that applies both to the individual and to human social relationships. In this way, I claim, we can draw together the threads of Homer's influence, Nietzsche's rejection of love and compassion, and the importance of evolutionary biology in Nietzsche's thought. The result is a new interpretation of Nietzsche's ethics as a radical adaptation of contest in its application to intimate personal relationships.

Having argued that Nietzsche develops his ethics in the context of the value of adversity for human flourishing, I go on to discuss the value of adversaries. One particularly fruitful avenue for describing the value of adversaries is evident in the growing literature on Nietzsche's distinctive interpretation of friendship.[41] This literature describes the many influences that Nietzsche drew on as he developed his idea that higher friendship is a relationship built on contest. I claim throughout this book that by drawing on these classical ideas and incorporating new elements – into what I call his new Homerism – Nietzsche's distinctive vision of higher friendship emerges.

Moreover, I show that it is important to understand that this movement in Nietzsche's thought to incorporate scientific insights into a Homeric ethos is not a simplistic drive towards a purely naturalist and materialist, or strictly scientific, approach to psychology and ethics. If this were the case, it would be difficult to avoid charges of narcissism, solipsism, *Realpolitik* and even social Darwinism. Rather, this direction in his thinking retains its roots in the Homeric world of noble heroism. The concept of contest, of the ancient Greek *agon*, provides an anchor for his thought that ultimately, in my view, allows him to move towards this materialist explanation of human experience and avoid ugly extremes to which he may otherwise have fallen prey to. I argue that the signature features of Homeric contest that provide this protection are two elements of its architecture outlined in previous chapters: namely, the concepts of difference and of abundance.

Further, I show in Chapter 5 that the generative power of contest in fact arises from its emphasis on difference. In *Homer's Contest* he writes:

> The original function of this strange institution [contest] is, however, not as a safety valve but as a stimulant: the pre-eminent individual is removed so that a new contest of powers can be awakened: a thought which is hostile to the 'exclusivity' of genius in the modern sense, but which assumes that there are always *several* geniuses to incite one another to action, just as they keep each other within certain limits, too. That is the kernel of the Hellenic idea of competition: it loathes a monopoly of predominance and fears the dangers of this, it desires, as a *protective measure* against genius – a second genius.[42]

I argue that difference, here expressed as the continual emergence of new 'geniuses' to challenge established excellences, supplies the contest with two characteristics. Firstly, it refreshes society by producing new excellences through the friction of otherness: this is its character as a stimulant. Secondly, it protects society from the excesses of an individual taste, that is, from hegemony or monopoly. The victor is continually challenged, the excellences established are always provisional, subject to the next contest and its outcomes.

Finally, I claim that within Nietzsche's thought the idea of personal abundance acts both as a precondition and as an outcome of contest. The great individual who can engage in this kind of contest-based social relationship must first have deep personal reserves to draw upon. For Nietzsche, this is not only a corrective against Christian and Schopenhauerian assumptions of human deficit, but also the protective element for those that enter the arena, and it enables them to benefit from contest. The great individual must have personal abundance in order to engage in contest, and their abundance is enhanced by it, win or lose. It is this virtuous circle that makes contest a positive force both for the individual and for their social relations, and perhaps distinguishes it from simpler ideas such as mere competition or conflict.

I must note here something that I do not address in this book. Throughout this work I refer to Nietzsche's understanding of the agonistic spirit of ancient Greece. As shorthand, I refer to this as Nietzsche's 'Homerism', as his 'Homeric' ethos. As with all shorthand, this is convenient but a little inaccurate. The agonistic spirit of ancient Greece has been extensively researched.[43] The scope of ancient Greek agon is evident from this literature: it extended to the athletic contests of ancient Olympia, the rhetorical contests of the *polis*, the theatre of classical tragedy and clashes on the battlefield. It is something that seems to have been deeply embedded in that culture, from its rise to its decline, permeating many elements of daily life, and is sometimes credited as the wellspring of the incredible achievements – artistically, politically, philosophically and materially – of that time.

Tracing the influence of this idea is a complex task, and many critical questions have been raised. For example, one might ask whether classical agonistic spirit has been whitewashed in order to make it more palatable or accessible to a contemporary audience. In sport, the 'Olympic spirit' has become the stock in trade of the Olympic movement and risks underplaying the violence of the ancient world.[44] In the political realm, for example, theorists such as Arendt, Mouffe and Honig have drawn on agonism in order to reimagine democratic politics.[45] The legitimacy of otherwise of these appropriations of the Greek agonistic spirit is a matter of debate.

Nietzsche is one of many philosophers, politicians, artists and sportspeople who have been interested in, and influenced by, the ancient Greek spirit of agonistic contest. Nietzsche understands this agonistic spirit to have first come to consciousness through the Homeric poetry of *Iliad* and *The Odyssey*, and to be more generally expressed in Greek tragedy – in theatre, poetry, literature and philosophy. In this book I do not offer a critique of Nietzsche's understanding of this phenomenon. I do not analyse his exegesis of ancient texts or demonstrate the limits of his understanding of that period of history. I don't refer to contemporary advances in our understanding of that world to show the shortcomings of his approach, and I don't even go back to those texts myself to explore themes or ideas. My intention in this book is simply to understand how Nietzsche used his conception of the ancient world – however flawed it might have been – to develop his own agonistic ethics. In this I take my lead from other scholars – most notably Christa Davis Acampora and Herman Siemens – while at the same time acknowledging that, at least in the English-speaking world, there seems to be a need for more work in this area. Notwithstanding the validity of these questions and problems, this book does not address them. Rather, building on the work of Acampora and Siemens, I take Nietzsche's understanding as a given, and I work to understand how his ethics is built on this foundation. I understand this to be the essence of Nietzsche's renewal of ancient ethics: he takes concepts from the ancient world – most notably that of contest – and he reinvents them for his time and place. Thus, when I refer to the Homeric ethos of the ancient world, I refer to Nietzsche's particular understanding of the classical world's agonistic ethos, and his view that this had its origin in Homeric literature.

Having thus established the contours of Nietzsche's new Homerism in Chapter 5, in Chapters 6 and 7 I go on to explore this new Homerism in its ethical dimensions. In Chapter 6 I describe Nietzsche's distinctive understanding of an individual's psyche as the place where a subterranean contest between an individual's drives plays out. There is a significant literature on this aspect of Nietzsche's psychology – his emphasis on the drives and his effacement of a unified subject to organize these drives.[46] In this literature there is a surprising gap, which is the application of the Homeric agon to this understanding of the interplay – often conceived in agonistic terms – of an individual's drives. Chapter 6 aims to address this gap. In this context, I argue that, at least for Nietzsche, the life task of an individual is to bring these drives into some sort of order through self-overcoming.[47] The task itself demonstrates the twin themes of Nietzsche's new Homerism – difference with respect to the self (the individual is internally differentiated), and abundance as the result of self-overcoming.

GS §23 provides a useful introduction to the first step in this development of Nietzsche's ethics, his application of contest to the inner life of the individual.

In this text he counters an imagined argument that a society becomes weak when it becomes less focused on externalized contests such as war and sport and more interested in creature comforts. He argues here for a reconfiguration of these externalized contests into private, internal contests to avoid this kind of weakness setting in:

> a society in which corruption spreads is accused of laxity; and it is obvious that the esteem of war and the pleasure in war diminish, while the comforts of life are now desired just as ardently as were warlike and athletic honours formerly. What is usually overlooked, however, is that the ancient civil energy and passion, which received magnificent visibility through war and competitive games, has now transformed itself into countless private passions and has merely become less visible ... And thus, it is precisely in times of 'laxness' that tragedy runs through the houses and streets, that great love and great hatred are born and the flame of knowledge blazes up into the sky.

Here we see his thought that the energy of a community, once spent in performative agonistic contests such as athletics and war, can instead be expended in private contests that take the form of internal passions such as love and hatred. These internal contests are in turn transformed into social constructs: they become public as they 'run through the houses and streets'. This internalization of contest is, I argue, essential to Nietzsche's understanding of the drives, and is the foundation, we see here, for the social expression of contest that is explored in Chapter 7.

In Chapter 6 I argue that this conjunction of internal drives and Homeric *agon* is further developed by his reimagination of another classical theme, namely, Epicurean and Stoic ideas about self-cultivation.[48] We can see this emerging in, for example, *D* §560, where he uses the metaphor of a garden and gardener to describe how an individual relates to their internal drives:

> *What we are at liberty to do.* One can dispose of one's drives like a gardener and, though few know it, cultivate the shoots of anger, pity, curiosity, vanity as productively and profitably as a beautiful fruit tree on a trellis...

This text suggests a fairly straightforward process: a gardener decides what type of garden they want to cultivate, and then they proceed to cultivate that type of garden, which might seem to a modern reader to be a rather naïve take on personal development. Nietzsche's idea of self-cultivation is, however, far more developed than indicated in this text alone. In particular, Nietzsche problematizes the idea that there is a thinking subject, a 'gardener', who is able to desire particular outcomes and direct the drives in order to achieve them.

Rather, he asserts in a text of the same period that the drives order themselves organically and 'naturally', through a process of victory and defeat, a kind of internal psychic Olympia (D §109):

> *that* one *desires* to combat the vehemence of a drive at all, however, does not stand within our own power; nor does the choice of any particular method; nor does the success or failure of this method. What is clearly the case is that in this entire procedure our intellect is only the blind instrument of *another drive* which is a *rival* of the drive whose vehemence is tormenting us ... While 'we' believe we are complaining about the vehemence of a drive, at bottom it is one drive *which is complaining about another*.

Thus, the Nietzschean task of self-overcoming is achieved through self-cultivation, and yet, confusingly, without a clear view of what this 'self' might be, other than a momentary coalescence of competing drives.[49] If we put this complication to one side, however, we can see one important component of Nietzsche's psychology here. The task of self-overcoming is not achieved by capitulating to a single and overpowering drive but by a rich variety of drives, including aversive emotional experiences, coming together into a finely calibrated state of harmony and integration. Nietzsche is specifically opposed to the idea that self-cultivation and self-overcoming involves removing internal friction: when an overly vehement drive 'torments' us, he says, we need our other drives to rise up and moderate its effects.

In Chapter 7 I show how Nietzsche applies this understanding of the individual to personal relationships, and especially to higher friendship. I argue that, on Nietzsche's understanding, the behaviours of friends towards each other are determined as each person develops an appreciation of the other's internal contest and learns how best to enhance their friend's self-overcoming. The result is that a friend is also inevitably a contestant, an adversary.

I develop the ideal of higher friendship from Nietzsche's drive psychology in the following way. I argue that Nietzsche's ideal of heroic friendship is one where individuals develop an understanding not only of their own psychological requirements for a flourishing inner life, but they also develop this understanding of others. We will see that Nietzsche considers that this knowledge of oneself and of others is incomplete and that it is therefore continually clarified, refined and deepened. In this context – of an ever-changing, ever-renewing appreciation of one's own constitution and the constitution of others – higher friendship presents a unique opportunity for the landscape of a person's internal contest to be brought to conscious awareness and reflection. Through this process people are able to develop a profound understanding of the best conditions through which desirable drives might flourish and undesirable ones might weaken, both within themselves and within others. This allows friends to respond freely and ethically to one another with a wide range of emotions and actions: with love *or* hatred, compassion *or* cruelty, generosity *or* withholding. These responses are all ethical in the sense that they are a response designed to promote the other's flourishing, albeit based on an emergent understanding of the individual and of the self that is contingent and provisional.

I go on to argue that this description of higher friendship is entirely consistent with Nietzsche's understanding of contest. Specifically, it relies on the two major themes in relation to contest described throughout this book: difference and abundance. In Nietzsche's account of higher friendship, a friend's responses are tailored to the specific circumstances of each person. It depends on a deep appreciation of difference – the ways in which one person is animated by a unique constellation of drives and a specific set of requirements for nourishing them. It also depends upon, and results in, an overflowing personal abundance. I will show the contours and possibilities of this idea of abundance and its importance for higher friendship in the chapter – for now it is sufficient to say that agonistic engagement with a friend requires at least some level of personal abundance because it is, in a profound and surprising way, an act of giving, of generosity. Thus, we will see in Chapter 7 that it can be ethical to respond to a friend by creating adverse circumstances or generating and responding to aversive emotional experiences.

The claim of this book is that Nietzsche's ideal of higher friendship emerges from his understanding of contest and his application of contest to the individual first, and then to the individual in their social relationships. Throughout this book I argue that we can understand Nietzsche's interest in contest through the complementary ideas of abundance and difference, and it is this understanding of contest that allows us to frame Nietzsche's sometimes confronting and abrasive attitudes to social relationships as a distinctive ethics. In this way Nietzsche's ethics avoids the charges of narcissism or solipsism. This great individual involved in higher friendships does not need to take advantage of, demean or diminish others in order to elevate themselves. On the contrary, they are able to support others in their own practice of self-overcoming. In this kind of relationship, the range of available strategies available is very wide, so wide that it includes elements not normally attributed to friendship – hardness, indifference, combativeness and opposition, for example. It also includes within the scope of an intimate relationship a range of aversive emotional experiences that are often devalued: hatred, indifference and enmity, for example. This kind of friendship does not devolve into dominance, violence, aggression or narcissism, because each person is able to act and respond out of their own abundant personal resources, and each person acts without the desire to erase difference but rather to enhance and support it.

This is the basis for intimacy and mutual inspiration within higher friendship. The specificity of an individual's constitution is respected: 'At bottom, all our actions are incomparably and utterly personal, unique, and boundlessly individual' (GS §354). Abundance arises from an individual's inner contest of drives: 'To "give style" to one's character – a great and rare art! It is practised by those who survey all the strengths and weaknesses that their nature has to offer and then fit them into an artistic plan' (GS §259). The great individual can now be seen as someone who has experienced their own self-overcoming to such a degree that they are able to engage in agonistic exchange with their friends, not on the basis of need but on the basis of the personal abundance that they generate for themselves and that overflows towards others.

My conclusion, then, is that Nietzsche develops a deeply personal and intimate portrayal of friendship, one that licenses a range of emotions and behaviours that can be problematic in more traditional approaches. Friendship here includes not only love and compassion but also enmity, envy, indifference to suffering and other aversive emotions and adversarial behaviours. By incorporating these into friendship, Nietzsche offers an ethically productive understanding of social relationships that are capable of benefiting from the full range of human experience, producing stronger, more energetic and more highly developed individuals in the process.

2

Against Christian love

In this chapter and the next I examine two approaches to morality that Nietzsche rejects. These are the morality of love that is based on the Christian idea of *agape* (self-sacrificial) love and the morality of compassion proposed by the early nineteenth century German philosopher Arthur Schopenhauer (1788–1860). By looking at these approaches and the reasons for Nietzsche's rejection of them as a basis for ethics, we can begin to see at least the outline of his commitment to the agonistic ethics of ancient Greek culture, and higher friendship specifically. In this analysis we will see the importance of two themes in Nietzsche's renewal of the concept of contest, namely, the themes of abundance and of difference. From Nietzsche's perspective, both Christian *agape* love and Schopenhauer's idea of compassion contradict the classical ideals of personal superabundance and the generative power of difference. In this chapter I demonstrate this with regard to the Christian morality of self-sacrificial love.

In analysing Nietzsche's response to Christian morality, it is clearly not possible to address the whole topic of Christian morality in all its forms over two millennia in a single chapter. To sharpen the focus of this analysis, I address Christian morality on the understanding that Christian morality centres on the concept of love. I do this because I think this resonates most strongly and coherently with Christian doctrine as a whole, as we will see later in the chapter. Further, I am not alone in thinking this way about Christian love: Simon May, one of few contemporary philosophers who writes specifically on the philosophy of love, argues that love is a theme of singular importance in the Christian tradition: '[Christianity] turns love into life's supreme virtue and moral principle.'[1]

The result of this, he argues, is the fetishization of love as the single most important aspect of social and/or moral behaviour in Western societies, a phenomenon that has (somewhat paradoxically) become more pronounced as these societies have moved away from their religious foundations. He argues that, having lost their concept of God, people in these societies now seek to divinize themselves by incorporating this concept of love into their moral frameworks: 'In the wasteland of Western idols, only love survives intact.'[2]

Given the significance of love as a moral ideal, it is clearly going to be both controversial and complex to establish that Nietzsche offers a viable ethics that rejects it. What I aim to show here is that, while there may be different ways of understanding love within the Christian tradition, Nietzsche's response to Christianity is shaped to a significant degree by his rejection of a specific version of love, namely, self-sacrificial or *agape* love.

In what follows I will demonstrate Nietzsche's rejection of *agape* love in two different ways. One is general: Nietzsche rejects Christianity's proposition that love can function as a singular moral standard against which everything must be judged. This is the Homeric principle of difference at work: Nietzsche rejects Christian love as a singular moral standard because this would preclude the possibility of the coexistence of multiple moralities, perhaps wildly different from each other. This, in turn, diminishes the possibility of contest, and therefore constrains the process that contest fuels, namely, the establishment of new values and the overthrow of old ones. In this way, love becomes a kind of tyranny that opposes and suppresses, it does not stimulate or celebrate the particular characteristics of individuals. For Nietzsche, this follows directly from Christianity's monotheism. Love as the only moral standard is proposed by a theological system that includes only one God. Nietzsche rejects the sheer homogeneity of this perspective as life-denying. His proposal for an agonistic ethics requires different perspectives to be tried against one another, in order to stimulate new standards of excellence.

The second part of Nietzsche's rejection of Christian love is more specific. I will show that he rejects the idea that love involves self-sacrifice. This, for him, is another reason why love (as self-sacrifice or self-abnegation) cannot serve as a moral standard against which other actions can be judged. This is a complex idea to unpack because it takes us into the very depths of the Christian understanding of God. I will outline the idea of self-sacrificial love by considering its development in the first few centuries of the church, and how this finds expression in Protestant – and especially Lutheran – philosophical theology. I will show that this Christian emphasis on self-sacrificing love both borrows from and contrasts with the world of ancient Greece which included not only *agape* love but also *philia* (brotherly love) and *eros* (passionate love). In both the Christian and classical contexts, *agape* love has the characteristic that it is beneficial for the beloved and it requires sacrifice for the lover. I show that Nietzsche rejects it because it conflicts with the second of our key themes, namely, the ideal of abundance. What we will see is that Nietzsche proposes an alternative to *agape* love that allows him to retain the ancient ideal of abundance. He calls this 'great love', which he thinks is primarily experienced in friendship.

Understanding Christian love

Before outlining these two components of Nietzsche's rejection of Christian love and his proposal for great love, we must first consider the complexities of the concept of love and some aspects of the history of its interpretation. Simon May's *Love: A History* is an excellent overview of the topic from a philosophical perspective, from ancient to contemporary times.[3] In order to explain the obsession with love in contemporary societies, May looks to both secular and religious sources including Plato, Aristotle, Lucretius and Ovid; as well as the Hebrew and Christian traditions.

May argues that while the Hebrew and Christian traditions can both be described by the double-barrelled injunction to love God and to love one's neighbour,[4] the Hebrew idea does not emphasize self-abnegation in the way the Christian ideal does.[5] For him, the Christian ideal, best captured by the Greek word *agape*, refers to a kind of 'unconditional, altruistic, obedient, humble selflessness'.[6] Other kinds of love are demoted or transformed to take on this fundamental posture. For example, while the Christian tradition includes *eros* as passionate desire to possess and to be possessed, this expresses itself not in its original terms – as a self-regarding desire to possess the beloved – but is transformed into a different concept that lends itself to the idea of self-abnegation.[7] In other words, for May, when Christianity deals with the concept of love, whatever its form, it focuses on the moral value of sacrificial behaviour.

The problem of self-concern and other-concern, and how these interact in the concept of love, is an important issue. According to May, love can be understood as the individual reaching out towards others in order to find their own ontological ground. As love arises from a feeling of insecurity in the world, it stimulates a corresponding desire to find security through others. This desire to secure one's place in the world May calls 'ontological rootedness'.[8] On his account, self-love and love of others can therefore be connected: to love others is to love oneself, that is, when we love others, we also satisfy our desire for 'ontological rootedness'. For him, this explains the paradoxical dynamics of love:

It involves seemingly contradictory attitudes: submission and possessiveness; generosity and selfishness; intense gratitude and – not least – the disrespect that is easily fostered by need when it becomes overwhelming and even violent.[9]

According to May, these forces and counterforces in the idea of love lead to very different approaches in the history of its development. For him, Christianity presents love as a possibility for participation in a transcendent divine power, or, even to become divine.[10] Nietzsche, according to May, interprets Christian love on this basis as a desire to transcend human experience itself. He argues that Nietzsche took this to mean that Christian love is, somewhat ironically, ultimately based on hatred for existence:[11]

> This is Nietzsche's most spectacular claim about the tradition of love that evolves from Judaism and Christianity: it grows out of hatred. He is not repeating the commonplace that love and hate go together – for example that love easily nurses hate when its hopes are disappointed, or even in anticipation of their disappointment. Rather, he is suggesting that hatred of nature, of strength, of life itself, drives 'the religion of love'.[12]

Nietzsche's solution to this specifically Christian problem, according to May, is *amor fati*, the love of fate. He presents Nietzsche's response as radical affirmation: where Christian love seeks transcendence beyond what actually exists – and is therefore a denial of it – Nietzsche seeks to describe a love that affirms *everything* that exists, including suffering, change and destruction.

On this view, Nietzschean love begins with self-love as an affirmation of everything about its object, the self. It then extends its reach to include the context in which the self exists, including other people. May sees Nietzschean affirmative love not as solipsism or narcissism that is purely self-directed but as love that starts with the self and works outwards to everything connected to the self. The Nietzschean individual comes to love other people *through* love of self. Using May's ontological terms, where Christian love seeks to ground people in a beyond, first reaching out to the divine in order to find their own 'rootedness', Nietzschean love seeks to ground people in themselves through radical self-acceptance, and then to reach out towards others. For May, this is how self-love, love for others, and the love of fate (*amor fati*) intersect in Nietzsche.[13]

This is good as far as it goes. However, there is one important element missing, namely, Nietzsche's emphasis on contest. Acampora and Hatab have recently offered further reflections on Nietzsche's concept of love that offer solutions to the riddle of love for self and love for others in Nietzsche's ethics by using Nietzsche's understanding of contest.[14] With May, Hatab emphasizes the importance of the love of fate but adds to this the concept of *agon*: love of fate includes love for the necessity of agonistic relations.[15] However, Hatab contrasts Nietzsche and Homer, arguing that the Homeric world allows for a greater emphasis on friendship, care and love than Nietzsche does. In his view, Homer's presentation of love and friendship is closer to the agonistic ideal, which affirms all of life – including positive attachments – than Nietzsche's was:

> Yet for all Nietzsche's celebration of passion, I regret that his approach to human attachments in the main seems to lack the kind of love and compassion expressed in the Homeric world.[16]

Acampora approaches this topic from a different perspective. She argues that we can't understand the ancient *agon* purely on the basis of dyadic relations, that is, relationships understood as something that happens between two individuals. She argues that the productivity of dyadic agonistic social relationships can only be understood in the context of the social systems that make them possible, and that adjudicate on outcomes. These include not only the individual contestants but also the institutional frameworks, the underlying systems that sustain these institutions, and a value economy that recognizes agonistic outputs.[17] Thus, dyadic contests (such as love and friendship) relate to an agonistically oriented social system that makes them possible. This helps move us even further away from an understanding of Nietzsche as someone who promotes a kind of narcissistic self-interest. We can see here the beginning of an idea about love and friendship as part of a broader political system that moves beyond the standard debates about Nietzsche's anti-egalitarianism or about the threat of political violence that some consider inherent in Nietzsche's explorations.[18]

These readings of Nietzsche on the topic of love offer insights into Nietzsche's capacity to affirm (or not) all of life's experiences, as well as insights into the self-sustaining nature of relationships and the social context in which they become not only operative but also generative. There is a sense in which, for each of these authors, the individual is constituted by their social relations, they *emerge* from their social relationships.[19] The generative principle at work in this conception of social relationships does not lie with the concrete reality of the individuals involved, but in the somewhat more abstract idea of the relationship itself. For May, ontological rootedness – the way in which a person *grounds* themselves in the world – arises from their love relations. For Hatab, the structure of the contest means that individual contestants are constituted by the relationship between them, their power only emerges or becomes real when it encounters resistance.[20] For Acampora, the field of relations that make agonistic engagements possible also constitute the contestants: 'with [these fields], agents *become who they are relationally*.'[21]

In my view, this is a significant mistake in understanding Nietzsche's ethics, and in approaching ethics more generally. In what follows I aim to demonstrate that Nietzsche's rejection of this idea – that relationships constitute individuals – is deeply embedded in his rejection of Christian *agape* love. For him, it is in solitude that an individual discovers themselves, signifying that the individual is themselves self-grounding.[22] It is not enough to simply accept that Nietzsche rejects *agape* love as an ethical idea, as many scholars do. Rather, in rejecting *agape* love, Nietzsche rejects a system of thought in which individuals are constituted, in a profound and ontologically basic way, by relations of love. The Christian idea of *agape* love, as I will show below, is not a pragmatic ethics based simply on ideas of what is best for people. It's based in a specific idea of personhood, which finds ultimate expression in the being of God himself as a unity composed of three persons. One of Nietzsche's basic problems with the Christian emphasis on *agape* love is precisely that within it the individual is erased. His counterproposal, great love, emphasizes the individual *qua* individual within a system of agonistic relationships. They are not constituted by these relationships. Instead, out of their individual 'genius', they contribute to them. We cannot, therefore, accept Acampora's and Hatab's proposals for relationally constituted individuals engaging in agonistic contest.

In what follows I aim to demonstrate this vital point. There is significant complexity here: we must dive into the depths of Christian metaphysics and seek to understand and even unravel one of the most obscure, but profound, elements of Christian theology, namely, the doctrine of the Trinity.

We begin by looking at a particular tradition of interpretation within Christian philosophical theology that privileges *agape* over other types of love, and especially over *eros*. For example, Anders Nygren, a prominent twentieth-century Lutheran theologian, provides a now typical description of *agape* love by contrasting it with *eros*. For Nygren, in *agape* love the lover does not respond to the inherent value of the beloved. Rather, the lover bestows value on the beloved by self-giving. This allows Nygren to make sense of the case where a beneficent lover gives their love to an unworthy and undeserving beloved: you can love the unlovable because, in this act of love, they become valuable. This is the conceptual space in which God loves sinful humankind, which, as we will see, is the archetypal example of *agape* love within this tradition of interpretation.[23]

Karl Barth, another prominent twentieth-century theologian but in the European Reformed tradition, which stands closely alongside the Lutheran tradition of Nygren, provides a complementary perspective. He understands *agape* love not only in terms of the bestowal of value on the beloved but also in terms of its costliness for the lover. Reflecting on the difference between *eros* and *agape*, he amplifies the experience of self-abnegation on the part of the lover. For him, from the lover's perspective, *eros* is an act of self-interest[24] and *agape* is an act of self-emptying.[25]

For Barth, both *agape* and *eros* are a pursuit of the beloved. In *eros*, this is based on the free and independent personhood of the lover, and in *agape*, it is based on the free and independent personhood of the beloved. For him, *agape* love is characterized by self-giving and surrender on the part of the lover. What is surrendered is the lover's sovereignty – their individuality and freedom – in the very act through which they recognize the reality of the beloved:

> We have equated the concept of love in a general way with that of self-giving … what we have here – in Christian love – is a movement in which a man turns away from himself [and] turns wholly to another, to one who is wholly different from the loving subject … Christian love turns to the other purely for the sake of the other … In Christian love the loving subject reaches back … to give itself away; to give up itself … [26]

We can put the perspectives of Barth and Nygren together in the following way. For Barth, the lover recognizes the otherness of the beloved as an individual and is motivated by this sense of otherness to seek after them, freely surrendering themselves and their interests in doing so. For Nygren, this involves the bestowal of value. In both cases, the orientation of *agape* love is towards the beloved and involves self-abnegation for the lover, that is, the free surrender of themselves as individuals to the otherness of the beloved. Thus, we see the outlines of a concept of *agape* love in which the lovers' 'ontological rootedness', to use May's term, is decentred. Both lover and beloved find themselves caught up in an act of self-abnegation, both emptying themselves in an attempt to ground themselves within a social relationship. The effect of this is that individuals only exist as products of their relations. Wolfhart Pannenberg is another influential Lutheran theologian who describes this understanding of love in terms of a distinctively Christian definition of personhood.[27] Here persons are understood as ontologically 'ecstatic' (think *ex-stasis*) in which the being of each person is found not within the person but outside of themselves in others.

It was the Scottish theologian T. F. Torrance who convincingly demonstrated the underlying connections between the concept of *agape* love as self-emptying and the foundations of Christian theology: namely, its understanding of the being of God as triune. Building on Karl Barth's work, he developed a line of interpretation that explores the ontological foundations for the Christian concept of love as the essence of Christian morality.[28] He claims that the creedal formulations of the fourth- and fifth-century ecumenical councils demonstrate that Christian morality is not simply a commandment to behave in a certain way or to adopt certain attitudes towards others. For Torrance, the Christian morality of *agape* love reflects the most elemental conception of reality in Christian philosophical theology, that is, the being of God.

These creedal formulations centre on two core doctrines and their ontological implications. These are the incarnation of the second person of the trinity in the human being Jesus Christ and the trinitarian understanding of God as Father, Son and Holy Spirit. The incarnation results in the crucifixion of Jesus Christ, which is held up within Christian theology as the supreme example of *agape* love. It is also interpreted as something that does not happen 'outside' the being of God, but rather, as an expression of the inner divine being of God, in which the three persons of the trinity exist not in themselves but in and for each other. Thus, in these two foundational doctrines, love as self-abnegation takes centre stage.

In developing this understanding of the origins of Christian morality, Torrance attributes particular importance to the ecumenical councils of Nicea (325 CE),[29] Constantinople (381 CE)[30] and Chalcedon (425 CE).[31] Developed against the background of theological controversy surrounding the doctrines of the trinity and of the incarnation, these creedal formulations describe the trinity by stressing the Father as creator, Jesus Christ as the simultaneously fully human and fully divine Son of God and the Holy Spirit as one who 'proceeds' from both the Father and the Son. In order to reach these formulations, and to preserve Christian doctrine from polytheism on the one hand and strict monotheism on the other, Torrance describes the development of technical terminology such as ὁμοούσιος (*homoousios*; 'one substance'),[32] ὑπόστασις (*hypostasis*; 'person')[33] and περιχώρησις (*perichoresis*; 'co-inherence').[34] These were deployed in order to maintain the idea that the Christian God was internally differentiated as three persons and yet was one God.

For Torrance, these technical formulations lead to an innovation that has far-reaching implications for human social relations:

> there developed out of the doctrine of the Trinity the new *concept of person*, unknown in human thought until then, according to which the relations between persons belong to what persons are … This onto-relational concept of 'person', generated through the doctrines of Christ and the Holy Trinity, is one that is also applicable to inter-human relations … [35]

In this conception of God, the story of creation and redemption including the incarnation and death by crucifixion of Jesus Christ do not take place in some imagined space 'outside' of God. Rather, this other-centred, self-giving and self-abnegating drama takes place within the internal dynamic of the life of God, an ultimate expression of the relationship between the Father and the Son mediated by the Holy Spirit.[36] The name given to this relationship within the being of God is love:

> since the whole Trinity is involved in our redemption [it] derives from and is grounded in the eternal Communion of Love which is in his one indivisible being as Father, Son and Holy Spirit ... our salvation is grounded immutably in the self-abnegating love of God which flows freely to us from the eternal Communion of Love in his Triune Being.[37]

In these theologians, who fall within the Lutheran and Reformed tradition that Nietzsche himself was influenced by, I think we see a compelling and comprehensive understanding of Christian orthodoxy that links the Christian metaphysics of a triune God with both a concept of personhood that is other-centred and the concept of *agape* love as its ethical outworking.

On this basis, it seems to me that when Nietzsche takes a stand against Christian love, he takes a stand precisely against this understanding of mutual co-constitution of individuals in their relations. Nietzsche's understanding of the individual in their love relations depends on a prior commitment to the individual as ontologically self-constituting. As we will see, for him value is not bestowed but self-generated, and individuals can only participate in great (agonistic) love on the basis of personal superabundance, not self-abnegation.

The essential point is this: we cannot consistently hold that Nietzsche rejects *agape* love *and* that Nietzsche believed individuals are constituted in their relationships to others. Acampora, Hatab and others do not address this problem. In my view, when Nietzsche rejects *agape* love, he rejects an entire metaphysical system of thought that has as its foundation this idea of relationally constituted personhood. Nietzsche's emphasis, as we will see below, is antithetical. It is an emphasis on the individual as genius, as self-constituting and self-defining.

Against the tyranny of love

Nietzsche's rejection of theistic belief is perhaps most famously captured in his pronouncements about the death of God.[38] It is a truism of Nietzsche scholarship that in these pronouncements Nietzsche is not simply referring to the Judeo-Christian God but rather to the function of the concept of God and its role in the formation of Western ethics.[39] In my view, while it is true that Nietzsche's attacks on these metaphysical and ethical commitments go far beyond a unifocal attack on Christianity, we must also not miss the continuing influence of the specifically Christian concept of God and the idea of *agape* love to which it is attached for Nietzsche's thought.

Christianity influenced Nietzsche throughout his life, both in enthusiasm for it and violent rejection of it.[40] Nietzsche's enthusiasm for Christianity as a young person raised in a pastor's house and his rejection of it through his teenage years are well documented.[41] Further, we can see that the importance of Christianity, at least as an enemy, continued to the end of his writing career in 1889. For example, in the preface to the revised edition of *The Birth of Tragedy* (*BT*, Preface §5; added in 1886), he writes about Christianity as 'the most excessive, elaborately figured development of the moral theme that humanity has ever had to listen to'.

In 1888, the last productive year of his philosophical life, he writes about himself as the anti-Christ in the book with that title, and in the last line of *Ecce Homo* (*EH* §9; also published in 1888), he includes a reference to the death of Christ in an attempt to summarize his philosophy: 'Have I been understood? *Dionysus against the Crucified*.'

That is to say, from his adolescence in the early 1870s right until the end of his productive life in January 1889, he was deeply influenced by Christianity as a singularly important instance of religious and moral commitment.[42] It is against this background of initial acceptance followed by maturing antipathy towards Christianity that his own ethical project was articulated and structured.

This specifically Christian articulation of God as trinity and, consequently, love as self-abnegation, is deeply relevant to help us interpret Nietzsche's more general response to monotheism and to the morality of custom. Against monotheism, the morality of custom, and their Christian instantiations, we see Nietzsche emphasize the individual and the importance of difference between individuals, as well as his understanding of the individual as personally abundant. These threads in Nietzsche's thought contradict any proposal, Christian or otherwise, that the individual is constituted in their relations to others and can live ethically only through self-abnegation.

Against monotheism

In *GS* §143 Nietzsche critiques monotheism by contrasting it with polytheism. Where polytheism allows proliferation and differentiation by celebrating individuality and difference, monotheism proposes a singular, normative and monoptical view of the moral field:

The greatest advantage of polytheism. – For an individual to posit his *own* ideal and to derive from it his own law, joys and rights ... The wonderful art and power of creating gods – polytheism – was that through which this drive could discharge itself, purify, perfect and ennoble itself ... Monotheism, in contrast, this rigid consequence of the teachings of a normal human type – that is, the belief in a normal god next to whom there are only false pseudo-gods – was perhaps the greatest danger to humanity so far...

Here we see Nietzsche propose that monotheism is tied to an oppressive moral hegemony, and that, by way of contrast, polytheism opens up the possibility of a polyphonous ethical heterodoxy.[43] The idea of a single normative type for all human beings, he argues, has monotheism as its 'rigid consequence'. For Nietzsche, monotheistic religious belief arises from a desire to establish moral hegemony, to establish an oppressive singular view of morally acceptable human experience. Thus, for Nietzsche, monotheism is a threat to humanity: it threatens humanity with 'stagnation' because human beings become unable to create and recreate themselves.

This critique of monotheism can be coupled with his general interest in promoting the individual, and, in so doing, promoting diversity as a touchstone for his ethics. This is expressed, for example, in *GS* §335 where he argues that ethical judgements must be tailored to the individual. Nietzsche's concern here is to emphasize the importance and generative power of difference. For Nietzsche, the specific circumstances of each individual are relevant to ethical judgements, not to promote a laissez-faire relativism but to discipline our thinking. In *GS* §335 he writes:

> No one who judges, 'in this case everyone would have to act like this' has yet taken five steps towards self-knowledge. For he would then know that there neither are nor can be actions that are all the same; that every act ever performed was done in an altogether unique and unrepeatable way, and that this will be equally true of every future act; that all prescriptions of action (even the most inward and subtle rules of all moralities so far) relate only to their rough exterior...

He also proposes a methodology for arriving at these bespoke ethical judgements, namely, (semi-)scientific observation as opposed to metaphysical speculation (*GS* §7). For him, this kind of observation is a kind of heroism because it requires the bravery to conduct, observe and reflect on moral experiments:

> *Something for the industrious.* – Anyone who now wishes to make a study of moral matters opens up for himself an immense field of work. All kinds of passions have to be thought through separately ... Has anyone done research

on the different ways of dividing up the day or of the consequences of a regular schedule of work, festivals, and the rest? Do we know the moral effects of foods? Is there a philosophy of nutrition? ... Has anyone collected people's experiences of living together — in monasteries, for example? Has anyone depicted the dialectic of marriage and friendship? ... If all these jobs were done ... then an experimenting would be in order, in which every kind of heroism could find satisfaction...

When read together these texts provide an insight into Nietzsche's emphasis on individual difference and how this relates to his rejection of Christian morality. The argument goes something like this: monotheism causes moral hegemony which in turns threatens human existence with stagnation (*GS* §143). The alternative, in which human beings flourish by celebrating difference, can be understood without the metaphysical speculations of polytheism by studying the relationship between the biological, social and psychological particularities of individuals as the basis for developing alternative ethical proposals (*GS* §7 and §335).[44]

It is clear in *GS* §7 that Nietzsche does not think that the appropriate methods had yet been developed to assist with this task, an observation appropriate to his time but perhaps less relevant today, where the social and psychological sciences are well-developed. There is, however, a clue as to his thought about the general shape that this task will take. This clue lies in his appreciation of Homeric contest as an antidote to the kind of moral stagnation that he writes against in these texts.

His 1872 essay *Homer's Contest*, which predates all the texts considered so far, also argues against tyranny in the form of a single dominant person or idea that leads to stagnation and decline.[45] In this essay he sees contest as a form of interaction that has the power to incorporate individual differences so that, when brought together in agonistic exchange, these differences act as a stimulant that refreshes otherwise stagnant human beings and provides a process for determining ever-new standards of excellence:[46]

> That is the kernel of the Hellenic idea of competition: it loathes a monopoly of predominance and fears the dangers of this, it desires, as a *protective measure* against genius – a second genius.[47]

This key insight about agonistic exchange – that it relies on individuals who are essentially different from one another, can be understood to underly his critique of monotheism and of the moral hegemony that follows from it: contest depends on individual difference for its generative power, and, at the same time, it uses this power to generate further difference. The diversity inherent in the contest-ethos is relevant to moral questions in that it rejects a singular view.

From this perspective, moral and ethical excellences are contingently established through a process of continual agonistic renewal. Note that this is not extreme individualism, a mistake that is often made in interpreting Nietzsche. Rather, these excellences have a form of authoritative or normative power in so far as they are recognized more broadly as the current-best perspective on human experience and behaviour. The contest is valued in precisely its capacity to overthrow a socially accepted current-best view for a socially acceptable next-best view. This process of the continual renewal of moral and ethical judgement is understood by Nietzsche as heroism, as the bravery to conduct moral experiments, to become a transgressor, to be an immoralist, for the sake of ethical discovery. Thus, for Nietzsche, the contest ethos of the Homeric age is directly contrary to the ethos of monotheism and specifically Christianity.

Against customary morality

Nietzsche's stance against Christian morality is expressed in a different way through his stance against the morality of custom.[48] He proposes an intimate relationship between the customary morality of European societies and the way in which Christianity monopolizes and universalizes its morality of love. Customary morality, as he saw it, requires the sacrifice of individual difference for the benefit of the collective (e.g. *HAH* §II.89, *D* §9, *GS* §149). For him, this is analogous to the way in which monotheism demands that individual differences be sacrificed to the 'normal' human type. This critique of self-sacrifice in the context of customary morality, once we take into account its close parallel to Nietzsche's rejection of monotheism, opens the door for us to more fully understand his critique of self-sacrificial love within the Christian tradition.

In *D* §9, entitled 'Concept of the morality of custom', he writes:

> morality is nothing other (therefore *no more*!) than obedience to customs [which] are the *traditional* way of behaving and evaluating ... The free human being is immoral because in all things he is *determined* to depend upon himself and not upon a tradition: in all the original conditions of mankind, 'evil' signifies the same as 'individual', 'free', 'capricious', 'unusual', 'unforeseen', 'incalculable'.

Here obedience to the morality of custom is taken to deny the expression of individuality and difference, so that difference is inevitably regarded as evil. The individual is clearly self-defining and solitary – she refuses to accept socially arbitrated ways of behaving and instead relies only upon herself. In this text Nietzsche goes on to claim that sacrifice is therefore the signature feature of these customary moralities:

> The most moral man is he who *sacrifices* the most to custom ... Self-overcoming is demanded, *not* on account of the useful consequences it may have for the individual, but so that the hegemony of custom, tradition, shall be made evident in despite of the private desires and advantages of the individual: the individual is to sacrifice himself – that is the commandment of [the] morality of custom.

Thus, for Nietzsche, the morality of custom requires the sacrifice of individuality as a moral duty. With this, individual differences are either erased or the individuals concerned acquire a bad conscience. We see in other texts that Nietzsche considers the morality of custom not only to deny difference but also to contradict the idea of personal abundance, which I argue throughout this book is central to his agonistic framing of ethical behaviour.

In *D* §18, entitled 'The morality of voluntary suffering', Nietzsche emphasizes that this morality of self-sacrifice is based on a deficit view of human nature. Because the morality of custom requires sacrifice, sacrifice itself – and the suffering that comes from it – turns into a moral act. Therefore, in a perverse reversal, the greater the deficit a person experiences, the more morally upstanding they become. In this system suffering and privation are valorized and the experience of personal abundance immoralized. Where in *D* §9 the individual was considered evil simply because of their individuality, here the individual arouses moral suspicion from the community because of their 'excessive well-being':

> thus there creeps into the world the idea that *voluntary suffering*, self-chosen torture, is meaningful and valuable. Gradually, custom created within the community a practice corresponding to this idea: all excessive well-being henceforth aroused a degree of mistrust, all hard suffering inspired a degree of confidence; ... Thus the concept of the 'most moral man' of the community came to include the virtue of the most frequent suffering...

This suspicion of individual well-being, a phenomenon he elsewhere calls the 'religious or philosophical blacken[ing] of existence' (*D* §238), he attributes here to the morality of custom. The morality of custom therefore crushes individuals in two ways: it erases individual differences, and places individuals into a downward spiral where suffering becomes a value in itself.

Against *agape* love

We have, then, a connection in Nietzsche's thought between the morality of custom and moralities based on monotheism, which can be understood against the background of his commitment to ideas he attributed to world of classical Greece, namely, the ideas of difference and abundance. Both monotheism and the morality of custom are, in Nietzsche's view, opposed to abundance and difference, and they therefore result in human stagnation that is perversely celebrated, which leads in turn to a general suspicion of well-being.

These criticisms are important for understanding his critique of *agape* love. We have seen above that the valorizing of self-sacrifice and the morality of self-abnegation have a foundation in ancient Christian philosophical theology. We have also seen that this theological discourse is prominent in the Lutheran and Reformed traditions that Nietzsche and his family participated in. And we have seen that Nietzsche understands this morality, having grown out of a monotheistic religion that forbids difference in the moral field, to have been translated into the morality of custom that leads to stagnation and decline.

We turn now to begin our sketch of his alternative. This, as we will see, is to promote individuality, and the fostering of individual excellence by generating personal abundance precisely through the differences between individuals. This is the whole purpose of agonistic exchange, of contest. That is to say, when individuals who are on this path encounter one another – even in their most intimate and positive interactions – they encounter one another as contestants determined to discover new excellences. This fundamental idea leads us to his alternative to *agape* love, which he calls 'great love', which sits within his understanding of higher friendship.

Higher friendship as great love

We have seen that Nietzsche's rejection of a morality where love is the singular standard for moral action. We have also seen his rejection of self-sacrifice as the highest moral value promoted by the morality of custom. These ideas, I have argued, would have come to Nietzsche originally through the Christian understanding of *agape* love, which achieves its vaunted status in the Christian pantheon of ethical possibilities because it has its foundation in the distinctively Christian understanding of God as Father, Son and Holy Spirit. In this understanding, personhood is decentred by incorporating social relations into the ontological ground of the individual. This 'ecstatic' understanding of personhood[49] gives added meaning to the Christian morality of love as specifically *agape* love. In this kind of love, persons live not for themselves but for others, freely sacrificing themselves and in doing so they bestow value on an otherwise unworthy beloved.

We turn now to see how Nietzsche's understanding of love responds to *agape* love. What I aim to show is that Nietzsche proposes higher friendship as an alternative that is diametrically opposed to it. This antithesis can be seen in Nietzsche's response to the highest example of *agape* love within Christian theology. This is the *agape* love demonstrated in the death of Christ, which is simultaneously, and somewhat mysteriously, the death of God himself. This death is presented in Christian theology in clearly *agapic* terms: in the death of Christ, God himself sacrifices himself for the underserving.[50] Further, it is clear that Nietzsche understood this connection. For example, in *GM* II.21, discussing questions of metaphysically motivated guilt and punishment, Nietzsche ridicules the idea of God dying for humanity out of love:

> we find ourselves standing in front of the horrific and paradoxical expedient ... that stroke of genius on the part of *Christianity*: God sacrificing himself for the guilt of man, God paying himself off ... the creditor, sacrificing himself for his debtor, out of *love* (are we supposed to believe this?—) out of love for his debtor!

While *GM* is a later text that sits outside the direct interest of this book, we see similar ideas woven together in *Thus Spoke Zarathustra*. There we see a complex interplay between ideas of compassion, friendship, great love and Christian love. In several texts Nietzsche contrasts great love with the *agape* love supposedly exemplified by the death of Christ/death of God. As with any reading of *TSZ*, these themes are layered into a series of texts that we must weave together, each of them unfortunately obscure in their own way.

First, in 'On the Pitying', we see an explicit contrast between great love and love that is based on either compassion for the suffering or forgiveness for wrongdoers. Being caught in this kind of love is to be caught up in a kind of hell:

> Thus speaks all great love; it overcomes even forgiveness and pitying ... Thus the devil once spoke to me: 'Even God has his hell: it is his love for mankind.' ...

In the section 'Retired from Service' this concept of *agape* love as a special kind of hell is explicitly connected with the death of Christ. Zarathustra, the main character, is speaking to a retired priest about the death of God and the conversation unfolds as follows:

> 'You served him up until the end,' said Zarathustra, pensively, after a deep silence. 'Do you know *how* he died? Is it true, as they say, that pity choked him to death, – that he saw how *the human being* hung on the cross, and couldn't bear that his love for mankind became his hell and ultimately his death?'

The old priest goes on to describe the love of God in terms of reward and retribution, and, therefore, as inferior. He infers here that, by way of contrast, great love is not concerned with questions of sin, judgement or divine justice:

Whoever praises him as a god of love does not think highly enough of love itself. Did this god not also want to be judge? But the loving one loves beyond reward and retribution.

Thus, the contrast between great love and Nietzsche's understanding of Christian love as self-abnegation continues. For Nietzsche, the Christian ideal of self-sacrifice, exemplified by the death of God for undeserving human beings that is required because of retributive justice against sin and the sinner, does injustice to the concept of love itself.

One way to make sense of this contrast between the ideal of *agape* love and Nietzschean great love is to consider the role of self-concern in great love. Unlike *agape* love, Nietzsche's understanding of great love is that it is generous, creative and bestowing. It does not require self-abnegation or sacrifice. On the contrary, the exercise of great love requires intense interest in one's own well-being. In order to have the personal resources required for the creative generosity required by great love, an individual must be intensely concerned with themselves. This is the idea of abundance so prominent in Nietzsche's conception of the heroic contest: when entering into contest relationships, the contestants must first overflow with personal abundance.

Further, when it bestows, it does not *bestow* value on the beloved. Instead, great love is a response to someone that recognizes their inherent personal value, without the need to appropriate it. Nietzschean bestowing comes out of the lover's excessive abundance and flows into the beloved's excessive abundance. Neither needs the other, which is how Nietzsche can characterize this kind of bestowal as freely given, an intriguing inversion of the Christian concept of grace.

Nietzsche explores ideas of love and friendship in many different ways throughout *TSZ*. In 'On the Bestowing Virtue' section 1, Nietzsche contrasts holy selfishness, with leads to bestowing love, with sick selfishness that is perpetually inward looking, rectifying personal deficits:

> This is your thirst, to become sacrifices and gifts yourselves, and therefore you thirst to amass all riches in your soul ... You compel all things to and into yourselves, so that they may gush back from your well as the gifts of your love ... hale and holy I call this selfishness. There is another selfishness, one all too poor, a hungering one that always wants to steal; that selfishness is of the sick, the sick selfishness...

Throughout *TSZ* Nietzsche uses the concept of neighbour-love to further draw out the difference between great love and *agape* love. We can see this by reading the two sections 'On Love of the Neighbour' and 'On the Friend' together. In the former, Nietzsche rejects selfless love of the neighbour as an example of the bad conscience imposed by Christian morality:

> I say to you: your love of the neighbour is your bad love of yourselves. You flee to your neighbour to escape yourself and you want to make a virtue of it: but I see through your 'selflessness' ... Do I recommend love of the neighbour to you? I prefer instead to recommend flight from the neighbour and love of the farthest! ... I do not teach you the neighbour, but the friend.

Here, love of the neighbour is presented negatively, as a compensation for not having first learned to love oneself. Neighbour-love distracts a person who is dissatisfied with themselves, from themselves. Nietzsche proposes the opposite: instead of flight from oneself into love of one's neighbour, he promotes flight from the neighbour and towards the friend. That is, neighbour-love based in self-sacrifice as opposite to friendship love, based on personal abundance.[51]

In 'On the Friend', friendship love is not only love of the furthest but also love of the future. Importantly, in this text friendship plays an important role in self-knowledge and self-overcoming because it takes the form of contest. Describing himself as a hermit in constant dialogue with himself, Zarathustra says:

> I and me are always in eager conversation: how could I stand it if there were no friend? For the hermit the friend is always a third: the third is the cork that prevents the conversation of the two from sinking to the depths ... If one wants a friend, then one must also want to wage war for him: and in order to wage war, one must be *able* to be an enemy. One should honour the enemy even in one's friend ... In one's friend one should have one's best enemy. You should be closest to him in heart when you resist him.

The purpose of friendship as contest is described in a subsequent text by an unusual piscatorial metaphor. In this metaphor the beloved is underwater, looking upwards at a cork that floats on the surface and to which she is tied. This prevents her from sinking into the depths as she would if she were alone. Thus, the purpose of higher friendship is to allow the individual to flourish, to 'become what they are' through self-creation, which involves staying buoyant, held up by the lifeline offered by one's friends.

In *TSZ*, then, Nietzsche presents great love as love of the farthest and love of the future, which is the signature feature of higher friendship. It involves love for what the beloved is in the process of becoming – of their future, of their farthest self. Great love is love exercised towards an emergent person, a person from the future, as it were, created by the beloved themselves out of hardship as much as out of comfort.

The role that a friend can play in this process, as we will see in later chapters, depends on the circumstances. Sometimes the friend provides comfort, or even *agape* love. But at other times it is their role to provide hardship, opposition, resistance. In higher friendship, people see in one another a vision of what they might be, in addition to the naked truth of what they are now, and they work through the relationship to bring that future, their furthest being into present existence. As we will see later in this book, this is the very essence of the ancient Greek contest in which agonistic forms of social relationship bring new excellences into existence.

Conclusions

This Nietzschean picture of great love between friends contrasts strongly with the idea of Christian *agape* love. Seen from the perspective of the lover, we have a picture of a superabundant individual who, thanks to their own self-concern, is able to love their friend as a true 'other', as someone from whom they need nothing and for whom they desire nothing but their own flourishing. This flourishing itself requires that the beloved is also concerned with themselves, with their self-creation. Seen from the perspective of the beloved, the lover provides an environment in which self-concern and self-creation are enhanced. If both parties, from their own internal largesse, are able to provide this for each other, then both parties flourish without the Christian requirement of costly sacrifice or humble recognition of personal disvalue. Where in both the Christian and the Nietzschean picture the lover loves from abundance, in the Christian picture this is based on an ecstatic personal ontology, in which self-concern is forbidden and in which the inherent value of the beloved is denied. In the Nietzschean picture, it is self-concern that makes personal superabundance possible in the first place. As this abundance flows outwards towards the beloved, it does not deny their inherent value but it responds to it, not necessarily as something immediately present but as the possibility of what that person might become.

GS §14, an important text on love and friendship that I will return to throughout this book, provides a useful conclusion to this chapter. It considers love of the neighbour, love of knowledge, love as compassion and love as eroticism. Nietzsche's argument is that each of these examples of love can be interpreted as the desire for possession, as greed (see also *D* §532 and *GS* §363). He concludes this passage by presenting friendship as the expression of a higher love that does not seek to possess the beloved, but rather to support them, whether through compassion or cruelty, on their pathway to becoming what they are:

> Here and there on earth there is probably a kind of continuation of love in which this greedy desire of two people for each other gives way to a new desire and greed, a *shared* higher thirst for an ideal above them. But who knows such love? Who has experienced it? Its true name is friendship.

This ethos, in which personal abundance and the preservation of individual difference are central themes, stems from the ethos of Homeric contest and it puts Nietzsche profoundly at odds with his Christian heritage. When he stepped out of Christianity and the ethos of *agape* love in his teenage years, he immediately embraced Schopenhauer's morality of compassion. This proved to be a step out of the Christian frying pan and into the metaphysical fire. His dedication to Schopenhauer, and the vehemence with which he ultimately rejected both Schopenhauer's pessimism about human experience and his monistic reductionism of all things to Will, are the subject of the next chapter.

3

Against pitiful compassion

In the previous chapter we saw how Nietzsche's ethics of higher friendship breaks with his Christian heritage, and how the themes of abundance and difference within that ethics help us to understand his rejection of the Christian morality of love. Biographically speaking, when Nietzsche rejected Christianity, he moved on to embrace the philosophy of Arthur Schopenhauer, a German philosopher writing in the early nineteenth century.[1] His engagement with Schopenhauer's philosophy, and the reasons he ultimately rejected it,[2] provide further insight into his ethics of agonistic friendship.

Importantly, Nietzsche's interest in and rejection of Schopenhauer establishes a trajectory for his philosophical project. Both Christianity and Schopenhauer propose a metaphysical basis for ethics. The trajectory that he establishes by moving away from them both is to move away from metaphysical foundations for ethics and towards a naturalist approach. This is a trajectory that, in my view, is complete by the time he writes *Daybreak* in 1881.[3] What I will later call his 'new Homerism', which emphasizes a naturalist ethics based on contest, comes about, at least in part, as a negative response to Schopenhauer's metaphysical monism. In what follows I aim to show how the two themes that occupy this thesis – abundance and difference – relate to his rejection of Schopenhauer and play a role in conceptualizing his own distinctive ethics of contest that is best understood against that background.

One reason to focus on Schopenhauer is that he clearly articulates a connection between ethics and metaphysics in his philosophy. He asserts that the only actions that have moral value are those that spring from compassion (*Mitleid*) and compassion, in turn, is based on metaphysical monism.[4] For Schopenhauer, the experience of separation and of differentiation between individuals is an illusion created by the process of representation, as opposed to direct experience of the underlying reality. This underlying reality is the metaphysical unity of all things as will (*Wille*). Cartwright summarizes:

Thus we find that Schopenhauer viewed compassion as the motive for morally valuable actions. He also saw it as the only motive which conferred moral worth on an action. The ultimate end of *Mitleid* is another's well-being … *Mitleid* is possible because the separation between individuals is only apparent; metaphysically we are *Wille*.[5]

In my view, Nietzsche rejects Schopenhauer's ethics of compassion not because he is against compassion as an element of human experience. He rejects this ethics because he sees in it a vision for human life that contrasts strongly with the Homeric ideals that he was attracted to. Schopenhauer's metaphysical monism and his pessimistic conception of existence contrast strongly with the ancient Greek idea contest. Against monism, Nietzsche's new Homerism emphasizes difference, and against pessimism it emphasizes personal abundance. Nietzsche's interrogation of Schopenhauer goes beyond a disagreement about preferences for this form of human life or for that one. Rather, it is a critically important shift in terms of the foundation for ethics. Nietzsche responds to Schopenhauer's ethics at its ontological base, which is its metaphysical monism, and in doing begins to chart a completely different course in his ethical project where metaphysics is discounted and the biological, natural and material are elevated.

What we will see in this chapter is that understanding Nietzsche's interest in Schopenhauer as part of a broad movement away from metaphysical systems is vital to contextualizing Nietzsche's understanding of the individual and their social relations. We see that Nietzsche's alternative vision for social relationships, which is ultimately built on a reimagined Homeric contest, is diametrically opposed to Schopenhauer's metaphysically grounded ethics of compassion in ways that reflect his rejection of the Christian morality of *agape* love. With respect to Schopenhauer, he proposes difference rather than monistic metaphysical union, and he proposes abundance rather than privation, deficit and suffering.

The question of Nietzsche's naturalism will be addressed in the next chapter and his project to build this alternative vision for social relations is the subject of subsequent chapters. Here I aim to demonstrate that his response to Schopenhauer's metaphysics of will and the associated ethics of compassion includes elements that turn out to be essential for that project. Firstly, Schopenhauer's monism proposes that the experience of individuality is an illusion because, metaphysically speaking, all beings are one. This contrasts strongly with Nietzsche's understanding of the individual along naturalist and materialist lines. Secondly, Schopenhauer's pessimism, in which he understands suffering to lie at the heart of existence, contrasts strongly with the joyful embrace of human possibility that Nietzsche saw in the Homeric ideas of strength and personal abundance.

Schopenhauer's metaphysics of will

The relationship between Schopenhauer's monistic metaphysics and his ethics is not, however, as straightforward as it may seem from the descriptions of it I have offered thus far. What seems at first glance to be a reasonable structural parallel between an underlying unity of all things and the expression of compassion for someone who suffers turns out to be a complex problem. David E. Cartwright has provided extensive analysis of these issues in Schopenhauer and presents two key problems. This first is the problem of motivational pluralism. Cartwright argues that there is an inherent tension in the idea that there are many motivations for an action at the experiential level (altruism, malice, egoism) and yet a singular metaphysical reality underneath. It is unclear, even in Schopenhauer's original presentation, how the individual can be differentiated at the motivational or experiential level and unified with all other individuals at the ontological or metaphysical level. The second problem that Cartwright raises involves the two different (and perhaps competing) explanations to resolve this problem, one psychological and the other metaphysical.[6]

For Cartwright, the tension between motivational pluralism and metaphysical monism[7] arises because Schopenhauer provides a catalogue of four basic incentives for action: one's own well-being, one's own woe, another's well-being and another's woe.[8] We might call these motivations egoism, asceticism, compassion and malice. In Schopenhauer's approach, only compassion has moral worth. The question at hand is how Schopenhauer describes the transition between his monistic metaphysics and these four motivations for action in the world. In seeking a solution, Cartwright uses the terminology of 'character':

> [According to Schopenhauer] The behavior of evil characters, which expresses that others are nonegos, is not metaphysically warranted, since individuality is merely apparent. Good characters, whose conduct expresses that others are an 'I once more', engage in conduct that is metaphysically warranted.[9]

The four motivations described above therefore become grounded in two character types: good and evil, only the first of which is metaphysically warranted. These occur in the realm of everyday experience, but only the good character types are expressed behind the veil of everyday experience, that is, in the metaphysical world.

We can see in Cartwright's interpretation the idea that the individual stands with one foot in each of these worlds, so to speak. They stand at the interface of metaphysics and ethics, one foot in the invisible world of metaphysical monism and the other in the experienced world of human action. Cartwright invokes a complex set of ideas to explain this interface: character, conduct and metaphysical warrant. What is clear is that the individual has a functional role in translating between metaphysics and ethics. If the individual is of good character, they will express the unitive metaphysics of will by acting with compassion, through which they recognize the other person to be an 'I once more'. Thus, their conduct is more or less a direct expression of metaphysical monism – the other and the self are the same. If they are of bad character, they will not allow this metaphysical monism to be passed through to the world of appearance, so to speak. This is manifested in acts of malice or egoism by which they deny the underlying metaphysical union between themselves and the other. Interestingly, asceticism isn't addressed using this approach.

In *World as Will and Representation* (*WWR*) Schopenhauer addresses this question of character directly. He uses three categories in his analysis: the 'good', the 'just' and the 'bad', outlined in *WWR* Volume 1, sections 65–67. Here a person's character determines their response to others. The just person will refrain from injuring others while seeking their own well-being because

> He *again recognises* his own inner being, namely the will-to-live as thing-in-itself, in the phenomenon of another.[10]

The good person goes one step further. They actively seek the well-being of others even at personal expense. This is expressed as a feature of their innate character through which they are capable of 'self-conquest'. They do not merely refrain from injuring others but actively seek 'positive benevolence and well-doing'.[11] This is because the good person has an intuition that the experiential distinction between themselves and others is a deception. They do not merely recognize themselves *in* the other, as with the just. They recognize themselves *as* the other. Schopenhauer defines the person who gives to others out of benevolence, even injuring themselves in the process, as follows:

> he *makes less distinction than is usually made between himself and others* ... He recognises immediately, and without reasons or arguments, that the in-itself of his own phenomenon is also that of others ...[12]

The good and the just respond this way because each possesses, in their own way and to varying degrees, an intuitive experience of an underlying, noumenal 'reality' of metaphysical union between themselves and others. This accounts for both compassion for others and asceticism towards oneself, similar to the Christian idea of self-sacrifice we considered in the previous chapter.

The person of bad character, by contrast, lives only in the phenomenon of difference, which contradicts the underlying metaphysical 'reality' of union. This manifests in

> an excessively vehement will-to-live [that is] involved in the *principium individuationis* [and] confines itself to the complete difference, established by this latter principle, between his person and all others.[13]

The person of bad character is involved only in the world of appearance (the *principium individuationis*), which is by definition the world of differentiation. Their lived experience, therefore, contradicts their underlying metaphysical unity.

Thus, we find that in Schopenhauer's analysis a person's character is evaluated by the degree to which their response to others aligns with the underlying metaphysical union of all brings. People of bad character are unaligned: *despite* the metaphysical reality of the ontological union of all things, they act with malice. The just are somewhat more aligned with this metaphysical reality in that they do not actively seek another's woe. They act with egoism, namely, for their own benefit and aiming to do no harm. The good person, on the other hand, actively seeks the well-being of others even at his or her own expense. This represents maximal alignment with reality and can therefore be accorded moral worth and it incorporates compassion that receives its highest expression when combined with personal sacrifice, with asceticism.

This, then, helps us to understand Cartwright's idea of metaphysical warrant.[14] For him, Schopenhauer's schema assigns moral value to action on the basis of the degree to which it is aligned with the underlying metaphysical union of all beings. I make the observation that that this approach places the individual at the intersection of metaphysics and ethics, as a kind of conversion or translation point. Because of the individual's innate character, the metaphysical reality of ontological union is passed through to experience to different degrees. Bad character obstructs this passing through of metaphysical reality into experienced reality.

The idea that the individual is a construct that stands at the intersection of the experienced world and the 'real' world to mediate alignment between moral action and metaphysical structures can be seen directly in Schopenhauer. His metaphysics of the will establishes a strict separation between experience and reality. Moral conduct belongs to the former and the underlying metaphysical ground for evaluating such conduct belongs to the latter. Sections 63–67 of *The World as Will and Representation* (vol. 1) apply this dualism to the individual:

> the eyes of the individual are clouded, as the Indians say, by the veil of Maya. To him is revealed not the thing-in-itself, but only the phenomenon in time and space, in the *principium individuationis* ... In this form of his limited knowledge he sees not the inner nature of things which are one, but its phenomena as separated, detached, innumerable, very different, and indeed opposed.[15]

This text presents the individual as a participant in both metaphysical and experiential worlds, but with limited knowledge of the metaphysical. In order to access metaphysical reality, the individual requires a transcendent experience in which the illusion of difference and separation is overcome and replaced with a direct perception of this underlying union. This union is constituted by a metaphysical understanding of will: 'the will is the in-itself of every phenomenon'.[16] Whatever things may appear to be in experience, metaphysically speaking, everything is will.

This unitive, monistic metaphysics has consequences not only for how the individual experiences things other than themselves but how they experience and understand their own reality. The unique personhood of the individual as different from and separate from other individuals is a deception. Schopenhauer goes even further: the deceptive character of experienced reality actually constitutes personhood:

> the person is mere phenomenon, and its difference from other individuals, and exemption from the sufferings they bear, rest merely on the form of the phenomenon.[17]

In my view, we find here an irreconcilable tension in Schopenhauer's presentation of the individual. On the one hand, the individual stands at the boundary that spans the real and the experienced, and they translate the underlying metaphysical union of all things into moral action to varying degrees dependent on their character. On the other hand, the individual does not exist in reality, but is merely part of the experienced world, and is constituted through the deceptive character of the experienced world. Thus, Schopenhauer effectively denies the existence of the individual while relying on the translational power of the individual's character for evaluating action. The individual becomes able to realize moral action in the world and, in a sense become real themselves, only at a moment when they do not actually exist.

We find, then, that mystical self-destruction lies at the heart of Schopenhauer's morality. At this point one might pause to reflect on the pessimistic nature of Schopenhauer's philosophy in general: the metaphysical idea of an underlying union of all things is not benign. It is, in Schopenhauer's words, 'evil'.[18] The will to live is by definition the will to suffer. The ultimate solution for suffering is withdrawal from life, and, indeed, from all others. Personal annihilation is the outcome of Schopenhauer's presentation of the individual.

In this respect Cartwright's description of the problem of motivational pluralism is not so much a problem as it is a recognition of Schopenhauer's pessimism, in which difference itself is the source of the deception that underlies the destruction of personality. In the experienced world there are many motivations for action. Also in this world, there are many different individuals separately expressing their various motivations through a multiplicity of actions. In reality, according to Schopenhauer, these individuals do not exist separately: they are part of a single, suffering being. The degree to which a person's character allows them to be deceived by the experience of difference corresponds to the degree to which a person acts morally. Presumably, however, these actions themselves and the motivations that underlie them only happen in the world of experience, and therefore are themselves not real. The only thing that is real is a unitive experience of suffering that lies at the heart of all existence. Not only is the individual suspended in the crucible of their self-destruction, which is actually not real, the only thing that is real is the metaphysically grounded experience of suffering.

The issue highlighted above, where the individual is both required by Schopenhauer for understanding moral action and declared not to exist in reality, has been identified by Cartwright as a difference between psychological and metaphysical explanations of Schopenhauer's morality:

> Schopenhauer believed that the phenomenon of pity could not be explained psychologically, [it can] only be explained by his metaphysics. *Mitleid* is possible, he argued, because the separation between individuals is only apparent; ontologically we are all one—expressions of the singular metaphysical will. There is, according to Schopenhauer, no ontological gap between beings.[19]

For Cartwright, the relation between self and other in Schopenhauer is best understood in metaphysical terms, through his idea of metaphysical warrant, which itself depends on an understanding of the individual as translating metaphysical reality into the world of experience through acts of compassion. As we have seen, however, this idea rests on a paradox where the individual both exists and does not exist.

Reginster offers an alternative view, in which Schopenhauer's explanation of the process through which an individual identifies with the other and thereby develops a response to their suffering is entirely psychological.[20] He proposes that Schopenhauer sees the self as will inasmuch as the world is will. From this premise, he develops Schopenhauerian concepts of knowledge, resignation, diversion and reflection. For him, the Schopenhauerian individual is not determined by mystical access to their own annihilation but rather by their cognitive relations. Here, the individual relates to themself differently to the way they relate to all other things:

> Schopenhauer certainly seems right on one central point: if some object is to count as me or mine, I must have a special cognitive relation to it — whether it is special by virtue of being 'immediate,' or in some other way, I shall leave undecided — that is to say, there is, in the individual, 'a difference between the relation of his knowledge to this one object and its relation to all others.'[21]

Reginster analyses several psychological constructs in this context. In particular, he analyses resignation and contemplation as experiences that express two different relationships between the will and knowledge. On the one hand, knowledge of the inevitability of frustration brings about resignation. On the other hand, knowledge as the capability to observe oneself objectively leads to contemplation. In resignation the will is quieted through self-suppression, in contemplation the will allows knowledge momentary respite from its servitude.[22] Where Cartwright's analysis leads down a mystical path to the recognition of one's own ontological annihilation, Reginster's analysis leads to a similarly pessimistic outcome: either the quieting of the will to live in resignation or release from the demands of the will to live in contemplation.

This leads to what Reginster calls 'the paradox of reflection.'[23] In reflection knowledge releases the self from self-imprisonment by negating that 'special' mode of cognition by which the self is differentiated from other objects. Knowledge breaks down the distinction between self and the world. The paradox that arises here is that the individual experiences at one and the same time alienation from themselves and alienation from the world. This leaves the self with nowhere to 'be'. According to this theory, the self is not annihilated but rather excluded. In other words, in his attempt to understand Schopenhauer's theory of the self on purely psychological grounds, Reginster arrives at a conclusion that is as pessimistic as the metaphysical approach, at least with regards to the possibility and reality of the individual.

Both Reginster and Cartwright provide an account of Schopenhauer's philosophy in which the reality of the individual comes into question. From Reginster's psychological perspective, the individual is caught in an unresolved paradox, where the experience of self-reflection works so as to annihilate the self. From Cartwright's metaphysical perspective, the self stands between the metaphysical and the experienced worlds and translates between them to the extent that they recognize they do not exist. Interestingly, this approach might provide a solution to the problem of self-reflection articulated by Reginster. Perhaps self-reflection can be understood not as a cognitive or psychological activity of a 'self' but as an intuitive mode of knowing in which the annihilation of the self comes to consciousness.

In any case, there remain complex problems if we are to try to develop a coherent picture of the individual from Schopenhauer's philosophy. Indeed, this problem can be understood to lie at the core of Nietzsche's rejection of it. For Nietzsche, it is important to articulate in naturalistic terms what an individual is. We will see this in later chapters. For the moment, I suggest that many of the problems in analysing Schopenhauer's philosophy are made easier if we foreground Schopenhauer's mysticism. By consistently emphasizing the place of mystical experience in Schopenhauer's philosophy, we can resolve, for example this problem of cognition and self-reflection. In my view, Schopenhauer bases his morality on a primary, direct experience of a metaphysical reality that arises in mystical-ascetic practice. By definition, this experience cannot be thought rationally or expressed verbally.

For example, in discussing the value of ascetic self-denial in *WWR* Volume 1, Schopenhauer contrasts the intuitive knowledge of the ascetic with their creedal or rational knowledge. For him, intuitive knowledge of metaphysical union trumps creedal variations:

> Different as were the dogmas [of the Christians, Hindus and Buddhists] that were impressed on their faculty of reason, the inner, direct and intuitive knowledge from which alone all virtue and holiness can come is nevertheless expressed in precisely the same way in the conduct of life.[24]

This non-rational and non-verbal experience of underlying metaphysical union takes precedence over cognition and provides the interpretive framework for rational expression. For him, all empirical data is evaluated against metaphysical criteria. Schopenhauer's mystical approach is sceptical of experience and explicit knowledge of that experience. Therefore, against

Cartwright, his philosophy cannot be considered truly empirical.[25] This is further expressed in the value Schopenhauer ascribes to asceticism and self-renunciation. It is a withdrawal from, and rejection of, the experience of life:

> Thus it may be that the inner nature of holiness, of self-renunciation, of mortification of one's own will, of asceticism, is here for the first time expressed in abstract terms and free from everything mythical, as *denial of the will-to-live*.[26]

Schopenhauer may have a drive to explain the phenomenon of asceticism empirically, which, as we have seen before, takes place as the individual translates between the metaphysical world and the experienced world. However, his metaphysical interpretation of existence undermines the value of empirical experience and, further, places the highest value on precisely its opposite. However, against Reginster, this cannot be considered a psychological or rational process either. Rather, for him, mystical experience of the union of all being leads to an implicit appreciation of the moral value of compassion and the realization within individuals that they do not exist *qua* individual. They exist, instead, as part of the metaphysical monad that is the will to suffer. This is a fundamentally pessimistic stance on human experience at many levels as described above, and it comes to its highest expression in ascetic practice.

Against monism

There are several important themes here that shape Nietzsche's thought as he begins to develop his own distinctive ethics based on Homeric contest. I will focus on just two ideas that rise to prominence as we investigate his critical response to Schopenhauer. These are 1) Schopenhauer's privative and ascetic stance, which is expressed as a pessimism in which suffering stands at the heart of all existence and 2) his annihilation of individuality through the monistic metaphysics of will. I show here that Nietzsche's new Homerism responds directly to these two ideas by proposing abundance instead of privation and difference instead of monism. Further, I show that not only does he respond to these practical implications of Schopenhauer's theory, but he also rejects its metaphysical basis.

This contrasts with Cartwright's understanding of the relationship between Nietzsche and Schopenhauer. For him, Nietzsche's critique of Schopenhauer is unsuccessful because it focuses too narrowly on psychological explanations for compassion and does not address the underlying metaphysics.[27] What I aim to show is that Nietzsche addresses both the metaphysical and psychological aspects of Schopenhauer's annihilation of the individual. Nietzsche's concern is to restore the individual without relying on metaphysics, and to do so in such a way that the individual can be conceived as a superabundant Homeric hero.

Nietzsche's relationship to Schopenhauer is complex, and it developed over the course of his philosophically productive years. Despite this change and development, we can see that Nietzsche's concern with Schopenhauer's metaphysics was pervasive. While the focus of this thesis is the period 1881–7, we can see in very early writings, even during his most fervent Schopenhauerian period in the 1860s, that Nietzsche harboured serious doubts about Schopenhauer's metaphysical project. For example, in notebook writings from the period 1867–8, in a discussion of will and the 'thing-in-itself', Nietzsche writes:

> Schopenhauer's supporting tissue becomes tangled in his hands, least of all as a result of a certain ineptitude of its maker, but mainly because the world cannot be fitted into the system as comfortably as Schopenhauer had hoped ... [28]

Nietzsche was never an unthinking devotee: from the beginning of his Schopenhauerian conversion in 1865, he thought that Schopenhauer's metaphysics and its obliteration of difference was problematic. This concern runs right through Nietzsche's responses to Schopenhauer up until the publication of *HAH* in 1878, where he confirms for his readers his complete rejection of Schopenhauer. Nietzsche's more detailed responses to Schopenhauer, which include his reassertion of the individual and rejection of asceticism, spring from this underlying issue: Nietzsche could not support metaphysical monism or, indeed, any kind of metaphysics at all.

The reality of the individual

There are several texts during 1881–7, the period most relevant to this book, that discuss, either obliquely or directly, this distinctively Schopenhauerian question of the dissolution of the individual into a metaphysical monad. There is a positive and a negative aspect to this. On the positive side, Nietzsche proposes that the individual truly exists.[29] On the negative side, Nietzsche rejects all attempts to dissolve the personal identity or particularity of an individual through ideas such as compassion and altruism.

GS §99, *Schopenhauer's followers*, demonstrates key elements of this critique. The text aims to show that Richard Wagner,[30] while claiming to be

Schopenhauerian, was only attracted to parts of Schopenhauer's philosophy. Wagner's heroes embody a philosophy that was, in Nietzsche's view, quite opposed to Schopenhauer's pessimism. In the course of this discussion Nietzsche explains Schopenhauer's philosophy by connecting his metaphysics to his dissolution of the individual and its outworking in an ethics of compassion premised on a pessimistic view of existence:

> Schopenhauer's mystical embarrassments and evasions in those places where the factual thinker let himself be seduced and corrupted by the vain urge to be the unriddler of the world; the indemonstrable doctrine of One Will ... the *denial of the individual* ... *development* [as] only an illusion ... his ecstatic reveries on *genius* ... the nonsense about *compassion* and how, as the source of all morality, it enables one to make the break through the *principium individuationis* ... these and other such *excesses* and vices of the philosopher are always what is accepted first of all and made into a matter of faith ....

In this text Nietzsche programmatically outlines the logic of Schopenhauer's approach, connecting metaphysics, the individual and ethics, and he expresses his opposition to Schopenhauer's attempt to connect metaphysics with ethics as a set of 'mystical embarrassments and evasions'.

In the critique that follows he goes on to focus on the issue of the destruction of the individual by pointing to Wagner's inconsistencies as a disciple of Schopenhauer. Nietzsche's argument is that, despite claiming to be an altruistic Schopenhauerian, the heroes that Wagner creates demonstrate 'the innocence of the utmost selfishness', which he sees as irreconcilable with Schopenhauer's annihilation of the individual and his emphasis on sacrifice and pity:

> nothing goes so directly against the spirit of Schopenhauer as what is genuinely Wagnerian in Wagner's heroes: I mean the innocence of the utmost selfishness...

For Nietzsche, against Schopenhauer, Wagner's art celebrates the individual in all the particularity of their personal identity. They are 'heroes', a term that invokes a Homeric context. Further, Nietzsche claims that Wagner himself embodies this problem. His artistry is based on his own particularity as a heroic genius, and yet his thought had become captivated by Schopenhauer's errors:

> Let us remain faithful to Wagner in what is *true* and original in him — and especially, as his disciples, by remaining faithful to ourselves in what is true and original in us ... Enough that his life is justified before itself and remains justified ... *Our* life, too, shall be justified before ourselves! We too shall freely and fearlessly, in innocent selfishness, grow and blossom from ourselves!

In Nietzsche's view, this contradiction between Wagner's heroic artistry and his intellectual 'delusion' as a follower of Schopenhauer is grounds for optimism. Despite the powerfully seductive nature of Schopenhauer's destruction of the individual, Wagner was able to celebrate the individual through his art. Nietzsche concludes this text with a quotation from his own 'Untimely Meditation' on Wagner's art, writing that the freedom of the individual is such that 'being honest in evil is still better than losing oneself to the morality of tradition'. In contrast to Schopenhauer's dissolution of the self and denial of the individual, Nietzsche here outlines with extreme brevity his nascent concept of an individual who is unique and self-generated, and for whom difference from others is to be preserved and celebrated.[31] This foreshadows a fuller description of the Homeric theme of difference and its role in Nietzsche's ethics of heroic friendship.

Another important text in Nietzsche's response to Schopenhauer is *GS* §127, *Aftereffects of the most ancient religiosity*. Here he provides three propositions that are explicitly developed in order to refute Schopenhauer:

> Against him I offer these propositions: first, in order for willing to come about, a representation of pleasure or displeasure is needed. Secondly, that a violent stimulus is experienced as pleasure or pain is a matter of the *interpreting* intellect, which, to be sure, generally works without our being conscious of it; and one and the same stimulus *can* be interpreted as pleasure or pain. Thirdly, only in intellectual beings do pleasure, pain, and will exist; the vast majority of organisms has nothing like it.

The context for this section is a general critique of what he thinks is an overly simplistic concept of will in which it is turned into an absolute given and is considered as a simple and effective cause. In critiquing Schopenhauer's doctrine of will, Nietzsche attempts to provide a materialistically oriented psychological explanation of will. In short: against Schopenhauer's simplistic metaphysics, Nietzsche presents willing as a complex natural phenomenon.

Given the critique already outlined in *GS* §99, this passage can be understood as an inversion of Schopenhauer's concept of will so that it is grounded now in the empirical reality of an individual. Will is not given as a metaphysical absolute from which the individual derives their existence in the observed world. Rather, willing is derived from a physical stimulus that an individual intellect interprets either as pleasure or as pain. Here will is a phenomenon based on the experiences of an individual as an embodied being in the world of experience and observation. Further, it applies only to intellectual beings and cannot necessarily be attributed to the 'vast majority' of organisms that do not possess an 'intellect'.

Where Schopenhauer proposed a metaphysical explanation, Nietzsche proposes an empirical one, and where Schopenhauer dissolved the individual, Nietzsche asserts its existence as a natural phenomenon.[32] This emphasis on observed reality, where the differences between individuals are evident, is a critical element of his Homeric ethos of contest that arises, at least in part, from his turn against Schopenhauer.

Against asceticism

Not only does Nietzsche oppose Schopenhauer's dissolution of the individual, but he also opposes his pessimism. In *GS* §370, entitled 'What is romanticism?', Nietzsche explains his following Schopenhauer in search of a solution to the problem of suffering as a mistake. He differentiates his approach from Schopenhauer's by identifying two types of sufferers and two corresponding types of philosophical inquiry:

> Every art, every philosophy can be considered a cure and aid in the service of growing, struggling life: they always presuppose suffering and sufferers. But there are two types of sufferers: first, those who suffer from a *superabundance of life* ... then, those who suffer from an *impoverishment of life* ... All romanticism in art and in knowledge fits the dual needs of the latter type, as did (and do) Schopenhauer and Richard Wagner ...

The two types of sufferers are those that suffer from personal superabundance and those that suffer from personal impoverishment or privation. The kind of art and philosophy that suits the former is Dionysian and the kind that suits the latter is Schopenhauerian/Wagnerian. He goes on to explain his view that both the desire for immortalizing (for 'being') and the desire for destroying ('becoming') are ambiguous. Each might arise either from abundance or from impoverishment:

> Nowadays I avail myself of this primary distinction concerning all aesthetic values: in every case I ask, 'Is it hunger or superabundance that have become creative here?' ... The desire for *destruction*, for change and for becoming can be the expression of an overflowing energy pregnant with the future (my term for this is, as is known, 'Dionysian'); but it can also be the hatred of the ill-constituted, deprived, and underprivileged one who destroys and *must* destroy because what exists, indeed all existence, all being, outrages and provokes him ...

The will to *immortalize* also requires a dual interpretation. It can be prompted, first, by gratitude and love ... spreading a Homeric light and splendour over all things. But it can also be the tyrannical will of someone who suffers deeply, who struggles, is tortured, and who ... takes revenge on all things by forcing, imprinting, branding *his* image on them, the image of *his* torture. The latter is *romantic pessimism* in its most expressive form, be it Schopenhauer's philosophy of will or Wagner's music — romantic pessimism, the last *great* event in the fate of our culture.

Here the difference between the Dionysian and the Romantic is that the former arises from abundance and the latter arises from privation. The Dionysian sufferer may desire destruction because of 'an overflowing energy pregnant with the future', or they may desire immortalization prompted by gratitude and love, a 'Homeric light and splendour'. The Romantic sufferer may desire destruction because of their hatred of existence and desire to escape it, or they may desire to immortalize something by seeking to 'stamp as a binding law and compulsion' their own particular suffering on the world at large. In order to avoid this ambiguity Nietzsche proposes his evaluative criterion for 'aesthetic values'. They are evaluated positively or negatively depending on whether they arise from abundance or from impoverishment.

We are now in a position to see more clearly, and more profoundly, Nietzsche's stance against asceticism. For Nietzsche, Schopenhauer's asceticism arises from the intersection of his annihilation of the individual and his privative assumptions about human existence. That is, in the Schopenhauerian scheme, when the individual finally and intuitively grasps their ontological unity with the world as will, they discover the infinitude of suffering that arises directly from existence. The ascetic relieves this suffering either destructively through resentment or passively by 'quieting the will to live'. In either case, they end up opposing existence itself. Nietzsche's response to this is opposite: the great individual responds to suffering from the deep well of their personal superabundance. This does not eliminate suffering but rather the need to alleviate it, precisely by asserting the ontological primacy of the self-grounding and overflowing individual. He explains it as follows:

> He who is richest in fullness of life, the Dionysian god and man, can allow himself not only the sight of what is terrible and questionable but also the terrible deed and every luxury of destruction, decomposition, negation; in his case, what is evil, nonsensical, and ugly almost seems acceptable because of an overflow in procreating, fertilizing forces capable of turning any desert into bountiful farmland.

Both Schopenhauer's altruist and Nietzsche's hero are confronted with the question of suffering. The former sinks into oblivion in the face of it because of their personal privation, the latter makes it productive and luxurious from their inner bounty.

We see this approach to suffering developed throughout Nietzsche's work. The most important development of this theme for the purposes of this book is its expansion to include not only Schopenhauer's metaphysics specifically, but metaphysics in general. One example of this that is particularly relevant is the section titled 'On the Hinterworldly' in *TSZ*.[33] In this text, Nietzsche brings together his critique of Christianity and his critique of Schopenhauer into a general critique of metaphysics. Despite the characteristic opacity of the language in this text, and the occasional unreliability of Zarathustra as a mouthpiece for Nietzsche's own ideas, in my view we see here that as Zarathustra rejects the idea that anything lies 'beyond mankind in reality', he expresses Nietzsche's desire to abandon metaphysics:

> Oh my brothers, this god that I created was of human make and madness, like all gods! … Believe me, my brothers! It was the body that despaired of the earth – then it heard the belly of being speak to it. And then it wanted to break head first through the ultimate walls, and not only with its head, beyond to the 'other world.' But 'the other world' is well hidden from humans, that dehumaned, inhuman world that is a heavenly nothing. And the belly of being does not speak to humans, unless as a human.

Nietzsche's target here seems to be very general. He is alluding, through Zarathustra, to his brief enchantment with Schopenhauer's philosophy and also the Christian ideas of the afterlife. That is, in seeking an answer to the problem of suffering both posit a metaphysic, an 'otherworld' or 'hinterworld'.

In this context the obscure phrase 'the belly of being' appears to mean something similar to the 'thing-in-itself'.[34] In the search for a solution to the problem of suffering the sufferer, 'the body that despaired of the earth', hears 'the belly of being' speaking. That is, the metaphysically understood 'thing-in-itself' seeks to address the problem of suffering and in doing so proposes a 'heavenly nothing'. Thus, this text expresses Nietzsche's scepticism about the metaphysical enterprise in both its Christian and Schopenhauerian forms as they seek to address real human beings in the context of their experience of suffering.

Zarathustra goes on to propose an alternative. Instead of heavenly nothings, Zarathustra speaks about the 'meaning of the earth' and its relationship to the body, that is, to natural existence. I take this to mean that Nietzsche's alternative to the metaphysical proposals offered by Schopenhauer and Christianity is a thoroughly naturalistic one. In critiquing the Hinterworldly Zarathustra claims that their belief is

> Indeed, not in hinterworlds and redeeming blood drops, but instead they too believe most in the body, and their own body is to them their thing in itself. But to them it is a sickly thing: and gladly would they jump out of their skin. Hence they listen to the preachers of death and they preach hinterworlds themselves. Hear, my brothers, hear the voice of the healthy body . . . it speaks of the meaning of the earth.

This text echoes the sentiment of *GS* §370 and its discussion of two different types of sufferers in that the Romantic and the Dionysian are here recast as the sick and the healthy, respectively. Further, we see the terms 'heavenly nothing' and the 'meaning of the earth' appear in structural symmetry with the ideas of the 'sickly' body and the 'healthy' body. The problem with the 'heavenly nothing' is with those who formulate it: their experience of embodied life is that of the sickly, they want to flee from themselves, and so they devise the afterlife, or an invisible world 'beyond' mere experience, they devise 'hinterworlds'. By way of contrast, the healthy body is capable of honest speech (unlike the 'belly of being') and it 'speaks of the meaning of the earth'. If we combine all of these metaphors, similes and binary symmetries, we see here that Nietzsche proposes as his alternative the embrace of embodied experience, including its suffering, as a healthy alternative to the sickliness of metaphysics.

Conclusions

Nietzsche's analysis of Schopenhauer's philosophy includes criticism both of Schopenhauer's dissolution of the individual on the basis of metaphysical monism and his pessimistic interpretation of the experience on an assumption of personal privation. Against Schopenhauer, he asserts his concept of an abundant and heroic individual as the foundation for ethics. His rejection of Schopenhauer means that the question of suffering is no longer the critical question for ethics to answer. In Nietzsche's alternative approach, an abundant individual can embrace even the ugliest or most painful elements of experience. Thus, the themes of his new Homerism – personal superabundance and individual difference – stand against Schopenhauer's philosophy, in similar ways to the ways in which they enabled him to turn away from the Christian morality of love.

More than a rejection of metaphysical monism, however, we see in Nietzsche's turn away from Schopenhauer a rejection of metaphysics in general and, specifically, metaphysics as a foundation for ethics. We can see in the arguments he mounts against metaphysically grounded ethics that his alternative will include an emphasis on abundance and on difference in the realm of actual human experience. In the following chapter I begin to describe how Nietzsche develops this positive alternative by drawing on evolutionary biology in order to 'update' Homeric contest with the most contemporary empirical tools he had available to him. We will see, at the end of this, that Nietzsche's alternative is a naturalistic ethics based on personal superabundance and difference between individuals within a framework of heroic contest. The relationship in which these dynamics are best expressed will turn out to be a form of friendship based on a profound understanding of each person's internal contest and a desire to see them flourish. It is difficult to imagine an outcome more opposed to Schopenhauer than this one.

4

A naturalist alternative

I have argued in the preceding chapters that Nietzsche rejects both Christian and Schopenhauerian morality and the metaphysical enterprises they are founded on. Moral ideas such as the Christian valorizing of *agape* love and Schopenhauer's morality of compassion are problematic for him. I have proposed that his alternative approach breathes the air of heroic contest, and that he develops from this classical Greek context ideals such as personal abundance and individual difference to support an agonistic ethics, and I have foreshadowed that this ethics features friendship. These ideals, at least as far as Nietzsche is concerned, stand directly opposed to the privative pessimism and monistic reductionism of Christian and Schopenhauerian metaphysical moralizing.

In this chapter I argue that in order to develop this alternative approach Nietzsche drew on the scientific methodologies of his day, as well as incorporating elements of materialist classical and contemporaneous philosophy. Most significantly, in my view, he adapted the classical notion of ancient Greek *agon*, or contest, by incorporating developments from the field of evolutionary biology. By bringing these influences together, I aim to show that Nietzsche develops a new interpretation of contest as an ethics in which friendship emerges as the ideal form of social relationship. As we examine the influence of the then-emergent field of evolutionary biology on Nietzsche's ethics, we see that he both affirms and rejects different elements of it and is especially antagonistic towards the figure of Charles Darwin. While this ambivalent stance complicates the picture, I will show that Nietzsche nevertheless incorporates important elements of evolutionary thinking into what I call his new Homerism as he tries to free his ethics from any kind of metaphysical foundation.

The question of Nietzsche's stance on metaphysics, and the related question of his naturalism, is not settled in the scholarly literature. There is a significant tradition of interpretation in which Nietzsche is thought not to reject metaphysics but to develop it. Perhaps most influentially, Martin Heidegger, writing in Germany in the early to mid-twentieth century, proposed that Nietzsche was the last great metaphysician in the Western tradition. He argued that this was demonstrated in the doctrines of the will to power and the eternal return of the same. For Heidegger, Nietzsche completes the circle of Western metaphysics that began with Plato.[1] Significant figures following Heidegger have argued similarly, particularly with reference to Nietzsche's idea of the will to power.[2]

A contemporary scholar in this tradition is Tsarina Doyle who, while disagreeing with Heidegger's views on the specifics of Nietzsche's approach, nevertheless argues that Nietzsche does not reject metaphysics in favour of naturalism and instead offers a metaphysics that is heavily influenced by Immanuel Kant. She claims that Nietzsche develops a distinctive approach to metaphysics that illuminates its continuities with naturalism. In responding to the problem of nihilism, she claims that Nietzsche proposes a metaphysics of the will to power that emerges from an implicitly understood continuity between mind (conceived metaphysically) and the world (conceived naturalistically). This, she argues, is how Nietzsche proposes values, which demonstrates that he is not a nihilist after all.[3]

Church is another scholar who sees an affinity between Kant and Nietzsche, and on this basis takes issue with the claim that Nietzsche is a naturalist.[4] In looking at Nietzsche's relationship to ancient classical ideals, Church argues that Nietzsche's ethical ideal includes ideas about individuality, agency and human aesthetic capacities that cannot, at least in Nietzsche's conceptual universe, be derived from a naturalistic account of human being.[5]

It seems to me that there is a lot of value in further developing the relationship between Nietzsche and Kant, particularly in developing a concept of Nietzsche as an ethical idealist and understanding Kant's influence on him. However, it also seems to me that these scholars who emphasize Nietzsche's interest in metaphysics can't fully explain the breadth and depth of Nietzsche's critique of metaphysics. While there is little doubt that there are some texts that admit a metaphysical interpretation, there are many more that stand against metaphysical enterprise in philosophy and ethics. In my view, when understood together and as a whole, Nietzsche's works present a philosopher seeking to move away from metaphysics towards a materialist and naturalist approach.

There are many scholars who, like me, question metaphysical interpretations of Nietzsche and assert that Nietzsche rejects metaphysical thinking.[6] These interpreters tend to refer to Nietzsche's approach as a form of 'naturalism' that is either post- or anti-metaphysical, whether Kantian or otherwise. Among this group of scholars there remain different ways of understanding 'naturalism' and, at least in my view, not all of them successfully exclude metaphysics in a strict way.

In what follows I consider some of these different ways of understanding Nietzsche's naturalism as a context for his response to the field of evolutionary biology and his developing understanding of a renewed agonistic ethics.[7] I have argued in the preceding chapters that Nietzsche's rejection of metaphysical approaches to morality reflects his interest in classical ideas of abundance and difference. However, in order to successfully reject metaphysics and retain these ideals, he requires a new foundation for them, one that does not rely on metaphysical ideas such as the gods and fate (*moira*), as was common in the classical period of Greek literature. What we will see in examining his naturalism is a certain ambivalence towards this question that can be understood with reference to the two touchstones of Nietzsche's new Homerism – abundance and difference.

While evolutionary biology satisfies the requirement for difference in that it proposes a naturalistic explanation for the diversity of biological life, Nietzsche understands evolutionary biology to assume a privative understanding of nature, which does not satisfy his commitment to abundance as a precondition for his ethics. While he welcomes the evolutionary explanation of difference through the idea of genetic mutations that take effect over long periods of time, he rejects an understanding of natural selection in which individuals within a species are caught in a downward spiral, a fight to the death as it were, struggling simply to survive.[8] That is, by placing the natural sciences in a subordinate relationship to an overarching and thoroughgoing philosophical naturalism, Nietzsche thinks that he will be able to account for higher forms of cultural and individual expression, for example, in artistic accomplishment, which are not about mere survival.[9]

His counterargument to the privative understanding of nature presented by Darwinism is the ideal of abundance as it is expressed in contest. In his view, nature (including human life) is not characterized by privation but by abundance. For him, the distress that arises because of the conviction that living within nature as a human being is to live with deprivation and deficit is a peculiarly human trait. Further, for Nietzsche this is a peculiarly human distortion of the evidence. According to him, a truly scientific understanding of human beings as natural beings within the natural world would take as its basis the same underlying premise of abundance that a scientist observes within the rest of the natural world. Nietzsche outlines this argument in GS §349:

today's natural sciences have become so entangled in ... Darwinism with its incredibly one-sided doctrine of the 'struggle for existence' ... As a natural scientist, however, one should get out of one's human corner; and in nature, it is not distress which *rules*, but rather abundance, squandering – even to the point of absurdity. The struggle for survival is only an *exception*, a temporary restriction of the will to life; the great and small struggle revolves everywhere ... around power and in accordance with the will to power, which is simply the will to life.

This seems like a straightforward denial of Darwinism because of his objection to the idea of a 'struggle for existence'. However, what we will see is that Nietzsche also, and often without explicit recognition, adopts those elements of Darwinism that suit his interest in providing an anti-metaphysical description not only of natural diversity, but also of the kind of personal abundance that is required for higher human beings to successfully engage in higher friendship.

Nietzsche's naturalism

I characterize Nietzsche's naturalism as an attempt to unify pre-scientific ('Homeric') and scientific ways of understanding the natural world. One starting point for this is the observation that he approaches both scientific and ancient Greek thought as vulnerable forms of naturalism. For Nietzsche, both ways of thinking are readily deflected from their attempt to explain empirical phenomena in natural terms. When this happens, they unnecessarily (at least from Nietzsche's point of view) incorporate metaphysics. The Homeric literature can, for example, rely on metaphysical concepts such as the gods and *moira* in order to provide the outer limits of permissible behaviour for its heroes (*GS* §130).[10] Similarly, he claims that scientific thought can arise from a mistaken desire to establish completely objective truths and, in doing so, it can begin to draw on metaphysical concepts such as 'bodies, lines, planes, causes and effects, motion and rest, form and content' that are not empirical but rather 'articles of faith' (*GS* §§121, 112).

This ambiguous relationship to both scientific and ancient naturalism can be further understood by differentiating naturalism from materialism. This distinction in ancient thought is described by Irwin.[11] He demonstrates that the various forms of naturalism found in ancient Greek philosophy are not synonymous with materialism. With regard to early Greek thought in Homer and his immediate successors, Irwin writes:

Apparently, then, we might suppose, a complete naturalist, believing that everything is determined by the nature of the stuffs [read: material world] and their interactions, will have no need and no room for gods. This supposition, however, is far too simple to capture the naturalists' attitude to the divine. For in fact they say quite a lot about gods.[12]

Irwin gives the examples of *moira* within the Homeric tradition, the concept of the Forms in the Platonic tradition,[13] and the conception of the soul in the Aristotelian tradition.[14] Naturalism in antiquity, according to Irwin, can be thought of as an impulse to describe phenomena as ordered, a desire to outline laws or patterns that govern the existence of phenomena and their interactions. In describing such a system, a naturalist may or may not utilize metaphysical components. By way of contrast, a materialist will explicitly avoid including any metaphysical elements.

These strands of naturalism and materialism in classical thought provide a complex set of influences on Nietzsche. Tracing these influences is made even more difficult by the intellectual climate of nineteenth-century Germany, which itself included a significant materialist movement.[15] Nietzsche was no doubt influenced by this movement, both by its protagonists such as Feuerbach and by its critics such as Lange.[16]

One particularly important influence that relates directly to the scientific thought of Nietzsche's day and his interest in Homeric contest is the contribution of Wilhelm Roux and his biological notion of struggle.[17] Soderstrom has demonstrated that Roux contributed to the evolutionary idea of struggle for survival by thinking about it at a cellular level.[18] He shows that Roux's idea of a cellular struggle within an individual member of a species influenced Nietzsche's approach both to the body and to history, locating both within his idea of contest. For Nietzsche, the struggle within an individual's body is a physiological mechanism for interpreting experience, which is otherwise chaotic and devoid of structure. According to Soderstrom, Nietzsche understands these biological and historical mechanisms as cyclical movements of assimilation and resistance, leading first to wounding and then to re-emergence as newer and stronger beings. Further, on Soderstrom's reading, Nietzsche is understood to extend Roux's description of cellular struggle to the psychological and personal struggles within the individual and also between societies across history.

Taking this approach and elaborating on it, we can see that through his reading of Roux[19] Nietzsche adapts concepts from biological science to the conceptual world of the Homeric hero. In doing so, a new understanding of the function of contest within the life of the individual emerges. As we will see in

Chapter 6, one result of this is that heroic contest can now be internalized as a psychological phenomenon. For the moment, however, what is important is the more general point that Nietzsche incorporates elements of evolutionary biology into an overarching contest-based schema in order to replace the metaphysical elements of Homerism with (quasi-)scientific alternatives. In doing so, we will see that he reinterprets concepts such as natural selection, species change over time and random genetic mutation within this new schema.

Naturalism as scientism

We move now to consider some scholarly approaches to Nietzsche's naturalism. One school of thought relates Nietzsche's naturalism to his general interest in science and scientifically empirical analyses of human experience. For these scholars, the purpose of Nietzsche's naturalism is to extend scientific analysis of natural phenomena into the realm of social and psychological analysis, which would have been a novelty at the time. One proponent of this approach is Brian Leiter, who differentiates between a scientific naturalism that offers substantive explanations for phenomena and one that has strictly to do with the application of a scientific method to the question at hand.[20]

Leiter argues that Nietzsche's concern as a naturalist is not to do with substantive explanations but rather the application of scientific methodologies to philosophical questions.[21] Leiter's Nietzsche does not propose, for example, that only physical things exist (as a materialist might). Rather, Leiter's Nietzsche asserts that proposals for describing phenomena such as human social relationships ought to adopt a scientific method of analysis and description.[22] Leiter claims that Nietzsche's critique of morality achieves this by developing and applying his genealogical method to these kinds of questions. Nietzsche's genealogical method is understood here as something that Nietzsche creates in order to extend the methods of the hard sciences to personal and social concerns. Thus, if the methodology proved successful, Nietzsche would then be able to apply the method of genealogy to moral/ethical questions, and he could do so scientifically.[23]

This approach has limited value for this book. In my view, Nietzsche frequently makes substantive as well as methodological claims, a problem that Leiter himself acknowledges.[24] In failing to provide a basis for substantive claims about ethics in Nietzsche's work (such as the claim that he values heroic friendship as the highest form of social relationship), Leiter makes Nietzsche's naturalism irrelevant to resolving ethical dilemmas. On this view, Nietzsche's claims are to be evaluated merely in terms of how he got there, rather than what those claims actually are. This book is concerned with the substance of Nietzsche's claims.

There is, however, a second and perhaps more important problem with Leiter's approach that, once recognized, helps to advance our general understanding of Nietzsche's naturalism and his ambiguous relationship to science and scientific methods. When Leiter refers to Nietzsche's extension of scientific methods to social and psychological phenomena, he refers to this as Nietzsche's genealogical method. However, I would argue that Nietzsche does not always ground his substantive moral or ethical claims in his genealogical method. Further, there are times when Nietzsche opposes scientific methods to his genealogical method of analysing social and psychological concerns. This opposition to scientific methods can be seen in such aphorisms as those in *The Gay Science* which discuss the importance of error, subjectivity and passion for human survival and flourishing.[25]

The importance of error is emphasized in *GS* §37. Here Nietzsche argues that three errors have provided the foundation for the promotion of science: 1) the idea that science is compatible with theism, 2) that its truths are useful for life, and 3) that it is objective and dispassionate. Nietzsche's understanding of science is opposite: he understands it to promote atheism (*GS* §§109, 123), he thinks that scientific truth may in fact be harmful to human life and flourishing (*GS* §§111, 344), and that it arises from passions and individual dispositions rather than purely objective observations (*GS* §§113, 151).

Nietzsche's interest in the dual roles of error and emotion in scientific judgement provides the conceptual background for those aphorisms where he expresses scepticism about the value of scientific methods in general. This scepticism is not entirely consistent: there are texts in which Nietzsche is positively disposed to scientific approaches (*GS* §§46, 113, 293, *TSZ*, *Of the Tarantulas*, *Of Science*). There are also, however, important texts where Nietzsche criticizes science as something that commands commitment from people in the same way that religious faith does (e.g. *GS* §§344, 347, 373).[26]

In *GS* §151, for example, Nietzsche argues that scientific thinking stands in a complex relationship to questions of objectivity, truth and knowledge. As a result, scientific thinking is as susceptible to fulfilling humankind's metaphysical need as religion once was. The loss of religious foundations for the 'other world' does not mean the loss of the 'other world' altogether. The conclusion he comes to is that scientific thinking can be taken to furnish a person with an alternate 'other world', which, without a religious foundation, is 'this time only a metaphysical one and not a religious one'. For Nietzsche, this substitution of a religious-metaphysical world with a naturalist-metaphysical world is an error because the religious-metaphysical world was originally 'an error in the interpretation of certain natural events, an embarrassing lapse of the intellect'. There is, therefore, no intellectual virtue in providing a substitute for something that was inherently faulty to begin with.

Against Leiter, it seems to me that Nietzsche's naturalism is not a simple matter of extending an accepted scientific method to questions of social and psychological significance. The relationship between the natural sciences and the social sciences, as it may be understood today, is expressed by Nietzsche not as a simple application of the methods of the former to the data of the latter. There is, rather, a complex interplay between these domains, and the spectre of lapsing into metaphysics remains even when scientific methodologies are privileged.

This thought is expressed in an early form in *D* §427 and §453. In *D* §427 Nietzsche argues that philosophy is not simply an extension of scientific method but rather a transformation of the natural sciences into 'entertainment' through their beautification. In other words, the methods of the natural sciences establish provisional truths that can be transformed by philosophy so that they are brought into the light of ordinary human experience. In *D* §453, Nietzsche makes the argument that sciences such as psychology and sociology may well be an extension of the natural sciences, but that the methods and conclusions of the science of his day were not developed enough to provide a basis for these new forms of inquiry. Here he considers that scientific methods are in need of development and transformation in order to be applied to social and psychological phenomena.

These texts reveal a complex web of continuities and discontinuities between the scientific naturalism of the hard sciences and Nietzsche's quasi-scientific naturalistic equivocations in the domain of social and psychological analysis. Despite these complexities and ambiguities, there are notable themes that recur throughout. I will highlight one continuity and one discontinuity. The continuity is that Nietzsche clearly sees value in paying attention only to observable phenomena. This method of post-hoc observation and analysis is something that he sees in the natural sciences and that he wishes to apply to social and personal questions. It is also, at times, crucial to his critique of science. Nietzsche rejects scientific analysis when it abandons this principle (as, for example, in the concept of cause and effect). The way in which Nietzsche thinks this principle can be applied to social and personal questions is through the conduct of moral and social experiments (*D* §§164, 432; *GS* §§7, 41, 51, 324, 335, 356).

The discontinuity between Nietzsche's thinking and scientific methods relates to the problem of meaning, as opposed to mere description. The connection between Nietzsche's interest in the meaning of human existence and his naturalist approach has been taken up by a number of scholars who describe his naturalism specifically in terms of meaning-making. This offers an alternative to the emphasis on science and its role in his naturalism, exemplified by Leiter. In this alternative approach Nietzsche's naturalism is construed in terms of human experience exclusively: it is deeply and only concerned with human affairs and has as its goal the development of appropriate methods (i.e. 'naturalistic' methods) for exploring human experience and the embedded question of meaning. These scholars claim, in one way or another, that Nietzsche achieves this through a kind of intersection with scientific methods but not as an extension of them. Rather, his examination of human affairs involves discovering or creating methods of enquiry through a critical reflection on the nature and value of scientific methodologies, which results in a different set of those methods that are typically applied to the natural sciences.

Richard Schacht is one scholar who takes this approach.[27] For Schacht, Nietzsche's naturalism is an attempt to explain phenomena that are not well-suited to scientific analysis. He argues that meaning-making experiences are frequently the subject of Nietzsche's naturalistic interpretation of the world, encompassing cultural, linguistic, musical and other artisanal endeavours. His analysis focuses on Nietzsche's later use of the German term for 'sensibility'. This usage, he argues, is evidence that Nietzsche's naturalism cannot be narrowly construed as an extension of the natural sciences:

> In sum: for Nietzsche no naturalism is worth taking seriously that ignores or is clumsy in dealing with all that gives depth and richness to human reality—such as the dimension and character of human reality I have been discussing in terms of 'sensibilities' and what they make possible.[28]

It is these sensibilities (for example, appreciation of art) that Schacht uses to avoid reducing human experience to the domain of the natural sciences. This includes an assertion that even experiences that are not at all amenable to scientific investigation can still be explained naturalistically. As he puts it, naturalism in this sense is the idea that

> everything that comes to be in this world is the outcome of developments occurring within it that are owing *entirely* to its internal dynamics and the contingencies to which they give rise.[29]

For Schacht, Nietzsche's naturalism consists in the idea that the natural world is the only legitimate domain of investigation and that it contains within itself all of the explanatory resources for human (and other) experience. In contrast with Leiter, Schacht argues that the methodologies relevant to the social and personal domains of human experience are distinct from the methodologies of the natural sciences. For Schacht's Nietzsche, these domains are unavailable to science and cannot be the object of scientific methods of investigation:

> [Nietzsche] strongly objects when scientific thinking—and especially natural-scientific thinking—is taken to provide us not only with considerable knowledge of many things, but with the whole story with respect to everything, human reality and the whole panoply of the human world included.[30]

Schacht has here raised a question of fundamental importance in Nietzsche's attempt to understand human experience – and the meaning of human experience – from a naturalistic perspective. A naturalism that is unable to address social and cultural institutions in terms of meaning, that mechanistically reduces them to scientific phenomena, is not sufficient for Nietzsche as Schacht understands him.

In my view, the idea that Nietzsche critiques the natural sciences as reductionistic when it comes to questions of meaning is well supported by texts such as GS §373. There Nietzsche decries a scientific interpretation of human artistic experience as absurd, precisely because it is disconnected from the question of meaning. Addressing scientists, he writes:

> That the only rightful interpretation of the world should be one to which *you* have a right; one by which one can do research and go on scientifically in *your* sense of the term (you really mean *mechanistically?*) – one that permits counting, calculating, weighing, seeing, grasping, and nothing else – that is a crudity and naiveté, assuming it is not a mental illness, an idiocy. Would it not be quite probable, conversely, that precisely the most superficial and external aspect of existence – what is most apparent; its skin and sensualization – would be grasped first and might even be the only thing that let itself be grasped? Thus, a 'scientific' interpretation of the world, as you understand it, might still be one of the *stupidest* of all possible interpretations of the world.

Nietzsche, then, is attempting to create a space for philosophical analysis in between his rejection of metaphysics and his rejection of scientism. Further, and somewhat contrary to Schacht, it also seems to me that Nietzsche's rejection of scientific description in the field of artistic endeavour and meaning-making cannot be directly transferred to his development of a methodology for ethical analysis and description. In *GS* §7, for example, Nietzsche seems to value at least some form of systematic (if not mechanistic) description of human social life. In contemporary terms, the text reads like an appeal for the development of what we now consider to be the social sciences:

> So far, all that has given colour to existence still lacks a history; where could you find a history of love, of avarice, of envy, of conscience, of piety, of cruelty? ... Has anyone collected people's experiences of living together – in monasteries, for example? Has anyone depicted the dialectic of marriage and friendship? ... Everything that humans have viewed until now as the 'conditions of their existence' and all the reason, passion, and superstition that such a view involves – has this been researched exhaustively? ... If all these jobs were done, the most delicate question of all would emerge into the foreground: whether science is able to *furnish* goals of action ... and then an experimenting would be in order, in which every kind of heroism could find satisfaction...

In this text we see Nietzsche express his desire for the development of a method of investigation that is appropriate to personal and social phenomena and yet one that is not completely distinct from scientific enquiry. It is clear he does not think that the natural sciences – at least as they existed in his time – are appropriate for this kind of investigation. Rather, he seems here to yearn for an as-yet unrealized analysis of human existence that incorporates the notion of experiment, the question of meaning, a systematic approach and a thoroughly naturalized understanding of human beings.[31]

Naturalism and evolutionary biology

Leiter's analysis helped to show us some of Nietzsche's scepticism with respect to science, and the role of emotion and error in scientific descriptions. Schacht's analysis highlights the importance of social and cultural experience for the question of meaning, and the unsuitability of scientific methods for analysing this kind of experience. By taking these thoughts together, the result seems to be that, for Nietzsche, some form of intersection between philosophical, social and scientific methodologies is needed in order to develop an appropriate mechanism for understanding human experience, which includes the question of meaning and the phenomena of artistic endeavour and cultural life. We have seen from texts in *The Gay Science* that Nietzsche questions the value of the natural sciences for describing human experience but at the same time searches for an ethics that is naturalist in its orientation and that works in parallel with the natural sciences, with a particular emphasis on the idea of experimentation.

To add further complexity to this question, but also to propose a way forward, we must acknowledge that the question of Nietzsche's naturalism cannot be understood apart from the development of evolutionary biology as a science in the second half of the nineteenth century. Many scholars have commented on Nietzsche's relationship to this then-emergent science, and to Darwinism in particular.[32] One insight common to these approaches is that evolutionary biology offers something of a bridge between the stricter 'scientism' of the natural sciences and the importance of topics such as meaning-making, sociability and ethics in human life. This seems to be because evolutionary biology is both science and history. It offers the opportunity to consider the historically observable development of both the species and of the individuals that constitute the species. Moreover, evolutionary biology offers the concept of natural selection as a framework for understanding this development. I claim that Nietzsche sees here the possibility to integrate a scientific method of experiment with the ancient Greek concept of contest as the basis for developing his ethics.

Attempts to understand Nietzsche's positive stance towards evolutionary biology are immediately complicated by the observation that Nietzsche does not adopt an evolutionary perspective uncritically. More specifically, he is highly critical of both Charles Darwin (e.g. *GS* §349) and Herbert Spencer (e.g. *GS* §373). However, this should not be taken to mean that he completely rejects the science of evolutionary biology. What I aim to show below is that within this critique there are several important concepts in evolutionary biology that Nietzsche adopts and adapts. These include biological adaptation for survival, species-level change over long periods of time and random genetic mutation. That said, there are also elements that Nietzsche clearly rejects. Importantly, he rejects an emphasis that he sees within Darwinism on *mere* survival. He rejects this because he thinks human life naturally strives for more than mere survival, it strives towards flourishing, something that is emphasized in classical philosophy.

One scholar who has commented extensively on Nietzsche's relationship to Darwinism and how this influences his broader philosophical project, is John Richardson.[33] He describes two important philosophical (and problematically metaphysical) ideas as the foundations of Nietzsche's naturalism, namely, teleology and will to power. Both concepts sit uneasily within a naturalist account: teleology because it seems to require a concept of intentionality or foresight in otherwise blind natural processes; and will to power because of a long history of interpreting it as a metaphysical element in Nietzsche's thought.[34]

Richardson attempts a naturalistic account of these ideas that resists metaphysical interpretations. He argues that Nietzsche uses the idea of will to power teleologically: an organism's will to power is the basis for understanding the purpose for its action in the world. When an organism acts, it does so in order to express its will to power. This can be understood through a biological notion of internal drives, which, for Richardson, allows both teleology and will to power to be naturalised:

> [Nietzsche's] core notion of will to power ... gives us a prospect or chance to *naturalize* these notions [i.e. 'drives' and 'instinct'] and especially to naturalize what may seem to be their most suspect aspect: Nietzsche's *teleological* use of them.[35]

The logic is as following: 1) a biologically determined organism acts in the world with the purpose of expressing its will to power and 2) this is a biological drive that is built into the organism as the result of the processes of evolution, which is structurally teleological.

In order to make this argument, Richardson defines two ways in which Nietzsche uses the concept of teleology: the narrow sense which illuminates this claim, and its general usage which does not. The narrow sense of teleology is based on etiology, an idea that Richardson argues allows the purpose of a design feature to be understood retroactively. This unusual definition of teleology commits Richardson to an unfortunate circularity where the purpose of a design feature (for example, a particular drive) is derived from its history of adaptation.[36] Looking forwards, drives emerge through the process of natural selection, which is a blind, purposeless process. Looking backwards, the drive to eat, for example, finds its purpose in survival of the species.

This is not the same as the usual understanding of evolutionary processes, which sees them as genuinely stochastic and where the history of adaptation alone explains what survives and what does not. Further, it seems to me that this historically adaptive and genuinely stochastic (as opposed to purposeful) approach is consistent with Nietzsche's reflections on chance and waste. These ideas are evocatively captured in, for example, his references to the 'dice box of chance' in *D* §130 and *GS* §109. In my view, Richardson does not adequately take account of Nietzsche's appreciation for the enormous waste of truly random, non-purposeful evolutionary processes, and, consequently, he does not give appropriate emphasis to the concept of chance in Nietzsche's understanding of nature. In my view, it is more consistent with Nietzsche's overall approach simply to acknowledge that he does not accept the idea of purpose but favours the Darwinian idea of randomness and its function within the process of natural selection.

This problem in Richardson's description re-emerges when he invokes a 'minority' interpretation of the will to power to support this narrow concept of teleology. He concedes (wrongly, in my view) that the will to power is a *mostly* metaphysical notion in Nietzsche but that Nietzsche sometimes uses it in a naturalistic way.[37] My view, perhaps somewhat controversially, is that the idea of the will to power is not as central to Nietzsche's thought as it is often taken to be, especially when it is understood metaphysically, as some kind of underlying force that drives the universe forward.[38] It can, I think, be understood as an outcome of more important ideas. In particular, we might see will to power as naturalistic way to describe interactions between individuals.

These are complex issues that cannot be fully addressed here. Their relevance to the present argument lies not in their application to evolutionary biology but in Nietzsche's application of them to human social behaviour. Despite the problems of Richardson's use of metaphysical and teleological concepts to describe Nietzsche's approach to evolutionary biology, he does helpfully build on the concept of evolution by natural selection by proposing two other kinds of selection that Nietzsche takes up, namely, social selection and self-selection.

This helps us to resolve the problem of the application of concepts from biological science to the domain of human social interaction and, correspondingly, to ethics. By organizing natural, social and self-selection around the central concepts of Darwinian evolution, Richardson offers us the beginnings of a Nietzschean method for moving between these domains and remaining true to his naturalist commitments. He explains these three levels of evolutionary analysis as

> different ways our behaviors have been selected: first the Darwinian, explaining the animal in us, then the social which explains our more peculiarly human behaviors, and finally a certain superhuman possibility we're pointed toward.[39]

Social selection operates through two quite different mechanisms: custom and morality. Both of these mechanisms are in conflict with the goal of natural selection. For example, one goal of social selection is homogeneity, which is achieved by imposing customary morality onto our natural inclinations

> Habits are selected to bind us to society, and the most effective means, under both the ethic of custom and morality, are habits that attack and undermine our drives and their natural 'healthy selfishness.'[40]

This conflict is resolved by self-selection. Richardson argues that this is characterized by the value of individual freedom.[41] Self-selection works in two ways. Firstly, natural desires are prioritized over social constructs: 'Nietzsche wants us to use the "taste" of our bodily drives to judge the social values laid over them.'[42] Secondly, choice is exercised not as a cognitive power exercised over one's own body, but through choosing one's environment: '[Nietzsche] insists that we pay close attention to the conditions—climactic, nutritional, behavioral—of our health as organisms.'[43]

This allows Richardson to integrate evolutionary history at the species-level with freedom for the individual

> A behavior is self-selected and free, not by what happens in the moment of choice itself—in that microsituation—but in the macrohistory by which the dispositions producing this behavior were designed.[44]

There is much to recommend in this approach. While Richardson has not, in my view, gone far enough in removing metaphysics from Nietzsche's thought, he provides a useful set of elements for integrating evolutionary biology into Nietzsche's thought. Richardson brings the strictly scientific elements of Nietzsche's approach (his 'Darwinism') together with his comments on human social behaviour and social and cultural institutions. He shows that Nietzsche's naturalism can be extended to the domain of social interaction and ethics as a genuinely scientific enterprise that incorporates insights from evolutionary biology by extending them from natural selection into social and self-selection. At the heart of this extension of naturalism into ethics lies Nietzsche's claim that the individual can be understood as a composite of natural drives and, further, that the species is a composite of these individuals and their interactions. These are subjects we will explore further in Chapters 6 and 7.

Considering Leiter, Schacht and Richardson together, it is clear that Nietzsche's naturalism sits in a complex and sometimes contradictory relationship with his views on the natural sciences. In my opinion, this complexity can be reduced by returning to Nietzsche's Homeric-heroic impulse. Richardson's approach, in which an individual's drives are brought into the evolutionary schema as a way of developing a naturalistic account of human social relationships, can be enhanced by understanding that Nietzsche saw a connection between the logic of natural selection and the logic of the contest. As we will see in the following chapter, Nietzsche does not approach agonistic contest simply on the level of brute competition. Rather, he internalizes it in ways that draw on the logic of natural selection.

This subtlety in his naturalistic approach enables him to connect scientific and heroic endeavour so as to avoid the simplistic brutality on the basis of which human social relations might be conceived as a competitive struggle to survive. In particular, as we will see, Nietzsche's reimagination of heroic contest, transformed by his consideration of the internal contest of drives within the individual, presents not brute competition but agonistic friendship as one solution to the problem of a naturalistic ethics.

We can understand this reimagining of heroic contest through a Darwinian lens by considering some of the key elements of heroic endeavour, at least as Nietzsche conceived it. Heroic endeavour is connected to the logic of natural selection in, for example, GS §318. Here, while arguing that most people respond to pain as a warning signal and make adjustments to avoid it, he makes the distinctly Homeric point that there is another kind of person – the hero – who welcomes pain. This heroic type is 'species-preserving' and 'species-enhancing':

> *Wisdom in pain.* – There is as much wisdom in pain as in pleasure: like pleasure, pain is one of the prime species-preserving forces. If it weren't, it would have perished long ago: that it hurts is no argument against it ... True, there are people who [don't resile] when great pain approaches and who never look as proud, bellicose, and happy as when a storm is nearing – yes, pain itself gives them their greatest moments! They are the heroic human beings, the great *pain-bringers* of humanity ... They are eminently species-preserving and species-enhancing forces, if only because they resist comfort and do not hide their nausea at this type of happiness.

Nietzsche advances this argument by transposing this species-preserving heroism into the search for knowledge. In GS §324, he proposes to apply the scientific notion of experiment to morality. Here the search for knowledge in the realm of morality can be understood as heroic experiment:

> And knowledge itself: let it be something else to others, like a bed to rest on or the way to one, or a diversion or a form of idleness; to me it is a world of dangers and victories in which heroic feelings also have their dance – and playgrounds. '*Life as a means to knowledge*' – with this principle in one's heart one can not only live bravely but also *live gaily and laugh gaily*!

Conclusions

The idea of heroic contest, when it is adapted to include intellectual and psychological elements, offers an opportunity to bring different threads within Nietzsche's thought together in a new way. Through it Nietzsche connects scientific experimentalism, heroism in the search for knowledge and the evolutionary concept of species preservation and enhancement. This heroism involves a certain kind of bravery – the bravery to eschew comfort, even to invite pain – in a quest for moral and ethical discovery.

This perspective on ethics is deeply influenced by the Homeric hero, and because of this, we find that the twin themes of abundance and difference, also at home in the world of evolutionary biology, are expanded to include the individual in themselves and the individual in their social relations. Natural selection relies on natural abundance, 'squandering to the point of absurdity' (*GS* §349). This abundant squandering happens through the production of difference, expressed as ever-new forms of biological life emerging from random mutations. Nietzsche's ethics, as we will see in the remaining chapters, involves individuals who also engage in abundant squandering, expressed as a contest in which ever-new forms of personal and social life emerge. What we will see in the final chapter is that, for Nietzsche, the highest form of social life, the one that most readily captures this spirit of adventure, of trial and error, and of the capacity to incorporate difficulty and opposition, is friendship. In the following chapters, I claim that Nietzsche bases this understanding of friendship on the classical Greek concept of contest. The next chapter takes us one step closer to this conclusion by exploring how Nietzsche understood the classical contest and its Homeric origins, and how he distilled from it the touchstone ideas of abundance and difference as key elements in his naturalism.

5

Nietzsche's new Homerism

In the preceding chapters we have seen Nietzsche's critique of metaphysics and of morality unfolding in several different ways. In Chapter 2 we saw that in his rejection of Christian morality he also criticizes the concept of *agape* love and self-sacrifice. In Chapter 3 we saw him reject Schopenhauer's morality of compassion. In these critiques we observed Nietzsche's desire to develop an ethics that emphasizes individual difference and personal abundance, elements that are, I claim, incompatible with *agape* love and Schopenhauerian compassion. Further, in the preceding chapter, we have seen how Nietzsche's move away from metaphysics towards naturalism leads him to draw on some elements of evolutionary biology while rejecting what he saw as Darwinism's pessimism in the idea of a struggle for survival.

I have claimed throughout that both in what he turns away from and in what he embraces, Nietzsche was formulating a new approach to ethics that is founded on the classical Greek notion of contest that would allow for individual difference and promote personal abundance.[1] My claim is that, as far as Nietzsche can be considered systematic, this emphasis on the idea of contest develops into what I call his 'new Homerism', that is, a systematic approach to ethics in which he integrates the practice of contest into the idea of higher friendship.[2]

It is time now to consider how Nietzsche understood this classical ideal of contest, and in particular, its roots in Homer.[3] In what follows I will outline Nietzsche's new Homerism, demonstrate how the themes of personal abundance and individual difference emerge from it and show that the idea of contest continued to influence Nietzsche throughout his active philosophical life. Here we also lay the groundwork for understanding how Nietzsche transforms the idea of contest so that it can be applied not only to war, competitive games, musical jousts and rhetorical sparring as in the ancient world, but to the contest of drives within an individual (Chapter 6) and to personal relationships (Chapter 7).

Individual difference and personal abundance

I begin with an overview of Nietzsche's treatment of individual difference and personal abundance as elements of heroic contest. At its core, contest involves two great individuals who vie for supremacy, and they do this within a social context that supports and promotes the outcomes of agonistic exchange. It is central to my argument that Nietzsche generalizes the ancient ideal by moving it away from the purely physical and performative contests of antiquity and including within it different forms of agonistic engagement, whether they be the internal *agon* of the individual, or a contest of ideas between individuals, or a contest of wills between friends.

First, let's consider the importance of individual difference for contest. In both forms of contest – the performative version and the personalized version – it is critical that the individuals involved represent genuine alternatives to one another. One cannot have a genuine contest between two people who are essentially the same, especially not in the personalized version. Individual difference is necessary for the possibility of contest. We have seen that Nietzsche rejects the drive to homogeneity common to Christianity and Schopenhauer. For him, human experiences in which difference, and the associated possibilities of variance, deviation and transgression, is not a rupture to some metaphysical fabric, nor is it sin that needs atoning, nor even a problem that need solving. The contest celebrates (and depends on) an understanding of human experience in which the contrary, the new and the different are signature features of the kind of contest that might produce human greatness. Here the pallid sameness of Christian monotheism and Schopenhauerian mystical union give way to multicoloured and multiform change, improvement and development, which are achieved through a clash between opponents as they test their differences against one another in order to see which features emerge as stronger, more vital, more alive. While Nietzsche found some support for this idea in evolutionary biology in natural selection, where we see a creative process in which truly new things emerge, it is the ancient Greek ideal of contest that allows him to develop this into an ethics.[4]

Another feature of these metaphysical systems is their pessimism about human potential. Nietzsche appears to have thought that both Christianity and Schopenhauer propose a privative view of human existence. Christianity does this through its understanding of *agape* love as self-abnegation and Schopenhauer does this with his metaphysical interpretation of suffering. Again, evolutionary biology offers some possibilities for Nietzsche, in particular the possibility to abandon this metaphysically grounded negativity and propose instead an understanding of nature, including human beings, as abundant. Through Darwin, Spencer and Rée,[5] he came to the view that the new science of evolutionary biology was inconsistent with the classical ideal in that it had not freed itself from privative assumptions. In particular, he rejected its characterization of the natural world as the stage for a mere struggle for survival. This struggle is conceived as a competition over meagre and diminishing resources in which the highest goal is simply to remain alive long enough to propagate. For Nietzsche, this view of the natural world cannot explain the variety, creativity and depth of human experience.

Nietzsche sees the Greek contest as premised on a different view of nature and, in particular, of human nature. This contest depends for its efficacy on the natural abundance of the individual. It is a creative, generative and innovative view of human possibility that suggests that human beings can adopt a higher standard for their lives beyond mere survival. For example, the personal abundance of great individuals provides possibilities such as the development of high culture including music, theatre and fine arts. For him, a privative view of nature cannot furnish a naturalist rationale for these aspects of human existence. It is the Greek *agon* that, for Nietzsche, gives expression to these creative and generative capacities in human life. Further, by insisting that the individuals who engage in contest are personally abundant, we find a heretofore unrecognized but, in my view, critical ingredient for sustaining contest. The relative equality of the contestants, and the absence of desire to annihilate or eliminate opponents, arises from the personal superabundance of the people involved. Abundant individuals can both win and lose with grace.

I will return throughout the remainder of the book to these two components of the contest and their importance for Nietzsche's ideals, fleshing them out, justifying them and reflecting on their presuppositions and implications. For now, I aim to show the textual and contextual elements of contest in Nietzsche's thought as it began to crystallize into one of the most important touchstones for his entire philosophical project.

Reconceptualizing Homeric ideals

In Nietzsche's early writings he reflects explicitly on the ancient practice of contest. In later writings, and in particular the writings of 1881–7, these ideas are pervasive but implicit, embedded in his descriptions of great individuals and human social relationships. When this implicit reliance on the ancient notion of contest is missed, Nietzsche can and has been cast as a philosopher purely interested in the flourishing of individuals at the expense of social or relational outcomes. He can become the philosopher of unrestrained egoism, selfishness, solipsism and *Realpolitik*. I aim to show that the contest, when understood on the basis of difference and abundance, allows for a new interpretation of his approach to social relationships that more than answers these charges. In the following two chapters this will become evident: he first transposes the contest so that it applies to the individual in their self-overcoming, and only then does he take it outwards towards others in social relationships. The importance of self-overcoming is one of the key elements in his idea of contest that prevents individuals from extreme egoism and solipsism: it introduces restraint and moderation. Further, we will see in the final chapter that higher friendship emerges as Nietzsche's preferred form of social relationship because it not only supports a contest ethos but is also able to draw on it to support both individual and social flourishing.

Recent interpretations

Several scholars have stressed the importance of contest in Nietzsche's thought. Particularly significant contributions have come from Christa Davis Acampora and Herman Siemens.

Christa Davis Acampora's *Contesting Nietzsche* provides a rich analysis of Nietzsche's thought through the concept of the ancient Greek *agon*. She considers four philosophical contestants that Nietzsche engaged with: Homer, Socrates, St Paul and Richard Wagner. She derives from these contests in Nietzsche's life and thought some general features of the *agon* as Nietzsche understood it, and she examines the resulting contribution to Nietzsche's overall project. From Homer she develops the function of the *agon* for revaluing values; from Socrates the function of the *agon* in understanding Nietzsche's naturalism; from St Paul the concept of decadence in the sense of personal and social decline, of decay, as an anti-*agon*; and from Wagner the idea of decomposing the subject into an internal *agon* of drives.

In doing so she identifies the concept of *agon*, translated as contest in English and *Wettkampf* in German, as a focal point for Nietzsche's thinking about the relationship between the individual and the community. She argues that Nietzsche understood this agonistic approach, even from its very foundation in the Homeric literature, to have elements of both individual greatness and social cohesion:

Nietzsche argues that Homer's valorization of the *agon* produced new forms of possible relations that allowed people to forge significant attachments among individuals and groups and between people, the city, and the powerful forces of the gods.[6]

That is to say, inasmuch as the contest focuses on the achievements of great individuals, it is also an inherently social construct in that the community moderates the process and outcomes of agonistic exchange:

> Thus it is the *community* and not any great individual competitor that founds this form of interaction. The community has this priority by virtue of the fact that it provides the conditions for the possibility of meaningful agonistic exchange ... [7]

There is a sense in which the true benefactor of agonistic exchange is not the victor only but also the community that sustains the possibility of agonistic exchange. The contest allows a society to grow and to develop as new standards of excellence are established.

Acampora has recently built on this idea by proposing that it is a mistake to overemphasize the contest as something that only takes place within the dyad relation of two contestants.[8] The social conditions for participation in the contest include four underlying systems that license the contest and enable its productivity: an agonistic value economy; the underpinning economic and societal sustainers of contest; the institutional framework within which contests are established and adjudicated; and the actual contestants themselves.[9] She describes the contest as sustained by the circulation of self-interest and social concern, in which the agonistic drive is disciplined and moderated by a societal context that relies on the production of contestants through education. This societal context emphasizes the importance of variety and of the need to maintain the conditions for contest as well as the mechanisms for incorporating of the productive benefits of contest into social life.[10]

In this way Acampora emphasises contest as a developmental and social process. Agonistic exchange repeats over long periods of time. Through it values are both established and overthrown, to the benefit of the victors in the short term and the community as a whole in the long term. Crucially, we can see in her analysis the idea that productive contest exists within a social context that provides the conditions and the parameters for it. This context, it seems to me, can best be described as a fragile agonistic equilibrium premised on the idea that the individuals involved in contest, and the social context within which it occurs, promote personal abundance and value heterogeneity. In order for agonistic exchange to maintain a long-lasting equilibrium, there must always be the possibility for a new contestant to arise and, from their own individual genius, to overthrow the established order. Contest eschews tyranny:

> a commitment to agonism – or an agonistic ethos – may ensure that any reigning performance in the *agon* maintains its superiority or mastery only by virtue of and so long as it sustains challenge or opposition.[11]

We can also connect Acampora's analysis with the understanding of Nietzsche's naturalism developed in the preceding chapter. In contest we see the essence of the analogy between evolutionary biology and ethics implicit in Nietzsche's approach: the contest is where values are revalued. Contingent values are established and then overthrown in an ever-improving cycle, analogous to natural selection. Thus, through contest a society is able to develop over time by venerating the success of its strongest. The situation of decadence, in which an individual or a society becomes locked in a struggle to survive by overseeing the diminishing vitality of its combatants with each bout is one in which the conditions for contest have failed, analogous to the Darwinian struggle for survival. The ancient ideal of contest, which begins with Homer, is fundamentally incompatible with mere struggle for survival: contest results in improvement and development over time, struggle results in decline towards *ressentiment* and decadence.

Acampora highlights not only the societal dimensions of Nietzsche's Homerism but also the psychological and relational dimensions of it, where we see the themes of abundance and difference clearly articulated. Acampora expresses the concept of difference as Nietzsche's way of integrating the Apollonian and Dionysian in social relations. The Dionysian is understood as the ecstatic dissolution of the individual into the whole and the Apollonian as the principle of individuation or separation of the individual from the whole.[12] In the contest 'Agonistic relations … quite literally *activate* the process of individualization, the basis of distinguishing one from the other.'[13]

In other words, the *agon* creates difference as the mechanism for establishing new excellences. It requires two unique and distinct competitors, 'individualization'. This process is based not only on the characteristics of each individual within themselves, but also by each individual's social context: 'Organizations form on the basis of their constituent parts (drives) and the kinds of possible relations are thereby circumscribed. They are also constituted in and through their external relations.'[14]

Other scholars share and elaborate on this view that context both requires unique individuals and constitutes them as a function of their social relations. Lawrence Hatab presents a neat summary of this interpretation of the contest:

> For Nietzsche, every advance in life is an overcoming of some obstacle or counterforce, so that conflict is a mutual co-constitution of contending forces. ... The self is constituted in and through what it opposes and what opposes it; in other words, the self is formed through agonistic relations ... Competition can be understood as a shared activity for the sake of fostering high achievement and self-development, and therefore as an intrinsically social activity.[15]

Thus, for both Acampora and Hatab, one contestant does not seek to annihilate the other, nor do they act without regard to the institutions that make contest possible. It is in this way that the *agon* is not destructive but rather constitutes a social order which is constantly improving itself and the individuals within it:

> Nietzsche argues that the *agon* emerged as a *cultivation* of more brutal natural drives in not striving for the annihilation of opponents, but arranging contests that would test skill and performance in a competition.[16]

Herman Siemens is another scholar who has made a significant contribution to the question of agonism in Nietzsche's ethics. Where Hatab and Acampora emphasize contest as competition, Siemens emphasizes contest as conflict. In describing agonism this way, Siemens covers the some of the same ground as Acampora and others. With these scholars, he claims that Nietzsche's contest arises from an understanding of the Homeric ethos, that it depends on human plurality and on personal abundance, and that it fosters human excellence:

> What Nietzsche values in the agon, then, is the way it fosters particularity and creative spontaneity among a plurality of individuals. In this regard, he sees the agonal polis as a kind of breeding ground or hothouse for human excellence, or rather, for human excellences, a regime of power that offers the best conditions for experiments in human excellence.[17]

Perhaps because Siemens focuses on this question of conflict and confrontation, he is much clearer on several dimensions of the contest than others. Particularly, he emphasizes the mutuality of the contest: opponents must be roughly equal and they do not seek to annihilate their opponents but rather to sustain and even promote them.[18] The result, for Siemens, is a creative complex of power relations between individuals that generate new values:

An important element of Nietzsche's lifelong project to transvaluate all values is to contest the Christian and post-Christian condemnation of conflict in favour of 'love', 'peace', or 'harmony', with the thesis that conflict has untold productive qualities.[19]

The result, for Siemens, is a self-moderating 'philosophical practice of hostile love'[20] where antagonists are continually overthrowing the standards of excellence, an organization of power that creates an equilibrium state for ascendant human life. Within this, the antagonists in fact require one other, if not for their existence, at least for their continued growth – resistance and power are mutually co-constituting.[21]

The analyses of Acampora, Hatab and Siemens provide us with many important elements of the Nietzschean contest, elements that are critical for the argument of this book. It incorporates both competition and conflict, and, in a sense sits above them as an overarching concept. It is interested in both the individual and in the social context. Ultimately, the contest ethos aims to establish an equilibrium that allows both individuals and communities to continually refresh themselves, overthrowing old values and establishing new ones.

However, these scholars do not go on to describe in significant detail the characteristics of the individuals who engage in these kinds of contest, or the structure and character of the relationships between them. Both Acampora and Siemens provide an analysis that goes beyond the mere dyad of two antagonists, pointing the way towards a systems-based social analysis of contest. And yet the dyad itself remains somewhat obscure. These are the matters I wish to address in the following chapters: the nature of the individual who engages in contest in Chapter 6, and a description of the kind of social relationship that can occur between these kinds of individuals in Chapter 7.

An important question to address here is the question of the ontological constitution of the individual person. We briefly touched on this topic in Chapter 2, where I argued that a rejection of relational ontology – that the self is constituted by its relationships – is already implied in Nietzsche's rejection of *agape* love. It seems that for Siemens, Acampora and Hatab, even the great heroic individual is constituted in their social relationships and context, not strictly within themselves as a biological fact. I have argued in Chapters 2 and 3 that Nietzsche seeks to ground the individual in themselves as a natural, self-sustaining entity, as a natural 'given'. Further, I have also argued in Chapter 4 that he resists any metaphysical attempt to explain or justify human experience.

In my view, by introducing the idea of individuals who find their being – who are constituted as beings – in their social relationships, these scholars require an ecstatically constituted self that is essentially metaphysically conceived.

To give an example of this in Nietzsche's thought, it is clear that this understanding of the individual as constituted by their social relationships stands in tension with Nietzsche's descriptions of an independently constituted individual who finds and knows themselves only in solitude. For him, it is often in solitude that the great individual is able to fully express or recover themselves (e.g. *D* §§323, 325; *GS* §§285, 359).[22] In my view, this difficulty is easily overcome. While the contest is essential to Nietzsche's understanding of interpersonal relations, the contest-relation is not essential to his understanding of the individual. For him, the individual is constituted by virtue of an inner necessity – the mere biological fact of their physical existence. Their existence as natural beings, however, invariably brings them into contact with others, and when this relationship to others is able to support individual self-expression, contest relations that support both the individual and their relationship to one another become possible. Thus, difference at a really fundamental level, one in which the individual can be understood and comprehended in all their specificity and particularity without reference to any other individual, is essential for the contest.

We also see in these scholars the idea that contest depends on an assumption of personal abundance at several levels. The competitors bring their own abundance to the contest and the society in which they participate is abundant enough to provide the conditions for seemingly endless victories and losses. Acampora stresses that the necessity for this kind of abundance makes the contest a fragile social institution. It can fail in various ways but perhaps most notably it fails when difference is eliminated: it fails in presence of tyranny.[23] Tyranny leads to failure of the conditions for contest because it limits the expression of abundance to a single individual, group or party. I think that this kind of personal abundance is connected in Nietzsche's thought to his emphasis on the self-grounding, self-defining and self-sustaining character of the individual, considered apart from their social relations.

For Siemens, the abundance of the individuals engaged in contest relationships is made clear through Nietzsche's concept of health:

> For our purposes, the next two features are crucial: the dynamic, energetic conception of health (as in GS 370), of abundant strength and vitality, able to thrive on obstacles as challenges in a dynamic of productive self-surpassing;

and then the more radical picture of a 'health in the teeth of sickness', or what Nietzsche calls 'great health', ... turning damaging forces into stimulants, to its advantage.[24]

Here the antagonist is able to channel impulses that might otherwise be destructive, such as hatred and aggression, into actions that involve them in an agonistic 'play of forces'. This, in turn, creates a therapeutic context for Nietzschean agonism.

In all of this, we can see a relationship between abundance and difference in Nietzsche's interpretation of contest. The development of the individual takes place through the friction that exists at the boundary between two distinct, differentiated beings. This becomes a virtuous circle as the individual learns to profit from engagement with others – abundance leads to difference leads to more abundance – so that we are left with a vision of upward-spiralling positive social relationships characterized by contest.

There is a curious tension in Nietzsche's thought here. This strong, ideal form of society characterized by abundance and difference, set on an upward-spiralling path by continual contest to produce every higher standards of value, is also fragile. Weak forms of social organization – the decadent society that is caught in a depowering cycle, such as that which privileges love and compassion, or the tyrannical, which is stuck in the hegemonic domination of a single individual taste – represent a threat to this supposedly ideal and strong form of social organization. Nietzsche recognizes, for example, the capacity of the Christian faith to overcome a strong society (e.g. *D* §71), or for a tyrant to emerge and dominate a society for their own individual ends (e.g. *GS* §23). There is a sense in which the strong society turns out not to be so strong after all.

The answer that Nietzsche seems to provide for this conundrum, unsatisfactory as it might be, is that these decadent and tyrannical forms of social organization achieve their victories by appealing to the worst rather than to the best. They are characterized as a kind of poison (*D* §321, *GS* §359) that weakens society by undermining it's best and brightest. The outcome – slave revolt and herd morality – is an ever-present possibility that threatens, in his view, to put human societies and individuals on a path towards annihilation.

This contrast, between the tyrant and decadent who seek to annihilate the other and the strong contestant who acts in opposition to the other, provides a useful context for thinking about Nietzsche's ethics. In particular, it is vital for our understanding of higher friendship that Nietzsche does not contemplate one-sided tyranny in social relationships. This will be elaborated in Chapter 7. For the present, it is sufficient to note that Siemens and Acampora have furnished us with the important ideas of abundance and difference as two essential elements of contest. Further, they provide us with the insight that contest is an inherently social idea in that it structures the relationship between the individual and their society, and that contest can be seen both interpersonally (in terms of social relations) and intrapersonally, where the individual is conceived as themselves the site of competing drives.

We now have a framework or developing Nietzsche's ethics: abundance and difference on the one hand and the transformation of contest to apply to both interpersonal and intrapersonal *agon* on the other. Before we examine these ideas in detail in the following chapters, we must first reckon with one difficulty that presents itself immediately. This is the observation that Nietzsche rarely discusses ancient Greek contest explicitly. In what follows I aim to show that what Nietzsche does say explicitly about contest in his early writings (1870–2) is extended and sublimated in such a way that it permeates his later published works implicitly.

Nietzsche's concept of contest

It is generally accepted that Homer was an important influence on Nietzsche, beginning with his academic career as a classical philologist and continuing throughout his life. The precise nature of this influence, however, is debated. I am not proposing here an analysis of his interpretation of ancient texts. What is important for this book is not whether Nietzsche got Homer (or any other ancient author) 'right'. What is important is how his understanding of those ideas shaped his ethics. I propose to consider the way in which themes that Nietzsche considered to be specifically 'Homeric' remained influential throughout his writing and, specifically, in his writings between 1881 and 1887.

In Nietzsche's early writings there is considerable evidence of Homeric influence. This influence is both implicit and explicit, and, in some texts, Nietzsche writes directly about the idea of contest. In these texts we see that Nietzsche starts with a concept of contest that is an amalgam of classical ideas (particularly from Homer and Hesiod) and Schopenhauerian metaphysics. However, we also see that by the time he published *Daybreak* he had decisively rejected metaphysics in favour of naturalism.

Thus, what emerges from these early texts is a system of thought strongly influenced by Homer but one that stands on a naturalistic foundation. This has significant consequences for his understanding of contest, as he now has to supplement the classical notion with naturalistic ideas that can be substituted for ancient metaphysics and yet keep the idea of contest intact. What we will see is that he developed his own version of contest that is essentially optimistic about human endeavour because it focuses on the ideas of abundance and difference, which stands in stark contrast to the metaphysically grounded concept of contest with which he began.

Three texts that demonstrate this transformation of the concept of contest are *The Dionysian World View* (1870), *The Birth of Tragedy* (1871) and *Homer's Contest* (1872). *DWV* sections 1 and 2 outline the basic structure of Nietzsche's early thought in which the metaphysical opposition of Apollonian and Dionysian is central. The Apollonian represents moderation ('measure') and limits, operates by means of dream-states and results in semblance (the 'veiling of truth'). For Nietzsche, this originates in Greek thought and is expressed in Homeric epic poetry, painting, sculpture and musical 'architectonics'. The Dionysian represents excess as opposed to moderation, operates by means of intoxication-states as opposed to dream-states, and results in direct access to truth rather than the veiling of it. It originates in 'Asia' and is expressed in lyric poetry, musical harmony and ecstatic dance. In Nietzsche's view, the genius of Greek thought was its capacity to integrate these two streams of thought, turning the Asian 'spring' of Dionysian thought into a Greek-Homeric 'river'.[25]

This dynamic tension was resolved in Greek culture by integrating the new Asian, Dionysian ideas with the old Homeric, Apollonian ideas, resulting in tragic-comedic art forms. The Dionysian ecstasy results in disgust for the mundane aspects of life that Apollonian thought consecrates. By integrating these two impulses, Nietzsche argues that Greek thought becomes able to live in between them, hovering between the Apollonian desire for beauty and the Dionysian lust for intoxication. This middle position is characterized by probability rather than certainty and by experiences of the sublime and the comical as responses to the absurdity of daily life.

Nietzsche overlays this union of Apollonian and Dionysian impulses in Greek thought with a Schopenhauerian interpretation. Here two drives – the Apollonian and the Dionysian – are interpreted as expressions of a singular underlying metaphysical unity, derived from a common goal:

> The struggle between both manifestations of the Will had an extraordinary goal, the creation of a *higher possibility of existence* and the attainment thereby of a yet *higher glorification* (through art).[26]

This understanding of the function of art and its relationship to will has a feature that is especially relevant to this discussion. Here Nietzsche discusses various forms of artistic expression (acting, musical harmony, rhythm, sculpture and painting) on the basis of their ability to mediate between the underlying metaphysical reality of Will and ordinary human experience. This expresses a theory of art, which is aimed at integrating the Homeric expression of (Western) Apollonian optimism with (Eastern) Dionysian pessimism, and which depends on Schopenhauer's unitive metaphysics of the Will. Thus, at this stage of his development, Nietzsche's concept of contest is tied up with a metaphysical binary of opposing forces and is essentially pessimistic. More positively, we also see here an emphasis on aesthetic experience that is infused with ethical considerations and that aims at ascendant forms of human experience.

This combination of ethics, aesthetics and metaphysics is sharpened in *The Birth of Tragedy*. In this book Nietzsche expresses the relationship between Dionysian excess and Apollonian moderation in an even more strongly Schopenhauerian way. The Apollonian is explicitly identified with the *principium individuationis* (the principle of individuation) and the Dionysian with the underlying metaphysical unity of Will. Individuality is the illusion of Apollo, self-abandonment and the annihilation of the individual in ecstatic performance is the truth of Dionysus. Homeric art is here completely identified with the Apollonian world of illusion: 'Homeric "naiveté" can be understood only as the complete victory of the Apolline illusion.'[27]

Nietzsche is here asserting several things at once. The function of Dionysian art – whether it be in music or in Attic tragedy – is to provide solace in the face of suffering: 'the solace that in the ground of things, and despite all changing appearances, life is indestructibly mighty and pleasurable'.[28]

This consolation is achieved by the dissolution of the individual into an underlying metaphysical monad and stands in opposition to the kind of solace provided by Homeric art. In Homeric art the gods justify ordinary human experience by participating in it ('the only satisfactory theodicy!').[29] There is here a form of Homeric excess which, in contrast to Dionysian excess, confirms and justifies all of human existence rather than merely offering consolation to the suffering:

> Nothing here [in the world of the Olympian gods] reminds us of asceticism, of spirituality and duty; everything here speaks only of over-brimming, indeed triumphant existence, where everything that exists has been deified, regardless of whether it is good or evil.[30]

While this text shows us a first hint of the Homeric idea of abundance, Nietzsche ultimately, at this point in his development, still subordinates Homer to Schopenhauerian pessimism.[31] The Homeric enthusiasm for existence, what Nietzsche here calls 'Homeric naiveté', pales in comparison to the mystical experience of the Dionysiac festivals of singing and dancing. This understanding of mystical experience is, in my view, directly derived from his reading of Schopenhauer. There, in ecstatic experiences, the true nature of reality (in which individuals are manifestations of an underlying Will that is characterized by suffering) breaks through into the world of appearance and experience. Despite his interest in the Homeric 'overbrimming' and 'triumphant' understanding of human existence, at this stage he remains wedded to his Schopenhauerian metaphysics.

There appears to be a radical change in his thinking on the merits of these Homeric ideals between these texts, which were written during 1870 and 1871, and the essay *Homer's Contest*, written in 1872. In this essay he praises Homeric contest both for its ethical function and for its aesthetics. Released from the obscurity of Schopenhauer's metaphysics of Will, Homeric optimism about human possibility combined with the 'Apollonian' drive to moderation and discipline is no longer dismissed as naïve. Instead, the Homeric impulse comes to the fore in Nietzsche's thinking as part of a conceptual move through which the world of appearance triumphs over the shadowy otherworld that supposedly moves behind some mystical veil. Central to this transformation in Nietzsche's thought is the idea that life itself can be conceived through the lens of Homeric contest, which becomes at once the foundation for art, ethics and the concept of the state.

The logic of this short essay is as follows. Nietzsche begins by arguing that Homer's concept of contest provides a mechanism for understanding the violence and cruelty of the pre-Homeric age. Without it the pre-Homeric age would appear nihilistic:

> The wake of that bloody [pre-Homeric] period stretches deep into Hellenic history ... the conclusions to which a continual exposure to a world of combat and cruelty led [were] nausea at existence, [and] the belief that existence and indebtedness were identical.[32]

These pessimistic conclusions he attributes to 'India and the Orient in general', a veiled reference to Schopenhauer and his 'Asian' influence. The Greek interpretation of combat and cruelty, he argues, was opposite. Rather than leading to nausea at existence, Hellenic culture was inoculated against this kind of nihilism by framing combat and cruelty within the concept of contest.

Nietzsche points to the dual character of *Eris* in Hellenism to further develop his idea of Homeric contest:

> In order to understand it, we must assume that Greek genius acknowledged the existing impulse [to combat and cruelty], terrible as it was, and regarded it as *justified* ... Combat and the pleasure of victory were acknowledged: and nothing severs the Greek world so sharply from ours as the resultant *colouring* of individual ethical concepts, for example *Eris* and *envy* ... [quoting Pausanias] 'One should praise the one Eris as much as blame the other ... One promotes wicked war and feuding [the other] drives even the unskilled man to work ... neighbour competes with neighbour for prosperity.'[33]

Here we see Nietzsche exploring two forms of *Eris*, one that is essentially destructive and another that is productive. We can characterize these as two different types of agonistic engagement. Nietzsche elaborates:

> And not just Aristotle but the whole of Greek antiquity thinks about grudge and envy differently from us and agrees with Hesiod, who first portrays one Eris as wicked, in fact the one who leads men into hostile struggle-to-the-death, and then praises the other Eris as good who, as jealousy, grudge and envy, goads men to action, not, however, the action of a struggle-to-the-death but the action of the *contest*.[34]

The distinction Nietzsche draws here between 'struggle-to-the-death' and 'the action of the contest' is important. The first form of *Eris* is life-negating and the second is life-affirming. In the former, the trajectory of the struggle is towards a minimum, death, where one party merely survives and the other is extinguished. By way of contrast, in the action of contest people are 'goaded to action'. This anticipates Nietzsche's reaction against Darwinism, in which the struggle for survival is assimilated to this life-negating struggle to the death and contrasted with the abundance both required and generated by Homeric contest.

We see here the emergence of abundance as a core motif for Nietzsche's concept of contest. This is based on his earlier view that the Homeric concept of life is one of overbrimming, triumphant existence. Where previously this view of life was considered naive, here it is legitimized as the prod that goads people to action through the action of contest, which in turn results in prosperity. Here this is cast in very general terms, we will see later how it is further developed by Nietzsche into his idea of the overflowing personal abundance of the great individual and their friendships.

In the remainder of this essay Nietzsche applies this concept of contest to the state and to culture. He uses this discussion of social institutions to articulate a second core idea that animates his later writings. This is the idea that contest depends on difference, which is expressed as the endless emergence of new competitors to oppose established champions. Through the contest that is generated by this process, society is able to refresh itself. Hegemony and homogeneity are antithetical to the proper, productive functioning of contest in social life:

> The original function of this strange institution is, however, not as a safety valve but as a stimulant: the pre-eminent individual is removed so that a new contest of powers can be awakened: a thought [that] assumes that there are always *several* geniuses to incite each other to action, just as they keep each other within certain limits, too. This is the kernel of the Hellenistic idea of competition: it loathes a monopoly of predominance and fears the dangers of this, it desires, as a *protective measure* against genius – a second genius.[35]

Thus, we see in this discussion of Homeric contest the core themes of abundance and difference.

Finally, I note that in this early period Nietzsche connects contest not only to individual flourishing, but also to communal life and cultural achievement. In this essay Nietzsche sees personal development through contest as integrally connected to the well-being of the state:

> for the ancients, the aim of agonistic education was the well-being of the whole, of state society. For example, every Athenian was to develop himself, through competition, to the degree to which this self was of most use to Athens and would cause least damage.[36]

He also connects contest to the development of art:

> the Greek knows the artist *only in personal struggle* ... What a problem reveals itself to us when we enquire about the relationship of the contest to the conception of the work of art![37]

These texts show that, at least for Nietzsche, the idea of contest cannot be reduced to individualism or solipsism, nor does it align well with the Darwinian idea of a mere struggle for survival because high culture and artistic endeavour are as much the outcome of contest as is the survival of the species. We find then that the important ideas of contest, abundance, difference and development towards higher goals all find expression in these early texts and, I would argue, they remain foundational concepts for the following series of publications beginning with *Daybreak*, published in 1881.

I conclude this analysis of the development of the concept of contest by noting a conspicuous and consequential absence. In *Homer's Contest* and other related writings of this period (late 1872–3),[38] we find Nietzsche develop the ancient concept of contest without reference to either Apollonian-Dionysian or Schopenhauerian metaphysics, which he relied on in earlier publications. It is especially noteworthy that the Apollonian-Dionysian distinction has lost its importance. This change of perspective reflects Nietzsche's growing impetus to reject metaphysical systems, whether classical or contemporary, and reinforces the notion that Nietzsche's ethics is an attempt to understand human experience on a naturalistic basis. The foundation for Nietzsche's new Homerism lies in the conceptual contrast between life-negating struggle and life-enhancing contest. This contest promotes the emergence of new standards of excellence over time, where 'life' is understood simply as the natural life of ordinary human experience.

Between writing these essays in 1870–1872 and the publication of *Daybreak* in 1881 Nietzsche continued to write and publish, culminating in *Human, All Too Human* volume one (1878) and volume two (1880). These writings represent a period of Nietzsche's development in which he continued to analyse and critique classical and contemporary philosophy and to develop his own approach. It is marked by an increasing interest in science and scientific method.[39] In my view, the publication of *Daybreak* marks a turning point for Nietzsche as he begins to focus more directly on a critique of morality. This critique draws on his earlier thinking but recognizes the limitations of the science of his day in its application to psychological, social and ethical questions. This culminates in 1886-7 with the republication of *The Gay Science* with the addition of its fifth section. In my view, in subsequent publications, from *On the Genealogy of Morals* onwards, Nietzsche becomes narrower and more aggressive in his approach, and is increasingly characterized by the intrusion of unhelpful features such as xenophobia and misogyny.

In his writings from 1881 to 1887 we find Nietzsche's most focused attempt to address questions of ethics and sociability in a (relatively) measured fashion that draws together the various strands of his earlier thought, and is particularly relevant to the question of contest and its place in his ethics. The important texts of this period, at least for my purposes, are *Daybreak* (1881), *The Gay Science* (Books 1–4 in 1882, Book 5 in 1887), *Thus Spoke Zarathustra* (1883–5) and *Beyond Good and Evil* (1886). The concept of contest that Nietzsche analyses and adapts in the early essays appears in these works in largely implicit ways. Explicit reference to Homeric contest moves into the background and derivative concepts such as heroism, danger, opposition, adversity and (self-)overcoming take centre stage. Throughout, however, we see the importance of abundance and difference as themes that make contest and adversity possible to conceive in positive terms.

Extensions of contest

Scholars in this field have pointed out the difficulty of analysing the concept of contest in these writings because of its embedded and implicit character.[40] Fully understanding the concept of contest in the later works is further complicated because not only does Nietzsche use the principle of contest in this indirect fashion, he also extends it to new domains. Whereas the original concept focused largely on a physical struggle between two athletes, Nietzsche extends it to include internal contest (Nietzsche's notion of a composite self) and interpersonal contest (contest in intimate relationships).

These extensions of contest mean that Nietzsche uses new language to describe it. Contest becomes, for example, power (*GS* §§297, 369), will (*GS* §347), war (*GS* §§92, 362), victory (*D* §571; *GS* §§258, 323), heroism (*GS* §§268, 283, 292, 318, 324, 333), error (*GS* §344), difference (*GS* §§143, 149, 260, 355), danger (*GS* §§303, 343, 375), suffering (*GS* §§48, 56, 302, 318, 37) and contradiction (*GS* §§297, 369). I will not attempt to fully describe all of these texts. Rather, in what follows, I will consider key texts in which contest is explicitly recognized as an ongoing inspiration for Nietzsche's thought and his attempt to internalize and/or extend it is discussed. Throughout, I will draw attention to the core themes of abundance and difference as integrative ideas.

GS §349 is an exemplary text in this regard. Here Nietzsche contrasts Darwinism with natural abundance along lines similar to the distinction I noted earlier between contest and struggle. He argues that creatures in a state of distress focus on self-preservation. In contrast, creatures that suffer from their own abundance focus not merely on self-preservation but on expansion, growth, power and dominance. This text is important because here he explicitly connects Darwinism with a view of nature that is premised on lack and privation. This is opposed to his own view that nature is abundant:

> The whole of English Darwinism breathes something like the musty air of English overpopulation ... but a natural scientist should come out of his human nook: and in nature it is not conditions of distress that are *dominant* but overflow and squandering, even to the point of absurdity. The struggle for existence is only an *exception*, a temporary restriction of the will to life. The great and small struggle always revolves around superiority, around growth and expansion, around power—in accordance with the will to power which is the will to life.

Here we see Nietzsche expanding on the contrast he drew in *Homer's Contest* between a struggle to the death and life-affirming contest by connecting it to his interest in evolutionary biology. That is, the struggle-to-death and the Darwinian struggle-for-existence together represent the negative aspect of contest conceived as competition based on scarcity. Conversely, the idea of will to power here represents the positive aspect of contest, which, using the analysis of his early texts, we can see is conceived in its Homeric form, based on abundance. Struggle is a negative form of competition that descends towards death and in which life becomes defined as mere survival. By way of contrast, contest is a positive form of competition that ascends towards the enhancement of excellence.

Not only does Nietzsche describe these two types of competition, he also describes their foundations. The negative form is based on pessimism about human existence (the 'human nook') that assumes lack, privation and threat, and then extends this negative picture to all of nature. The positive form is based on a naturalistic optimism about existence that proposes absurd squandering as the distinguishing feature of nature, and then extends this quality into human experience. This absurd squandering fuels the positive action of contest that produces excellence. That is not to say that excellence is necessarily produced by the naturally wasteful process of contest. Rather, the contest is able to produce excellence whereas struggle is not. This is one important example of how implicit reference to Homeric contest and its themes of abundance and difference continue to influence Nietzsche during this period.

We can also see in this period how Nietzsche takes the Homeric idea of contest and extends it to new domains. For example, in *GS* §23, Nietzsche describes the signs that might demonstrate that a particular society is in decline as the 'signs of corruption'. One sign of corruption is 'laxness':

> a society in which corruption spreads is accused of laxity; and it is obvious that the esteem of war and the pleasure in war diminish, while the comforts of life are now desired just as ardently as were warlike and athletic honours formerly. What is usually overlooked, however, is that the ancient civil energy and passion,

which received magnificent visibility through war and competitive games, has now transformed itself into countless private passions and has merely become less visible...

Here Nietzsche explicitly transposes the Homeric performative notion of contest – 'war and competitive games' – into a more personal and internalized expression. The examples he gives of this transposition are tragedy, love, hatred and knowledge. The point of the passage is that the accusation of laxness against such a society is false because the accuser is concerned only with this performative notion of contest and is unable to discern the subtler forms of contest, based on the personal abundance of the participants, in the arena of 'private passions'.

Another example of this can be found in GS §283. I quote below a long excerpt from this text because it is an outstanding demonstration of Nietzsche's weaving together themes and images derived from contest into more general themes such as the relationship between social and individual goals in terms of war, bravery, heroism and danger:

> I welcome all the signs of a more virile, warlike age approaching that will above all restore honour to bravery! For it shall pave the way for a still higher age and gather the strength that the latter will need one day – the age that will carry heroism into the search for knowledge and *wage wars* for the sake of thoughts and their consequences. To this end we now need many preparatory brave human beings... human beings profoundly predisposed to look, in all things, for what must be *overcome*; human beings whose cheerfulness, patience, modesty, and contempt for great vanities is just as distinctive as their magnanimity in victory and patience with the small vanities of the defeated; human beings with a sharp and free judgement concerning all victors and the share of chance in every victory and glory... For – believe me – the secret for harvesting from existence the greatest fruitfulness and the greatest enjoyment is – *to live dangerously*! Build your cities on the slopes of Vesuvius! Send your ships into uncharted seas! Live at war with your peers and yourselves! Be robbers and conquerors as long as you cannot be rulers and possessors, you seekers of knowledge!

This text demonstrates the extension of the idea of contest into new domains. For example, Nietzsche here extends the concept of heroic war to the search for knowledge. The echoes of Homer are abundant as Nietzsche describes a new age of war, victory, glory, pride, heroism and seafaring. However, rather than conceive this new age in terms of brute political or military actions, Nietzsche describes this age as one where wars are waged between peers on the basis of ideas and in the search for knowledge. This is clearly not a socio-political or geopolitical concept of war. It is the Homeric ethos extended into a more personal domain in an exhortation to 'live dangerously', particular in social life and in personal relationships. Further, the concepts of danger, overcoming, war and victory are connected to ideas of personal abundance. The human beings that can engage in this kind of war he describes as fruitful, happy, cheerful, magnanimous and patient (as well as modest!).

Finally, we can also see that Nietzsche extends the concept of contest to the internal constitution of the individual. In this period, he develops an idea of the individual as constituted by a complex interaction of internal drives. *D* §119 is a good example. Here Nietzsche describes the individual in terms of their drives, each of which is nourished by a particular set of experiences. Nietzsche seems to lament the chance nature of this nourishment, claiming that people are most often unaware of the laws that govern the growth or stunting of their drives:

> However far a man may go in self-knowledge, nothing however can be more incomplete than his image of the totality of *drives* which constitute his being. He can scarcely name even the cruder ones ... and above all the laws of their *nutriment* remain wholly unknown to him. This nutriment is therefore a work of chance: our daily experiences throw some prey in the way of now this, now that drive, and the drive seizes it eagerly; but the coming and going of these events as a whole stands in no rational relationship to the nutritional requirements of the totality of the drives: so that the outcome will always be twofold - the starvation and stunting of some and the overfeeding of others.

Here Nietzsche sees the individual not as a coherent, integrated whole or 'self' but as a composite of inner drives. In *Daybreak* §560 Nietzsche develops this idea further, proposing that it is possible to learn the laws that govern the growth of one's internal drives (see also *D* §§109, 143, 245 and *GS* §333). The metaphor is a botanical one.[41] The individual is conceived as a garden composed of many plants and personal development is likened to the fashioning of this garden:

> One can dispose of one's drives like a gardener and, though few know it, cultivate the shoots of anger, pity, curiosity, vanity as productively and profitably as a beautiful fruit tree on a trellis; one can do it with the good or bad taste of a gardener and, as it were, in the French or English or Dutch or Chinese fashion...

Not only does he see the individual as a composite of drives, but he also sees the individual as capable of using this fact to cultivate themselves, to determine the direction and character of their development by tending to their internal drives in particular ways. Indeed, this understanding of the individual as heterogeneous and composite is the basis for the very notion that a person can develop over time:

Do the majority not believe in themselves as in complete fully-developed facts? Have the great philosophers not put their seal on this prejudice with the doctrine of the unchangeability of character?

In these texts we see the ongoing but implicit influence of the ancient ideal of contest, extended into new domains: the interpersonal and the intrapersonal. In my view these are implicit references to the ancient ideal of contest, transposed and transformed as the basis of Nietzsche's ethics.

Conclusions

We have seen in this chapter the importance of the Homeric contest for Nietzsche's thought, and that he is prepared to reinvent it so that it can serve his purpose in developing his ethics. The transformation is manifold: he 'updates' Homeric contest by moving towards a naturalist approach and he extends it from the performative notion of athletic competition and political aggression to the interpersonal and the psychological. Despite these transformations, we see also that the important themes of abundance and difference remain and become embedded in his implicit use of the idea of contest in his later writings.

We have also seen how Nietzsche develops these ideas against the backdrop of numerous influences, including Christianity, Schopenhauer and evolutionary biology. Where Christianity and Schopenhauer present metaphysically grounded alternatives, evolutionary biology presents a naturalist alternative. And yet none of these are entirely satisfactory for Nietzsche, because each in their own way presents a view that, at least on his interpretation of them, opposes the core ideals of abundant individuals who flourish by maintaining and celebrating difference-as-opposition. Christianity empties the individual through *agape* love, Schopenhauer dissolves the individual into a metaphysical *Wille*, evolution allows for individual difference but posits mere survival as its goal and, in his view, Darwinism assumes privation and lack as nature's norm.

In other words, each of these three influences describe a life-denying struggle that contrasts with the life-affirming character of Nietzsche's new Homerism. In the final two chapters we will see how Nietzsche's commitment to abundance and difference in the context of contest is applied to his ethics. In the next chapter I will explore more fully his internalizing of contest through the concept of the drives, and in the following chapter I will show how this informs Nietzsche's ethical ideal of higher friendship.

6

The individual as contest

In the preceding chapters I have argued that Nietzsche constructs his ethics by adapting the idea of Homeric contest for his own purposes. These adaptions include the rejection of metaphysical grounds for ethics and the inclusion of some motifs from evolutionary biology. The result is an ethics characterized by contest between individuals that is naturalistically conceived and emphasizes personal abundance and individual differences.[1] This contest is modelled on the Homeric *agon*, resulting in an approach that is different to the metaphysical and scientific alternatives that Nietzsche rejects in two important ways: it assumes an overwhelming natural abundance both within the contestants and in their environment; and it celebrates genuine and radical difference as the engine room of contest. The outcome is an ethics that embraces change and adversity, especially in the realm of ethics and values.

Nietzsche's works published between 1881 and 1887 explore this kind of contest and the possibility of an ethics based on it in many ways. In the next two chapters I examine this from different but related perspectives. In this chapter I will begin with the individual in themselves and in the next I work outwards towards the individual in their social relations. I will show how Nietzsche conceives individuals as a site of contest, conceived through the lens on Nietzsche's new Homerism. The individual is conceived as internally differentiated (i.e. as a composite of contesting drives), with the contest between these drives as the source of an individual's personal abundance. In particular, I aim to show that the resulting idea of a great, self-concerned individual is not that of a narcissist or egotist. It is that of a person who through self-overcoming (rather than self-indulgence or licentiousness) is able to bring harmony and order to their internal world. For the great individual, contesting internal drives coalesce into an agonistic equilibrium. This brings with it a kind of internal resourcefulness, psychologically and emotionally speaking, which, in turn, allows this individual to engage in social relationships that feature what Nietzsche calls 'great love'.

The Nietzschean soul: music and city

That Nietzsche describes the individual as a composite of underlying drives is uncontroversial among Nietzsche scholars. However, beyond this initial premise there is little agreement. Nietzsche's view of the drives has been understood biologically, psychologically and even cosmologically; or in various combinations of these. I begin with two important contributions to this discussion. The first is that of Graham Parkes, who uses a musical motif in which the great individual brings harmony to their internal drives, using the analogy of a musical score. The second is that of Leslie Paul Thiele, who sees Nietzsche's conception of the individual as analogous to the Athenian *polis* (or city-state), in which social harmony is achieved through democratic contest.[2]

Parkes draws attention to the multiplicity of the self as a Nietzschean theme and contrasts this with the more usual assumption that the self is a unified, singular (often psychological or spiritual) entity:

> Although the topic of the multiple self has important ramifications in a number of fields of philosophical inquiry, it has been generally ignored. Many problems in philosophy and their putative solutions rest on an unquestioned conception of the unity of the self. [This is] an existential issue with far reaching psychological and ethical implications.[3]

In drawing out this picture of the composite self, Parkes provides extensive commentary on the influences that shape Nietzsche's conception of it, including the German philosopher Johann Fichte (1762–1814) and poet Friedrich Hölderlin (1770–1843).[4] He identifies ancient influences on Nietzsche's thought, including the distinctively Greek influence in which the individual is conceived as a society, with its own internal 'citizens'.[5] More importantly for this book, he also articulates a relationship between the Homeric idea of contest and the ancient Greek conception of self-cultivation, using the idea of integration. Parkes proposes an interpretation of self-cultivation that requires integrating these contesting drives in order to bring them into balance.[6]

Underlying this idea of an integrated set of drives are several important features. Firstly, the health of the individual depends not on extinguishing the drives but on nurturing them. For Parkes, this is crucially important because Nietzsche is here breaking with the Christian tradition and its largely negative relationship to the passions.[7] Harmonizing the drives – which includes bringing our passions into some kind of equilibrious relationship to one another – gives the individual the ability to construct an experience of the world that brings multiple imaginative and creative perspectives to bear. This harmony of drives does not take away from their fundamental differentiation, instead, it allows the individual to use the many perspectives presented by their drives and to form from them a single integrated vision of the world. This allows the individual to exercise their power over the world through imaginative interpretation: 'Insofar as [drives] imaginally interpret the world (as presented in nerve stimuli), the drives are manifestations of will to power.'[8]

Parkes's analysis has much to commend it, in particular his ability to bring together Nietzsche's concept of the drives, his naturalism and his experimentalism into a unified framework. He also provides something of a solution to one particularly thorny problem with Nietzsche's approach. The problem is that this discussion frequently requires the drives to be governed, for decisions to be made regarding their organization. But who is to make these decisions, exercise this government, if there is no unified 'self' that sits behind or beyond the drives? We will return to this problem later. For now, we can acknowledge that Parkes's solution is to consider the internal multiplicity of the great individual to be a kind of drive aristocracy, in which the totality of a person's drives is directed by a group of 'governing drives'.[9]

The ideas of personal abundance and individual difference that I have argued fuel Nietzschean personal development also play a central role in Parkes's interpretation. He considers the drives, quite apart from traditional ascriptions of positive or negative value, to be the source of an individual's energy. The abundance of the individual depends not on valuations of the drives as either positive or negative but on how harmoniously the drives are arranged.[10] For him, maintaining the differentiation of multiple drives within the individual is essential to their health, and, conversely, the tyranny of a single drive is a sure sign that an individual is in decline.[11] This sits squarely within the framework of Nietzsche's new Homerism that I have developed in the preceding chapters. Parkes sees the individual's development as the result of this confluence of drives shaping and directing an individual's life over time.[12] He also sees this development through the lens of self-cultivation,[13] which he refers to as a form of contest.[14]

Parkes extends this analysis of the individual into their social relationships, as I will do in the next chapter. He does so, however, in an unhelpful way. As we saw in the chapters on love and compassion, I think that Nietzsche resists any idea of the self as ecstatically oriented. That is, Nietzsche resists defining or grounding the individual in others or in their relationships to others. Parkes, however, sees the Nietzschean individual as ontologically composed by their relationships with others.¹⁵ He does this because, in his view, if, there is nothing else in the individual but a multiplicity of drives ungoverned by a 'self', then the individual does not, in fact, exist. It is the drives themselves that interact with the outside world – they are stimulated, nourished or deprived of their nutriment strictly because of the events of the external world.¹⁶ Therefore, for Parkes, the ego is constituted by others¹⁷ and its boundaries are dissolved: 'the soul is in a way all things, and so the boundaries between the inner and outer are dissolved'.¹⁸

Thus, Parkes's Nietzsche understands the great individual as a multiplicity of drives that are brought into order by governing drives, forming an internal aristocracy, the result of which is interaction with the external world, which constitutes the ego and is unmediated by a 'self'. For Parkes, this permeable boundary between self and world provides the ground for ethical action on the part of the great individual. For example, it results in generosity, a thought captured in metaphors of lakes, rivers, oceans and their overflowing: 'the hydrodynamics of Zarathustrian generosity depend on keeping the boundaries of the self permeable and the channels clear for a continuous influx and outflow'.¹⁹ The result of Parkes's analysis is a picture of a multiplex soul in a social context. In this soul the drives, through a process of internal contest fostered by self-cultivation, together create high culture, which is itself premised on social relations characterized simultaneously by contest and generosity.²⁰

Paul Leslie Thiele, in his *Politics of the Soul*, also provides an analysis of the Nietzschean individual in terms of the multiplicity of their drives. He develops a thematic study of heroic individualism across Nietzsche's writings that emphasizes this understanding of the inner world of the individual.²¹ With Parkes, he emphasizes the integration of an individual's various drives as the signature feature of Nietzsche's great individual. However, he takes a different route in developing this picture. Thiele conceives the multiplicity of the soul through the metaphor of the city, drawing primarily on Homeric and Platonic influences. He describes Nietzsche's great individual as able to create an internal aristocracy from the contest between their drives in which the dominant drives bring order and yet maintain the productive action of contest:

> The higher man, in short, is the man with an aristocratically ordered soul ... The good of the whole through the rule of the best is the aim of aristocratic society. To this end hierarchy provides the condition for harmony *and* the stimulus for struggle. Thus the soul remains both ordered and active.²²

Importantly, Thiele accounts for the drives in terms that are thoroughly naturalistic and explicitly non-teleological; and in doing so he models Nietzsche's depiction of the internal contest of the Homeric hero. Further, he recognizes some of the key themes of Homeric contest such as the importance of individual difference,[23] combined with what he sees as a Heraclitean emphasis on becoming and development.[24]

These are welcome additions to Parkes's analysis. However, in contrast to Parkes, Thiele claims that Nietzsche's great individual has no interest in, or even engagement with, their social context. Instead, Thiele proposes a radical individualism in Nietzsche, in which social relations are a threat to the great individual because they require norms for behaviour. For Thiele this runs against the essential idea of development over time, and encourages dependence on others, in contrast to the Nietzschean idea of personal abundance and a corresponding notion of self-sufficiency.[25] For Thiele, Nietzsche's great individuals refuse to act according to externally imposed behavioural norms. They are absolutely autonomous and self-possessed:

> The self-enclosure of the individual is complete ... all that exists are individuals, each enclosed in his own world, each a world unto himself ... To be an individual is to be autonomous is to be supramoral.[26]

Therefore, the Nietzschean great individual shuns community[27] and they consider political engagement a threat to their individuality:

> The higher man ... has no particular cause to which he devotes himself ... He fights, but under his own rules, for himself, and, paradoxically, against himself ... Human relations in general are seen as a threat to his allotted task ... Politics ... constitutes a threat to the individual.[28]

The result is a theory of the individual in which the individual has little or no interest in others except to help put them on a path towards their own solitude.[29] Yet, they are forced by circumstance to engage with others. The expectation of the great individual in this circumstance is not to win acceptance but to expect that only a small group of equally individualistic geniuses will understand them.[30] For Thiele, the heroic struggle of self-overcoming has no audience but the individual themselves and is not attended in any way by even the simplest recognition from others, let alone acceptance, affirmation or agreement.[31]

Despite this extreme position on the existential isolation of the individual, Thiele does leave a small opening for social engagement in his discussion of Nietzsche's idea of the 'eternal return of the same', one of the great Nietzschean 'doctrines' that has been extensively analysed in the literature. For Thiele, the idea of the eternal return of the same is thought to create a moment of self-awareness in the individual in which they are forced either to accept themselves absolutely or to fall into resentment and self-loathing.[32] The result of this moment of absolute acceptance provides the basis for ethics: every action now bears the 'heaviest weight', one asks whether this action is one that a person would wish to repeat eternally.[33] In this discussion, and somewhat inconsistently, Thiele recognizes that social outcomes depend on the egoism and self-love of the individual: 'The selfishness of the parts is to be encouraged and exploited for the benefit of the whole.'[34]

This inconsistency is resolved for Thiele by reversing what he sees as the usual relationship between the self and society. Rather than seeing a new and better world as the basis for improving individuals within that world, for him the development of better individuals through self-mastery is the basis for improving the world of politics and social relations: 'new and better human beings are the means to changed world views and moral regimes'.[35]

Thus, in terms of the internal composition of the individual, we see in Parkes and Thiele a similar understanding of the individual as a plurality in which drives compete with one another for ascendancy. For both, the well-ordered individual is organized internally along the lines of an aristocracy: certain drives achieve dominance in such a way that they bring order and harmony to the other drives.

There are, however, important ways in which they differ. For Parkes, much of the function and activity of the drives is conceived in cognitive terms ('[as] patterns of neural stimulation through the medium of imagination'[36]) whereas for Thiele, the operation of the drives is largely preconscious: 'With reason and intellect out of contention as motive forces, the entire spectrum of human action and thought must be accounted for in terms of instincts or drives and their (political) relations.'[37]

This is an important issue for several reasons. On the one hand, if bringing competing drives into order is the way to become a great individual, it would be useful to understand the way in which this ordering happens. For Parkes, it is possible to see this ordering take place through an individual's cognition. Thiele, however, cannot construe the individual as a cognitive agent making decisions about their drives. Decisions about which drives to feed and which to starve are not possible because decisions themselves are merely the mental outworking of another dominant drive. This is the first issue I will explore in detail below.

The second issue is about how this conception of the individual does or does not permit a discussion of ethical social relations. Parkes explicitly recognizes the relationship between the well-ordered individual and their social context, whereas Thiele denies the importance of social relations while at the same time, however grudgingly, admitting their possibility. In construing the great individual as someone who participates in social relations, Parkes makes the suspiciously metaphysical claim that the boundaries of the self must be porous. Thiele, in eschewing social relations, makes the opposite claim: the individual is absolutely self-contained, self-sufficient, self-sustaining and self-absorbed. Thus, with Thiele and Parkes, we have opposite outcomes when we think through this question of the individual as a composite of internal drives. We have either absolute existential isolation or this concept of mutual co-constitution of the self, something that I began to address in the preceding chapters discussing the contributions of Acampora, Hatab and Siemens, and Nietzsche's rejection of *agape* love and of compassion.

These two issues are deeply intertwined, as we can see in Christine Daigle, who attempts to integrate Nietzsche's conception of contest into an understanding of the individual self.[38] She focuses on the claim that Nietzsche's concept of the free spirit is specifically developed as an ethical concept oriented towards change and becoming rather than a static notion of being. In this context, she outlines an intersection between the consciousness of an individual, which is understood as an everchanging 'ambiguous multiplicity',[39] and the environment of the individual, which is also always changing and therefore requiring new and different things from people. Thus, for Daigle 'The multiple and ambiguous subject is constantly seeking its own unity while continuously shattering in a process of self-overcoming.'[40]

This process of self-overcoming involves a constant interplay of social, historical, cultural and physiological forces, leading Daigle to conclude that Nietzsche makes the 'human subject ontologically dependent on the other'.[41]

Daigle's emphasis on change and development both within an individual and within their environment is welcome, and her proposal to reconceive the self as something dynamic and emergent rather than defined at a particular point in time is a significant conceptual step forward in this discussion. However, we once again find ourselves required to believe the individual is not self-grounded or self-defining, but rather constituted at a very basic level by the relations to others. I have argued throughout this book that this idea of a mutually co-constituted self, or an ontologically 'ecstatic' idea of the self, is at odds with Nietzsche's conception of the great individual as self-contained, self-sustaining and self-concerned. At the same time, it is evident that Nietzsche is deeply interested in social relationships, and their value and importance for human life.

We need to chart a course that recognizes the importance of the individual as an individual, independent of their social relations, and the way in which social relationships impact on individuals both positively and negatively. If we collapse the individual into their social relations, then, from a Nietzschean point of view, they will become trapped in a downward spiral, unable to contribute generously to others from the wellspring of their unique personal genius.

I think we can return to the twin themes of abundance and difference to bring us towards a resolution of this issue. For Nietzsche, the personal superabundance of the individual is the result of an individual being able to bring their drives into a state of torsional and productive equilibrium, the result of an internal contest. This abundance is the basis for social engagement conceived as contest relations. This kind of abundant individual can enter social relationships of contest and sustain them in productive, torsional equilibrium because of an abundance that is independently sourced: it comes from their internal contest. This does not deny that the individual is impacted, and even transformed, through these social engagements. They are not, however, constituted by them. Before and after contest with others, the great individual exists in solitude, they take account of themselves, they accept or reject these transformations, and they rediscover their new, emergent selves before re-entering the fray. In other words, it is entirely possible to talk about an emergent self without also claiming that the self is constituted by the conditions in which it emerges.[42] I think we can say that is true that Nietzsche's individual is a deconstructed self, for whom drives emerge, gain ascendancy, harmonize, disharmonize, decline and disappear. There is no ego governing this process, only an ever-changing environment that calls forth this or that combination of drives within the individual. But while there is no mental 'ego' to oversee this process, there is always a body, whose biological reality will ultimately provide the guide rails and outer limits of this development and change over time.

This is at least consistent with Acampora's treatment of the theme of personal abundance, particularly in her discussion of Nietzsche's relationship to Wagner.[43] She asserts that Nietzsche proposes both that the drives operate in subterranean fashion, beneath or behind conscious awareness, and that the individual is able to reflect on and even determine their own future on the basis of internal and self-generated creative energies. The way forward, she proposes, revolves around ideas of innocence and necessity:

> becoming (Werden) of the sort Nietzsche finds interesting requires that one *not have the slightest idea what one is*. This opens a complicated set of concerns

about how Nietzsche thinks about what constitutes becoming and how one goes about it or how it occurs ... becoming what one is appears to turn, at least in part, on *making oneself necessary*.⁴⁴

The idea seems to be that by achieving a unity of the drives, that nevertheless maintains a certain productive tension between them, the individual becomes free to act simply according to their (biological) nature. That is, individuals operating in this way act according to their inner necessities, eliminating the need to weigh up options and make choices. Acampora goes on to describe the importance of the 'basic concerns of life' in this context but does not elaborate strongly enough the connection between the inner necessity of the drives and these basic concerns. I think there is room here for a strong materialist claim. The inner necessity – the law that governs and limits the individual's becoming – is the specific biological fact of their body and what it requires for mental and physical health. The great individual attends to the basic nutritional requirements of their drives and of their body, and then leaves nature to take its course. This seems to me to capture most closely what Nietzsche means when he refers to 'innocent selfishness' (GS §99). The great individual is to simply take care of the basic needs of their bodies and minds, to do what is necessary to develop their personal and material resources so that they can be generous in the various contests that their environment requires of them. This seems to be the kind of thing Acampora has in mind when she writes that

> development, is nevertheless possible by virtue of taking care of ourselves in very basic ways. These greatly affect our capacities to maximise our resources and become integrated rather than disintegrated.⁴⁵

She goes on to discuss the social dimensions of this kind of self-concern by contrasting different forms of love. On the one hand, there is love that arises from the internal abundance of the individual who has become unselfconscious through rigorous and exacting self-care, and on the other hand there is love that is premised on self-denial and other-person-centredness. Her discussion reflects my earlier consideration of Nietzsche's stance against *agape* love and against compassion. Acampora neatly summarizes: 'While love as *fatality* is fecund, love as selflessness is sterile, "chaste."'⁴⁶

Thus, Acampora provides an elegant, naturalistic account of abundance and difference as they relate to the individual's development over time. Further, she retains the possibility that this approach to ethics, premised on ideas of self-cultivation and self-concern, can also provide us with an ethics of social relationships. For Acampora, the individual is a composite self whose drives require integration; this integration is achieved through self-development focused on attending to the basic requirements of the body that allows the individual to focus on higher order concerns; and these higher order concerns include questions of social engagement as, for example, in relationships of love. If anything, she simply does not take this thought far enough – here we see the truly materialist elements of Nietzsche's approach to ethics, one that promotes pro-social behaviours amongst the self-concerned.

As elegant as this might be, it may also strike interpreters of Nietzsche as difficult to sustain exegetically. For example, one might reflect on Nietzsche's oft-expressed disdain for love relationships (e.g. *D* §§151–2, 415; *GS* §§72, 263), or the complexity of the problems that arise given his occasional positions against free will and conscious choice (e.g. *D* §130; *GS* §127), or some of the more intractable problems that arise when we move beyond love relationships in exploring the connection between the individual's focus on themselves and other kinds of social engagement, as in, for example, relationships of enmity. In what follows I aim to show how these concerns can be addressed and how Nietzsche's understanding of the individual as an internal contest of drives can be further developed as an ethical idea.

Internal contest and the drives

It is difficult to select a manageable set of texts to describe Nietzsche's theory of the drives. This is because, on the one hand, the idea is ever-present, particularly in *Daybreak* and *the Gay Science*. On the other hand, it is because texts that provide in-depth and systematic descriptions of the drives are, somewhat paradoxically, exceedingly rare. For the purpose of this chapter, I have identified several passages that I think could form the basis for a coherent description of his understanding of the drives in the context of his new Homerism and the concept of contest.

First, I will explore texts that touch on the relationship between the drives and the question of choice. Second, I explore aphorisms that discuss the relationship between this presentation of choice and Nietzsche's idea of development over time, captured in the notion of self-cultivation. Finally, I show how these two could come together so that the great individual's personal abundance and unique personal identity arise from their particular configuration of internally differentiated and competing drives. My preference in exploring these texts is to quote from Nietzsche frequently, and sometimes extensively, so that readers who are not particularly familiar with Nietzsche's writing can gain an insight into the tone and context of his presentation of the issues. I also do this because Nietzsche's style is famously fragmented and diffuse. Building the Nietzschean picture of any topic requires the putting together of many fragments into a philosophical kaleidoscope, or a mural made of found objects.

The drives and choice

We begin by looking at how Nietzsche presents the drives as a sub- or pre-conscious power that influences – and even determines – the choices that individuals make. *D* §109, a text about self-mastery, is written as a physician's manual for 'combating the vehemence of a drive'. Nietzsche proffers six methods to combat an overly active drive: avoidance, regulation, indulgence, negative association, distraction and self-harm. Whatever a contemporary reader might think of these methods for self-regulation, what is relevant here is the way that Nietzsche concludes this curative meditation with a reflection on the whole process of 'combating' one's drives. He writes:

> *that* one *desires* to combat the vehemence of a drive at all, however, does not stand within our power; nor does the choice of any particular method; nor does the success or failure of this method. What is clearly the case is that in this entire procedure our intellect is only the blind instrument of *another drive* which is a *rival* of the drive whose vehemence is tormenting us...

This text offers an insight into Nietzsche's understanding of the internal composition of the individual. For him the intellect is a 'blind instrument' for the drives, it is not an independent or regulative ego or self. Understanding the intellect in this way contrasts with an understanding of the intellect as a rational arbiter between drives, as the site of free will and decision-making. Nietzsche claims that it has no such function: somehow one drive is able to take over the function of the intellect and use it against a particularly strong drive in order to conquer it. Just in case we were left in any doubt, he goes on:

> While 'we' believe we are complaining about the vehemence of a drive, at bottom it is one drive *which is complaining about another*.

This is a significant move with far-reaching consequences. Here the intellect is not free to choose which drives to foster and which to stunt. More strongly, this implies that conscious choice and decision-making are illusory experiences. Seeing these as an illusion suggests that, for Nietzsche, concepts of moral responsibility and personal accountability are problematic at best. Here there is nothing within a person that stands apart from the drives, as it were, in order to direct the behaviour of a person in response to them, that can be held responsible or accountable. There is *only* an undirected contest between drives. The outcome of this contest, as opposed to some rational choice-making process, is what determines a person's behaviour. The concluding sentences of the text describe how it is that the intellect becomes the 'blind instrument' of a vehement drive:

> for us to become aware that we are suffering from the *vehemence* of a drive presupposes the existence of another equally vehement or even more vehement drive, and that a *struggle* [*Kampf*] is in prospect in which our intellect is going to have to take sides [*Partie nehmen muss*].

This text might be taken as a somewhat contradictory assertion that there is, in fact, an independent intellect that arbitrates between drives. Here the intellect seems to stand apart from the drives, deciding between them, 'taking sides'. The phrase *Partie nehmen muss*, however, admits a different interpretation. We could understand this to say that the intellect is part of this struggle and implicated in it, not simply standing on the sideliners and discriminating between them. The nature of this 'taking sides' Nietzsche has already described: the intellect is co-opted to one side rather than the other. The whole person, intellect included, is constituted by the drives. Behaviour is determined by the struggle (*Kampf*) between them, noting the allusion to contest, which is normally described using the term *Wettkampf*.

In *D* §115 Nietzsche goes further. Here it is not merely the intellect that takes sides with various drives to determine a person's behaviour, it is the entire ego, described as a 'co-worker in the formation of an individual':

> *We are none of us* that which we appear to be in accordance with the states for which alone we have consciousness and words, and consequently praise and blame: those cruder outbursts of which alone we are aware make us *misunderstand* ourselves ... *Our opinion of ourself*, however, which we have arrived at by this erroneous path, the so-called 'ego', is thenceforth a fellow worker in the construction of our character and our destiny.

He suggests here that conscious awareness of ourselves is fundamentally unreliable, particularly with regard to our sense of self (see also *GS* §11). Consciousness can here only become aware of those things for it is equipped to become aware, including being equipped with language. For Nietzsche, the actual underlying reality of a person's drivescape might include things for which consciousness is ill-equipped to become aware of, or for which it has no words. Thus, for Nietzsche, not only does the intellect play a questionable role in arbitrating between drives, but consciousness is unreliably selective with the things that it brings to forward for intellectual rumination.

In *D* §119, a lengthy and important text on this subject, Nietzsche give much greater detail about his understanding of the relationship between consciousness and the drives than he does elsewhere. The text is a meditation on dream-states and waking-states, and their relationship to conscious awareness and the drives. Here it is the drives, rather than the intellect or ego, that interpret experience by positing imaginative explanations for sensory ('nervous') stimuli. The result, for him, is that 'there is no *essential* difference between waking and dreaming'. He writes about dreams as follows:

> [Dreams are] interpretations of nervous stimuli we receive while we are asleep, *very free*, very arbitrary interpretations of the motions of the blood and intestines, of the pressure of the arm and the bedclothes, of the sounds made by church bells, weather cocks, night revelers and other things of the kind.

Here dreams are an internal projection built on sensory inputs from the outside world. Wakefulness, he argues, is essentially the same as dreaming because it relies on the same interpretive function, not of a conscious mind, but of the drives. Before we are aware of it our drives have interpreted the world around us 'according to their requirements'.

This understanding of the drives and their operation implies that conscious interpretation of sensory input, insofar as it occurs at all, occurs within a framework that has been pre-determined by the drives. This understanding is consistent with what we have seen so far in Nietzsche: for him, conscious reflection is not free. Here we see what it is that determines the structure and content of conscious reflection: it is the drives. As he writes elsewhere: 'Our thinking is superficial and content with the surface, indeed, it does not notice that it is the surface' (*D* §125).

Nietzsche concludes *D* §119 by extending the discussion of conscious reflection to morality. As in the case of waking and dreaming, it is the physiological processes of the drives that stand behind moral judgement and evaluation:

> our moral judgements and evaluations too are only images and fantasies based on a physiological process unknown to us, a kind of acquired language for designating certain nervous stimuli ... all our so-called consciousness is a more or less fantastic commentary on an unknown, perhaps unknowable, but felt text. ... What then are our experiences? Much *more* that which we put into

them than that which they already contain! Or must we go so far as to say in themselves they contain nothing? To experience is to invent?

In these texts Nietzsche subjugates conscious thought to the internal contest of the drives; he connects the operation of the drives with physiological processes; and he credits the configuration of a person's drives with the interpretation of their experience. The drives react to a person's external world and, in doing so, they create a person's internal experiences and responses to that world. We can again see here the strongly materialist underpinning of Nietzsche's drive psychology: nervous stimuli, the movement of the bowels, the pressure of a pillow against the arm – these are the sensory inputs that the drives, in sometimes unknown and unknowable ways, transform into the imaginaerium of human experience.

This understanding of the drives in *Daybreak* lays the conceptual foundation for Nietzsche's further description of them in *The Gay Science*. Here he introduces ideas from evolutionary science to support this understanding of the individual, the result of which is the sublimation of moral judgement to aesthetics. To act morally is to value the things that you find beautiful, and to continually bring them into experience. Given that the drives determine a person's experience prior to the intervention of ego, intellect or conscious thought, we will now see Nietzsche begin to argue that moral judgements are built into a person's taste by their personal and evolutionary history, which has a crucial role in forming the substructures of a person's internal drivescape.

In *GS* §23, which we have analysed previously, Nietzsche refers to the ideal of Homeric contest – war and athletic competition – to describe the operation of the drives. However, he also describes how, in contemporary times, this contest has been transposed into the internal arena of the passions:

> the ancient civil energy and passion, which received magnificent visibility through war and competitive games, has now transformed itself into countless private passions and has merely become less visible.

We also see in this text that Nietzsche sees the process of internalizing the drives as a way of extending the notion of contest using evolutionary themes.[47] Here the individual human being develops characteristics that are relevant to their preservation, including a particular set of drives. When a person acts, this can be interpreted mechanistically: an action is simply a drive discharging itself. Drives discharge themselves in a manner that has been predetermined by the way in which they have been cultivated.

This does not mean that human beings have no choice. Rather, for Nietzsche, that choice is exercised significantly in advance of an action through which a drive is discharged. The choice to behave in a particular way is made before the event, that is, when an individual decides which drives to cultivate and which to stultify.[48] The externalization of those drives in specific behaviours is simply the consequence of those earlier choices. An apt analogy might be that of athletic training and the idea of muscle memory: an athlete performs in competition in a way that is predetermined by their training. Their body just does what it has been consciously designed to do. Thus, a person evolves by cultivating their drives, and the species evolves in part as the cumulative effect of these individual choices. Particular actions are an inevitability, a piece of fate: the person simply does what her drivescape has been cultivated to do.

Evolutionary themes are especially prominent in GS §1 and §4. There Nietzsche argues that the evolutionary processes that preserve the species operate, at least in part, because of this necessity for human beings to discharge their drives, whatever the moral evaluation of those drives might be.

In GS §1 Nietzsche puts together an evolutionary economy in which the instinct to preserve the species has created individuals that nurture their drives in such a way that even if they were to pursue their 'worst' passions ('Hatred, delight in the misfortune of others, the lust to rob and rule'), the species stands to benefit. The drives that stand behind these aversive emotions and adversarial behaviours do not work against this economy. In fact, he argues, they are especially useful for strengthening the species: He writes:

> Whether I regard human beings with a good or with an evil eye, I always find them engaged in a single task, each and every one of them: to do what benefits the preservation of the human race. Not from a feeling of love for the race, but simply because within them nothing is older, stronger, more inexorable and invincible than this instinct ... Even the most harmful person may actually be the most useful when it comes to the preservation of the species; for he nurtures in himself or through his effects on others drives without which humanity would long since have become feeble or rotten. Hatred, delight in the misfortunes of others, the lust to rob and rule, and whatever else is called evil: all belong to the amazing economy of the preservation of the species, an economy which is certainly costly, wasteful, and on the whole foolish – but still *proven* to have preserved our race so far.

In GS §4 he continues this thought, but with an emphasis on the moral evaluation of these harmful passions:

The strongest and most evil spirits have so far done the most to advance humanity: time and again they rekindled the dozing passions ... time and again they reawakened the sense of comparison, of contradiction, of delight in what is new, daring, unattempted ... What is new, however, is under all circumstances *evil*, being that which wants to conquer, to overthrow old boundary stones and pieties ... In truth, however, the evil drives are just as expedient, species-preserving, and indispensable as the good ones – they just have a different function.

Here the strengthening of the species through moral innovation takes place through the discharge of drives and the awakening of the passions. During this process, there are people who begin to behave in new ways, ways that are called evil because they challenge an old order with new standards of excellence. This is the essential function of Nietzsche's new Homerism: contest refreshes society. The critical point here is that, for Nietzsche, this kind of ethical innovation works by analogy with natural selection. It is the discharge of natural drives that leads to new behaviours and, ultimately, to new standards of behaviour. The people that discharge their drives in this way are a select few who 'delight in what is new, daring, unattempted'. They are, in short, heroic, and are equipped by their drives for precisely this kind of contest.

As a final contribution to this line of thought in *The Gay Science*, we see in GS §39 that these heroic individuals are notable for their ability to change society's general outlook by their challenging behaviours. They do this in a way that is conceptually parallel to the process of natural selection. Change takes place over time by incorporation of new features into a 'shared taste'. This is the essence of how morality becomes translated into aesthetic judgements at a societal level:

> Change in common taste is more important than that in opinions; opinions along with proofs, refutations, and the whole intellectual masquerade are only symptoms of a changed taste and most certainly *not* what they are so often taken to be, its causes. How does common taste change? Through individuals – powerful, influential, and without any sense of shame – who announce and tyrannically enforce ... the judgement of their taste and disgust: thus they put many under pressure, which gradually turns into a habit among even more and finally becomes *a need of everyone*.

It is time to put these disparate observations together. For Nietzsche, the kinds of things that make for the preservation of the species are discovered through the discharge of carefully cultivated drives enacted by heroic individuals. As these take root in society, overthrowing the current outlook, they are incorporated as a new taste. Thus, the general taste changes over time in a non-cognitive fashion (see also GS §9) so that the species as a whole (or at least, a community or society) develops a taste for these new, successful strategies and behaviours. Further, we see that in this context it is important to Nietzsche that human beings are able to discharge their drives, irrespective of the prevailing morality (see also GS §§19, 35, 294, 305). Moral innovation requires great individuals who can act against taste, 'evilly', in order to enhance and strengthen the species by establishing new standards. This can be understood through the contest ethos: the great individual brings moral innovation to society by contesting an established set of moral evaluations, and by expressing emotions and behaviours that have been outlawed by the morality. These, for Nietzsche, are aversive emotions and behaviours that imply opposition to social norms.

In other texts Nietzsche goes further in describing this great individual. Not only must they be capable of acting evilly, that is, against the prevailing judgements of the time, but they must also be capable of acting erroneously. For example, in GS §110 Nietzsche reflects on the problematic relationship between consciousness and the development of moral judgement. One issue that he highlights here is the idea that conscious thought seems to strive for knowledge of the truth. This seeking for the truth has become morally determined: it has come to seem right that the human quest is a quest for the truth. This goes along with an assumption that knowing the truth will somehow turn out to be good for human beings both individually and as a species. This assumption is problematic for Nietzsche for several reasons. In this text he argues that error might be as important to human flourishing as truth. Once again, I note the conceptual parallel with what takes place in evolution over evolutionary time:

> Through immense periods of time, the intellect produced nothing but errors; some of them turned out to be useful and species-preserving; those who hit upon or inherited them fought their fight for themselves and their progeny with greater luck. Such erroneous articles of faith, which were passed on by inheritance further and further, and finally almost became part of the basic endowment of the species, are for example: that there are enduring things; that there are identical things; that there are things, kinds of material, bodies; that a thing is what it appears to be; that our will is free; that what is good for me is also good in and for itself.

Most important here, at least for this book, is the idea that useful errors are incorporated over evolutionary time into human experience both as individual beings and as societies, so that they become 'articles of faith'. This implies some kind of evolutionary model for conducting moral experiments so that new moralities can be developed and incorporated into the species over time that includes the possibility that these judgements are wrong. Whether they are right or wrong is, in fact, a secondary consideration. For Nietzsche, the contest itself may well simply select the next set of beautiful and/or useful errors through which human flourishing can be sustained. This understanding of error in moral judgement is, in fact, the very thing that licenses the continual overthrow of moral and ethical judgment in society.

He goes on to make further claims about this human obsession with the value of truth. He argues that this will to discover the truth is a late-arriving phenomenon in humanity, associated with the emergence of conscious thought. This will-to-truth is represented by the figure of 'the thinker' and the specific drivescape Nietzsche associates with this type:

> Gradually the human brain filled itself with such judgements and convictions; and ferment, struggle, and lust for power developed in this tangle. Not only utility and delight, but also every kind of drive took part in the fight about the 'truths'; the intellectual fight became an occupation, attraction, profession, duty, dignity—knowledge and the striving for the true finally took their place as a need among the other needs. Henceforth, not only faith and conviction, but also scrutiny, denial, suspicion, and contradiction were a *power*, all 'evil' instincts were subordinated to knowledge and put in its service ... Thus knowledge became a part of life and, as life, a continually growing power, until finally knowledge and the ancient basic errors struck against each other, both as life, both as power, both in the same person. The thinker – that is now the being in whom the drive to truth and those life-preserving errors are fighting their first battle...

Thus, we find in the thinker that the will to truth has become a drive. This drive is contested by other drives that are founded on useful errors and supported by the evolutionary drive, the will to life. For Nietzsche, this battle between the will to truth and the will to life is of ultimate significance:

> In relation to the significance of this battle, everything else is a matter of indifference: the ultimate question about the condition of life is posed here, and the first attempt is made here to answer the question through experiment. To what extent can truth stand to be incorporated? — that is the question; that is the experiment.

The 'thinker' in which this struggle[49] takes place participates in an experiment of ultimate significance. This experiment is conducted within the thinker, but not as an internal contest between conscious thought (which seek truth) and the drives (which express passions) as one might expect. Conscious thought, remember, is merely a tool with which drives struggle against each other. Here truth and error are incorporated as drives, they contest one another, and the winner of this contest will simply take the species into its next phase of development. This is not because of some inherent value in truth: it is simply the outcome of a contest between drives which may or may not have a species-preserving or life-affirming effect. The decision to follow what is true or what is false is, in actual fact, not a decision at all.

One way of making sense of this is to say that, for Nietzsche, consciousness is the mechanism by which the underlying process of decision-making and choice, a subterranean process conducted by contesting drives, comes into our experience. More precisely, consciousness is the means by which the *outcome* of this contest of drives rises to awareness, and we become erroneously aware of it as 'making choices'. He summarizes in GS §111:

> The course of logical thoughts and inferences in our brains today corresponds to a process and battle of drives that taken separately are all very illogical and unjust; we usually experience only the outcome of the battle: that is how quickly and covertly this ancient mechanism runs its course in us.

This interpretation of consciousness is expressed paradigmatically in GS §127. Here Nietzsche addresses the question of will and choice directly, in a context where he is presenting the individual as the site of sublimated drive-contests:

> Every thoughtless person believes that the will is effective, that willing is something simple, absolutely given, underivable, and intelligible in itself. When he does something, e.g. strikes something, he is convinced that it is *he* who is striking. and that he did the striking because he *wanted* to strike. He does not notice a problem here; the feeling of *will* suffices for him to assume cause and effect, but also to believe that he *understands* their relation. He knows nothing of the mechanism of what happened and the hundredfold delicate work that has to be done to bring about the strike, or of the incapacity of the will as such to do even the slightest part of this work.

This 'hundredfold delicate work' is the work of cultivating drives. For Nietzsche, then, the experience of making a choice is just that – an experience generated by consciousness. Choice, if we may even call it that, happens ahead of that experience, it is determined by an underlying, and often unknown, contest between drives.

GS §333 reinforces this idea. Here Nietzsche moves from the question of will to the phenomenon of knowledge. For him, knowledge is the coming-to-consciousness of a built-in aesthetic judgement, a 'taste', which is also derived from an often-unknown contest between drives:

> Before knowledge is possible, each of these impulses [to laugh, lament or curse] must first have presented its one-sided view of the thing or event; then comes the fight [*Kampf*] between these one-sided views, and occasionally out of it a mean, an appeasement, a concession to all three sides, a kind of justice and contract ... Since only the ultimate reconciliation scenes and final accounts of this long process rise to consciousness, we suppose that *intelligere* must be something conciliatory, just, and good, something essentially opposed to the instincts, when in fact *it is only a certain behaviour of the drives towards one another*. For the longest time, conscious thought was considered thought itself; only now does the truth dawn on us that by far the greatest part of our mind's activity proceeds unconscious and unfelt...

To summarize: in these texts Nietzsche conceives the individual as composed of underlying drives. These drives contest one another, striving for supremacy. The outcome of this contest determines the choices they will make and their experience of the world. This process takes place over long periods of time, analogous to evolutionary time, as individuals incorporate the outcomes of innumerable contests (both within great individuals and between great individuals) into their moral judgements. Moral judgements are, therefore, one example of how a new 'taste' can evolve in human beings as the outcome of contest. This process also results in the contest between truth and error in the figure of the thinker: Nietzsche does not concede that taste evolves by incorporating truths but rather that truth and error are simply contesting drives. All of this centres on the great individual, who is able to bring these internal contests onto a public stage, who is able to act evilly and erroneously in order to conduct experiments in the field of morality, the outcome of which may establish new values that support human flourishing. These great individuals are able to behave in this way because of an internal self-moderating alignment between their drives so that they reach towards a state of internal agonistic equilibrium, a state of productive tension that provides them with their personal abundance.

The drives and self-development

In what follows I aim to show that, for Nietzsche, this internal state of agonistic equilibrium is what creates the great individual's capacity for self-development. The way in which a drive gains ascendancy and then functions to organize subordinate drives into an equilibrious state is addressed in both *Daybreak* and

The Gay Science as a function of a person's environment. This 'environment' is broadly construed and includes everything from diet through to personal relationships and the broader social and moral context.

In *GS* §7, for example, Nietzsche longs for the construction of 'cyclops-buildings', by which he seems to mean the construction of methods for analysing the influence of an environment on a person's behaviour. There he wonders:

> where could you find a history of love, of avarice, of envy, of conscience, of piety, of cruelty? ... Is there a philosophy of nutrition? ... Has anyone collected people's experiences of living together – in monasteries, for example? Has anyone depicted the dialectic of marriage and friendship?

Notwithstanding that today this kind of work is done through the disciplines of the social sciences, this text, together with his general theory of the drives described above, raises further questions about Nietzsche's understanding of individual choice in the context of self-development. As we saw above, his proposal is one where action is determined through the outcome of an internal and often unrecognized contest between an individual's drives. This outcome results from the relative strength of the drives involved, and we see here some ways in which Nietzsche understands this environment: emotions, diet and social experiences. This takes us in two different directions. There is a freedom here: the drives play out their contest freely, without the intervention of a disciplining or constraining intellect or consciousness. There is also, however, a determinism here: the relative strength of the drives is determined by externalities. This tension between determinism and freedom in Nietzsche's proposal for understanding the drives is thrown into sharp relief by an overall assertion of his that stands at the heart of this book: the great individual is supposedly a free spirit able to contest social norms on the basis of their individuality, and yet this individuality is itself determined by factors that make their choices inevitable, even mechanical. Further, these factors include the very social norms that the great individual will seek to contest.

In my view, Nietzsche does not back away from determinism in his presentation of the great individual. Rather, his form of determinism includes a particular idea of chance that he combines with a subtle treatment of the ancient Greek concept of self-cultivation. For him, based partly on his understanding of evolutionary biology, natural processes operate purely on the basis of chance. The human desire for purpose – for a teleologically understood goal that brings order and causality into an otherwise random sequence – is untenable. For example, in *GS* §1, he writes:

> The ethical teacher makes his appearance as the teacher of the purpose of existence in order that what happens necessarily and always, by itself and without a purpose, shall henceforth seem to be done for a purpose.

Similarly, in *GS* §109, he writes that

> The total character of the world ... is for all eternity chaos, not in the sense of a lack of necessity but of a lack of order, organization, form, beauty, wisdom, and whatever else our aesthetic anthropomorphisms are called...

In these texts, Nietzsche expresses his view that natural processes have no intentionality, directionality or referentiality. Human beings have become accustomed to seeing the world with reference to themselves, for good or for ill. Nietzsche tries to disabuse his readers of this perception, presenting nature as blind with regard to human being and intention. Human beings are but one small part of a natural system and the actions of human beings are as blind as the activity of any other part of that natural system. To the extent that a theory of conscious choice and agency disturbs a stochastically materialist vision of the world, Nietzsche unequivocally rejects it.

This idea is explored at length in an earlier text, *D* §130. Here we see human action presented as an act of nature, that is, as the chance coming together of different elements to produce an outcome in such a way that the illusion of purpose is shattered. In this aphorism Nietzsche directly addresses the problems of teleology and of choice as two sides of the same problem, two realms. The one realm, that of purpose and will, is where people live consciously and build for themselves a 'spider's web of purposes'. The other realm is one that hangs above us, the realm of chance, filled with accidents, described here as 'monsters'. We fear these accidents for their ability to destroy the spider's web, the purposes, that we have laboured to create. We also appreciate their ability to break through the tedium of a life constrained by these constructed purposes. The realm of chance, what he calls 'the great cosmic stupidity', does indeed break into our lives to do just that, to destroy the illusion of purpose:

> This belief in the two realms is a primeval romance and fable: we clever dwarfs, with our will and purposes, are oppressed by those stupid, arch-stupid giants, chance accidents, overwhelmed and often trampled to death by them – but in spite of all that we would not like to be without the harrowing poetry of their proximity, for these monsters often arrive when our life, involved as it is in the spider web of purposes, has become too tedious or too filled with anxiety, and provide us with a sublime diversion by for once *breaking* the web — not that these irrational creatures would do so intentionally! Or even notice they had done so! But their coarse bony hands tear through our net as if it were air.

He goes on to discuss how, in his view, different cultures and religions have used metaphysics to describe chance: those unexplained phenomena that disrupt our sense of purpose are attributed to an invisible netherworld. For him, this distinction between the human world of will and purpose and the metaphysical world of chance and chaos is fundamentally flawed. It implicitly rejects his naturalistic assertion that human action comes about just as much by chance, with just the same destructive effects. It is the human world, the observed and experienced world, that is the world of chance and chaos:

> Let us therefore *learn* ... in our supposed realm of purposes and reason the giants are likewise the rulers! And our purposes and our reasons are not dwarves but giants! And our nets are just as often and just as roughly broken *by us ourselves* as they are by slates from the roof!

Nietzsche not only rejects the reality of purpose and will in the context of deliberative choice, but he also discounts their possibility. For him, the illusion of purpose and will is created by random natural activity when considered over infinite periods of time. From this perspective, random activity will necessarily coincide with precisely the kind of activity generated by purposeful or wilful agency, when considered at a particular point in time. As the saying goes, a stopped clock is right twice a day. For him, human action can be understood in the same way. It is not that some random acts break in to disrupt the ordinary human world of purpose and choice, it is that human acts of purpose and will are themselves random acts of chance, not the product of some considered, rational choice-making being, even though they may seem to be so at particular points in time. He continues in *D* §130:

> And if you want to conclude from this: 'so there is only one realm, that of chance accidents and stupidity?' – one will have to add: yes, perhaps there is only one realm, perhaps there exists neither will nor purposes, and we have only imagined them. Those iron hands of necessity which shake the dice-box of chance play their game for an infinite length of time: so that there *have* to be throws which exactly resemble purposiveness and rationality of every degree. *Perhaps* our acts of will and our purposes are nothing but just such throws – and we are only too limited and too vain to comprehend our extreme limitedness: which consists in the fact that we ourselves shake the dice-box with iron hands, that we ourselves in our most intentional actions do no more than play the game of necessity.

This 'game of necessity' can be understood by drawing on the analysis of the relationship between the drives and choice described above. The decision to act in this way or in that way is not so much a decision as it is the inevitable outcome of the contest of internal drives. It is a necessity because there is a particular drive, which must act in a particular way, that has gained its ascendancy within the individual. Thus, it seems to me that Nietzsche's determinism is the foundation for his understanding of the possibility of self-cultivation. The great individual is as much a piece of fate as any other natural phenomenon. It is as a necessity, a fatality, that the individual becomes a 'free' spirit who can challenge social norms by acting 'evilly' and experimentally. While this may appear to be a frustratingly circular depiction of the individual, in my view, its power lies in opening up possibilities for meaningful and practical application, and in reinforcing precisely through this circularity the idea of self-grounded but also emergent personhood.

The mechanism that Nietzsche proposes for an individual to engage in this circle of self-development is self-cultivation, an idea for which he draws heavily on ancient Greek philosophy. In *D* §560, 'What we are at liberty to do', Nietzsche pictures a person cultivating their drives as one might cultivate a garden:[50]

> One can dispose of one's drives like a gardener and, though few know it, cultivate the shoots of anger, pity, curiosity, vanity as productively and profitably as a beautiful fruit tree on a trellis.

This includes both cultivation and neglect, active and passive self-directed work:

> one can also let nature rule and only attend to a little embellishment and tidying-up here and there; one can, finally, without paying any attention to them at all, let the plants grow up and fight their fight out among themselves – indeed, one can take delight in such a wilderness and desire precisely this delight, though it gives one some trouble, too.

The point of the text is not to recommend either cultivation or neglect but rather to claim that few people realize their ability to perform these acts of self-cultivation. This lack of awareness is fostered by philosophies that consider the individual incapable of development over time:

> All this we are at liberty to do: but how many know we are at liberty to do it? Do the majority not *believe* in *themselves* as in complete *fully-developed facts*? Have the great philosophers not put their seal on this prejudice with the doctrine of the unchangeability of character?

So, we have then these elements of Nietzsche's theory: the great individual is composed of internal drives that compose themselves into an order without conscious reflection, they grow or wither dependent on chance interactions with their environment, and yet the great individual can cultivate their drives so as to produce certain effects. As noted above, these positions seem incompatible. On the one hand he seems to be saying that the individual does not include a choosing intellect or ego that can arbitrate between competing drives, and on the other he seems to be saying that conscious, deliberative self-development over time is possible.

Ansell-Pearson and Bamford, noting this problem, propose to resolve it by focusing not on the theoretical clarity of Nietzsche's argument from a psychological perspective, but from the perspective of Nietzsche's critique of customary morality:

> Nietzsche's remarks on subjectivity and the self are made fundamentally for critical-ethical purposes: Nietzsche's promotion of the conditions for ongoing development and self-cultivation of free-spirited ethical agency requires exposure of the presumptions of customary moral agency.[51]

They go on to argue for a concept of autonomous subjectivity that constitutes an implicitly emergent self, a self that is constituted by the process of self-cultivation, rather than existing as the object of self-cultivation.[52]

This is a useful step in the right direction. However, it seems to me that this argument could have been made more forcefully. For Nietzsche, it is not as though there is a choice between free moral agency and naturalistic determinism. The conditions of customary morality are themselves deterministic – slavery to customary morality is the problem. I would argue that Nietzsche's solution to this is his aesthetic ideals: the great individual is *by nature* free from the compulsions of customary morality, and a slave *only* to their own taste. Thus, acts of self-cultivation are the outcome not so much of conscious reflection and decision-making but as a piece of fate themselves, that is, as the development of an intuitive aesthetic judgement limited and determined by the biological necessities of mind and body. This aesthetic sense is directed towards the person one would like to become, towards one's future self, and it leads to a (admittedly self-reinforcing) process of self-cultivation. This aesthetic sense can be distinguished from intellect: it seems to emerge out of the particular combination of drives that form a specific person. The great individual, then, is the rare (and randomly selected) case of someone who grasps this possibility for self-cultivation and goes on realize it in their lives.

If we are to read these texts together and attempt to bring all of these ideas into one integrated notion of the individual, this picture would, I think, be something as follows. Individuals are composed of many drives competing with each other for ascendancy. Over time, due to the interaction of their natural constitution with their environment, certain drives gain ascendancy, and, in the best case, these bring other drives into some kind of subordinated alignment. This combination of ascendant and subordinate drives implies the development of a taste, the sense of an individual's preferred style of life. This taste is able to select the environments in which it finds the greatest satisfaction. The harmonization of the drives thus becomes an ongoing and self-reinforcing process in keeping with these developing and aesthetically motivated self-directed preferences. For the great individual, this is a virtuous cycle of alignment and reinforcement. Further, this individual can be thought of as both fully determined and constantly developing over time as a natural agent in a stochastic system. The personhood of this great individual is given not as a theoretical, point-in-time abstraction, but through this self-directed agency. The individual constitutes themselves as they work on themselves. They are both emergent over time and determined at a specific point in time.

This is the case of the great individual. The case of the lesser individual is one in which this self-organizing alignment of drives is not possible. They remain inwardly chaotic, their taste for themselves and their world is never defined and therefore cannot be refined over time. They are as much the outcome of inner necessity as the great individual, it is simply that this inner necessity does not lead to strength, harmony and increasing refinement. It leads to weakness, chaos and the impossibility of personal development over time. If there is a pessimism in Nietzsche's approach, it is the claim that individuals fall only into one of these two groups, and by virtue of this classification their fate is sealed. It might be possible, however, to reconceptualize this in less stark terms – I would be inclined to argue that this binary separation of types is an oversimplification and that people generally find themselves somewhere along a continuum of infinite depth and variety. This continuum runs between internal chaos and life-denying, misdirected attention either towards the self or towards others at one end, and internal alignment with self-supporting cultivation, both of oneself and on one's environment. We can, therefore, release ourselves from the value judgement about human types that seems so deeply embedded in Nietzsche's approach.

The drives and individuality

In the case of Nietzsche's great individual, the effect of this self-reinforcing internal system is the development of increasingly unique characteristics. Personhood emerges as an individual creates integration and harmony, albeit within an agonistic ecosystem, within their drivescape. This is the result of the particular and specific internal contests between drives that constitute them: this configuration of drives defines their uniqueness as a human being. Thus, for Nietzsche, the self is indeed emergent, but not on the basis of social relations external to them. Rather the relations that constitute them is that of their internal *polis*. The process by which this person emerges from the configuration of their drives is described by Nietzsche in various ways. What is important here is to understand how the drives are related to his idea of the individual as unique. This is central to the notion of difference in agonistic equilibrium: we get to know who an individual is by getting to know the intimate details of their drivescape, and how to become part of the environment in which some drives flourish and others whither. This understanding of the other person, as we will see in the following chapter, is essential to higher friendship.

The specificity of the drives and the manner of their integration is particularly emphasized in *The Gay Science*. For example, in GS §113, the integration of drives is described in terms of scientific enquiry where the success of the enquiry depends on the alignment of several drives at once. Similarly, in GS §288 it is described as a single elevated mood. But the most potent idea for understanding how the drives constitute a unique and emergent person appears in several texts throughout *The Gay Science*. This is the idea of a singular value standard.

The concept of the singular value standard arises in several texts in which Nietzsche focuses on the idea of nobility. In GS §3 Nietzsche links his notion of a great individual as a noble person with a 'higher nature' with the idea of internal drives that coalesce into a singular value standard (*singuläres Werthmaas*). His argument is that in the noble person 'several feelings of pleasure and displeasure' unite to create an overwhelming passion. The noble person submits to this passion, which is the outcome of otherwise conflicting drives that somehow coalesce into a defined aesthetic sense or 'taste' (*der Geschmack*). He describes this result, the taste of the noble person, as follows:

> The higher nature's taste is for exceptions, for things that leave most people cold and seem to lack sweetness; the higher nature has a singular value standard. Moreover, it usually believes that the idiosyncrasy of its taste is not a singular value standard; rather it posits its values and disvalues as generally valid and so becomes incomprehensible and impractical.

Nietzsche goes on to argue that by taking their idiosyncratic moral taste to be generally valid, the noble person perpetrates an injustice on others. To be 'just' in this situation, presumably, would be to recognize that these noble values are in fact specific to an individual's taste and therefore *not* generally valid. In any case, Nietzsche's emphasis is on the singularity and idiosyncrasy of values that coalesce as drives become integrated within a great individual.

This thought is expanded in *GS* §55, 'The ultimate noblemindedness'. Again, here we see the noble person as someone overcome by a single passion, which results in a singular value standard that they relentlessly pursue:

> So what makes a person 'noble'? Certainly not making sacrifices; even those burning with lust make sacrifices. Certainly not following some passion; for there are contemptible passions. Certainly not that one does something for others without selfishness: perhaps no one is more consistently selfish than the noble one. – Rather, the passion that overcomes the noble one is a singularity [*eine Sonderheit*], and he fails to realize this: the use of a rare and singular standard [*singulären Maassstabes*] and almost a madness … hitting upon values the scale for which has not yet been invented; a sacrifice on altars made for an unknown god; a courage without any desire for honours; a self-sufficiency that overflows [*Überfluss*] and communicates to men and things.

This text returns us to our core themes of abundance and difference, connecting the abundance of the noble person with their internal coherence and drive-harmony. For Nietzsche, each great individual (and their moral taste) is unique, even if they claim that they are universally valid. The great individual, as a result of this single-minded pursuit of personally bespoke values, becomes able to give to others out of their abundance, captured here in the metaphor of overflow.

To conclude this text, Nietzsche offers an optimistically democratic prospect:

> Note, however, that by means of this standard everything usual, near, and indispensable, in short, that which most preserved the species, and in general the rule of humanity hitherto, was inequitably judged and on the whole slandered in favour of the exceptions. To become the advocate of the rule – that might be the ultimate form and refinement in which noblemindedness manifests itself on earth.

Here Nietzsche creates an additional complexity for the interpreter by introducing the idea that the noble individual, even as a unique and incomparable judge of values, advocates for 'the rule'. On the one hand, it seems self-evident that Nietzsche is in favour of the rare type, the noble, higher person. On the other hand, he seems to argue here for the extension of nobility so that it comes to embrace not just the exception, the different and unique, but also the general and undifferentiated.

A resolution to this conundrum can perhaps be found by drawing together some of the threads of this discussion. On the one hand we have the idea of the great individual as the site of contesting drives that form an integrated impassioned interiority, and on the other hand we have the idea of absolute singularity, the difference(s) between one great individual and another. Perhaps the 'rule' that Nietzsche outlines here is that each individual is to develop the peculiar environment – moral, social and physical – that is best suited to their particularity. This, at least, would be consistent with the idea of self-cultivation described above. The great individual is someone who experiences self-overcoming to the degree that their passions are not unruly, their internal world is integrated and aligned. This, in turn, enables them to refine their personal identity, to fashion themselves into a work of art. This perhaps is Nietzsche's rule: great individuals ultimately advocate for all people to follow this path, to become their own unique work of art, to discover their own singular value and standard and the particular style of living that goes along with it.

In my view, the idea that values are created according to the idiosyncrasies of an individual is one that animates Nietzsche's understanding of emergent personhood. These value standards do not arise simply from the ratiocination of an individual over their lifespan but as drives that, when integrated with one another so as to create an internal equilibrium, provide the individual with their own personal abundance. The idea of integrated a continually self-constituting drivescape that makes the individual unique and the idea of self-overcoming by cultivating preferred environments come together so that the great individual becomes emergent as self-sufficient, self-reliant and self-defining. As a result of this, he or she has personal abundance which can be shared with others.

This is an important result for understanding Nietzsche's ethics as an heroic ethics. The independent (but emergent) constitution of the individual is not self-dissolution, solipsism or narcissism. It is self-overcoming: the taming and cultivation of passions, instincts and inclinations into self-creating drives. It is severe and exacting discipline, exerted over oneself, to create oneself *ex nihilo*, as it were. There is a sense in which the much-discussed trans- or re-valuation of values within Nietzsche's thought is, in fact, a process of constant self-evaluation, self-critique and a corresponding self-fashioning.

This is outlined in GS §290. Here Nietzsche describes how self-overcoming by submitting to the peculiarity of one's own values is an artistic act of self-creation:

> To 'give style' to one's character – a great and rare art! It is practiced by those who survey all the strengths and weaknesses that their nature has to offer and then fit them into an artistic plan until each appears as art and reason and even weaknesses delight the eye!

For Nietzsche, the great individual, conceived as a self-defining, self-sustaining person, is not free from rules or constraints. Rather, they are able to develop and implement the various constraints that are most appropriate to their own peculiar characteristics, to work under an 'artistic plan', and to cheerfully submit to it:

> In the end, when the [artistic] work is complete, it becomes clear how it was the force of a single taste [*des selben Geschmacks*] that ruled and shaped everything great and small – whether the taste was good or bad means less than one may think; it's enough that it was one taste! It will be the strong and domineering natures who experience their most exquisite pleasure under such coercion, in being bound by but also perfected under their own law...

Thus Nietzsche's great individual has the freedom to live as a self-determined, self-referential and uniquely constituted being not because of an excess of self-indulgence but rather through the severity of self-imposed restraint. Nietzsche's self-sufficient individual is able to harness the energy of their internal contest by submitting to its particular style, in order to develop their life as an ethical artwork, that is, according to an aesthetic taste. The weak character is one who is ruled by passions, only able to satisfy themselves in the absence of constraint, ironically becoming the victim of these passions. As a consequence, they are characterized by resentment and victimize others with their sheer ignobility and ugliness:

> Conversely, it is the weak characters with no power over themselves who *hate* the constraint of style ... they become slaves as soon as they serve; they hate to serve ... For one thing is needful: that a human being should *attain* satisfaction with himself – be it through this or that poetry or art; only then is a human being at all tolerable to behold! Whoever is dissatisfied with himself is continually prepared to avenge himself for this, and we others will be his victims if only by having to endure his sight.

In contrast to this domineering, wild and unruly individual, Nietzsche's great individuals exercise extreme constraint in pursuit of the artistic vision that they have developed for themselves, and in becoming satisfied with themselves, are able to give to others. Nietzsche's alternative to customary morality and social norms is not hedonism, solipsism or narcissism, but self-creation under the constraint of an individually defined style of living.

Conclusions

Thus, we find that the self-overcoming of the great individual that brings the drives into alignment and integration results in a form of magnanimous generosity towards others. The surprising dynamics of this generosity will be the subject of the following chapter when I look more closely at social relations. By way of anticipation and conclusion, we can consider several texts in which the personal abundance of the great individual is tied to their ability to give generously to others. This connection between abundance and generosity is characterized in various ways in Nietzsche's published writings, particularly after 1882. The themes of abundance (*der Überschuss, überschütten*) and overflow (*der Überfluss, überfluten*) are more pronounced in, for example, *The Gay Science* Book 5 (1887) than in either *Daybreak* (1881) or *The Gay Science* Books 1–4 (1882).

On the cusp of this thematic transition, *The Gay Science* Book 4 concludes with a description of the overflowing abundance of Nietzsche's great individuals (*GS* §342).[53] This text is imagistically connected with texts such as *GS* §289 where Nietzsche characterizes the great individual as able to create his or her own sun, by which he means his or her own bespoke ethical, social and personal climate. In this text we encounter Zarathustra musing on his relationship to the sun. In this musing, we learn that Zarathustra is weighed down by the personal abundance that this affords him, and he feels the need to go down from his mountain in order to engage with others. He does this to unburden himself of his largesse by giving generously to others:

> But at last his heart changed – and one morning he arose with rosy dawn, stepped before the sun, and spoke to it thus: 'You great heavenly body! What would your happiness be if you did not have those for whom you shine!... Behold, I am sick of my wisdom, like a bee that has collected too much honey; I need outstretched hands; I would like to give away and distribute...'

The idea that the personal abundance of the great individual flows outwards towards others is here presented as the unburdening of the great individual. This idea is reformulated in *GS* Book 5, on the other side of the thematic transition we are examining, from a much more positive stance. In *GS* §382, 'The great health', he writes

> Another ideal runs before us, a peculiar, seductive, dangerous ideal... the ideal of a spirit that plays naively, i.e. not deliberately but from overflowing abundance and power, with everything that was hitherto called holy, good, untouchable, divine; a spirit which has gone so far that the highest thing which the common

people quite understandably accept as its measure of value would signify for it danger, decay, debasement, or at any rate recreation, blindness, temporary self-oblivion: the ideal of a human, superhuman well-being and benevolence...

In this description of the overwhelming superabundance of Nietzsche's great individual, we find the ideas of naïve play and of human-superhuman benevolence (*menschlich-übermenschlichen Wohlseins und Wohlwollens*). Here the personal superabundance of the great individual is directed towards others as benevolence and playfulness. Great well-being (*Wohlsein*) and great benevolence (*Wohlwollen*) go together.

The ability of the great individual to engage productively and generously with others is, then, intimately connected to the agonistic contest that takes place within them and defines their unique identity. The twin themes of difference (here expressed as the particularity of the individual) and abundance (here expressed as overflow) are of decisive significance. By overcoming themselves, submitting themselves to the discipline of self-creation and focusing on themselves in all their singularity and peculiarity, the great individual becomes able to give to others in their social relations. This is not the self-sacrificial giving of Christian morality, nor is it the compassionate engagement with others that Schopenhauer outlines. As we will see in the following chapter, it is the Nietzschean ideal of higher friendship. As each individual is utterly unique, constituted by a specific configuration of drives that continually emerge in a given environment, higher friendship is built on an intimate knowledge of these processes not only for oneself, but also for another.

7

Friendship as contest

In the preceding chapters I have described the way that Nietzsche's ethics emerges in response to three important influences – Christianity, Schopenhauer's philosophy and evolutionary biology. Further, I have shown that his response to these influences is shaped by the ancient Greek ideal of heroic contest. As we have seen, Nietzsche's incorporation of these influences implies that, for all their significant differences, they share common features that contrast with this agonistic impulse. One of these is that, at least as Nietzsche understood them, they share a negative stance towards the natural world, a stance that emphasizes privation and deficit. Nietzsche saw in classical Greek culture, and particularly in early literature such as Homeric epic poetry, a positive attitude towards the natural world, including human life, that celebrated abundance. I have shown how Nietzsche developed his understanding of great individuals as personally abundant by applying this ancient idea of contest to a person's internal life, conceiving the self as a battlefield of competing drives. Nietzsche's view seems to be that personal abundance arises in great individuals as the outcome of this internal contest.

A second feature of Nietzsche's adaptation of Homeric heroism is his emphasis on difference. For Nietzsche, Christianity's monotheism and Schopenhauer's monistic metaphysics are oppressively reductionistic. Against these perspectives, he turns to the idea of ancient Greek contest to conceptualize an ethics that acknowledges and cultivates individual difference. For him, an appreciation of difference is essential for forming ethical judgements, at least if those judgements are about what is best for each individual to flourish in their particular circumstances. In this context, Nietzsche sees that evolutionary biology identifies natural mechanisms for generating difference, particularly in the idea of natural selection. Thus, the result of his attempt to integrate evolutionary biology into his Homeric ethos is an emphasis on the specificity of each individual person as a unique product of naturally stochastic forces. Nietzsche understands the specificity of each individual human being in terms of their drives: it is a specific set of drives and their interrelations that defines each individual against every other individual. His great individuals find themselves in an internal state of agonistic equilibrium, created by an ongoing process of self-overcoming. Further, Nietzsche claims, this process of internal contest between differential and opposing drives is actually what generates the personal abundance that is characteristic of a great individual.

This is the argument of the preceding chapters. We are now able to consider Nietzsche's ethics in terms of social relationships. I have noted above that some scholars think Nietzsche promotes an arch-individualism in which concern for others plays little to no part. This view is magnified when we consider Nietzsche's critical stance to ethical norms such as compassion and love. It is tempting to conclude that Nietzsche does not offer an ethics after all, but rather a justification for extreme individualism that fosters harmful behaviours and rejects nurturing, pro-social ones.

I have resisted this temptation, instead claiming that Nietzsche does not propose a narcissistic or solipsistic individualism. We saw in the previous chapter one protection against this charge: for him the great individual does not simply give him- or herself over to the passions at the expense of other people. Rather, this individual engages in a task of self-overcoming, which requires self-discipline in order to achieve a particular internal equilibrium within themselves, harmonizing their contesting drives. In this chapter, I will show how this process of self-overcoming extends into social relationships. Nietzsche's view, I claim, is that if we conceive individuals as unique arrangements of drives, who are on their own particular pathway to self-overcoming, we can also see how it is possible to develop positive social relationships where individuals understand each other's drivescapes, and work towards each other's flourishing.[1]

In this chapter I argue that, for Nietzsche, this is the essence of one particular form of social relationship, namely, higher friendship. One important feature of this kind of friendship is that it can incorporate aversive emotions and adversarial behaviours. This is because it is agonistic in its structure: it is a contest relation.

Further, I will show that we can contrast how Nietzsche describes higher friendship from other forms of social interaction where contest also plays a role, such as the relationships between enemies or neighbours. What we will see is that higher friendship is *the* form of contest in which 'great love' plays a vital role.[2] This understanding of great love as the hallmark of higher friendship means that within it individuals find not only a means to self-overcoming but also the means to benefit others. In particular, they benefit their friends by promoting the friend's self-overcoming. In higher friendship, great love uses every tool available – love, hate, compassion, opposition, enmity, authenticity, deception – in order to support the other's self-overcoming.

In this chapter I demonstrate how Nietzsche conceptualizes and argues for higher friendship as an expression of this kind of great love. Firstly, I will explain how Nietzsche broadens the concept of contest in order to ascribe a positive value to adversity in general and to shape his ethics so that it can include adversarial experiences. I then consider some alternative approaches to this topic in Nietzsche studies, which, for all their strengths, ultimately do not fully accommodate Nietzsche's interest in the connection between adversity and human flourishing. Secondly, I compare friendship, enmity and neighbourliness as forms of social relationship that incorporate adversarial components, but in different ways and on different foundations. I demonstrate that, for Nietzsche, while each of these has its higher and lower forms, higher friendship stands alone because of its capacity to fully embody the signature features of contest, namely, individual difference and personal abundance. As with the individual, in friendship, the contesting individuals find that they are able to enter into an agonistic equilibrium, where the push and pull of emotions and behaviours is sustainable and productive.

Contest and adversity

First, we will look at the idea of adversity and its importance for Nietzsche's ethics. Throughout this book I have emphasized the figure of the great individual in Nietzsche's ethics. It must be acknowledged, however, that Nietzsche's work includes not only his ideals but also their antitheses. These include what he considered to be 'decadent' individuals, who participate in 'lower' forms of social relationships.[3] There are texts where Nietzsche describes social interactions between decadents and great individuals. Perhaps the two most famous metaphors that he uses for this are those of master/slave (*GM* §I.10) and eagle/sheep (*GM* §I.13). The moral problems that emerge from these descriptions are manifold. Nietzsche seems to presuppose, for example, that the higher type should be free to instrumentalize the lower type for their own purposes. Further, he also seems to endorse their contempt for, or indifference towards, the 'lower' type's experience of resentment and animosity.

These texts raise significant questions that I do not propose to address here. It is sufficient to indicate that, at least in my view, these themes emerge most forcefully in Nietzsche's later writings. Many of his earlier texts, the ones I have focused on in this book, present a more balanced, moderate and integrated form of Nietzsche's philosophy in general and of his ethics in particular. While the seeds of these ideas are no doubt present throughout his writing, it is in the later texts that we find an increasingly strident emphasis on an anti-egalitarian order of rank between human types, resulting in social relationships that are construed in strictly hierarchical terms,[4] and which culminates in his so-called 'aristocratic radicalism'.[5] Noting these problems, in this chapter I limit my analysis to Nietzsche's presentation of his idealized individuals in their highest forms of social interaction. Limiting the analysis in this way is important because, as we will see, Nietzsche's concept of higher friendship includes the ability of the participants to withstand and profit from adversity, even in their intimate relationships. One the key elements of this is that the participants in the relationship are more or less equals.[6]

We have seen in the preceding chapter how Nietzsche transforms the performative notion of Homeric contest by internalizing it. In addition to this transformation, Nietzsche also adapts it to include a general understanding that the optimal conditions for human flourishing are adverse conditions. These include danger, pain, tension and opposition.[7] In contrast to Christian love and Schopenhauer's morality of compassion, Nietzsche formulates his ethics of great love within the context of higher friendship so that he can reject the idea that everyone should always feel compelled, in each and every circumstance, to alleviate the suffering generated by adverse conditions. Rather, Nietzsche suggests that it is the virtue of higher friendship to encourage or even intensify adverse experiences because it is through adverse conditions that individuals find their greatest opportunities for self-overcoming. This extended notion of contest shapes Nietzsche's ideal of friendship – it is in higher friendships that the widest array of strategies for personal growth can be brought to bear in an ethical way, including opposition and enmity. It is clear why this must take place between equals. If it is hierarchically construed the prospect of equilibrium vanishes and the likelihood increases that one of the participants will be annihilated.

Let us consider the relationship that Nietzsche sees between adversity and a certain kind of happiness before we consider its application to higher friendship. In GS §302 Nietzsche writes about Homeric happiness as the outcome of adversity. He first argues that Homeric happiness involves developing a refined taste, which includes the capacity to experience suffering and pain *exquisitely*.

The text ends, however, with the critique that this extreme refinement made Homer unable to endure the slightest failure:

> To have refined senses and a refined taste; to be accustomed to the exquisite and most excellent things of the spirit ... who would not like all of this to be *his* possession, his state! It was the *happiness of Homer*! ... But don't disregard the fact that with this Homeric happiness in one's soul one is also more capable of suffering ... [As] one becomes ever more refined in pain and eventually too refined; in the end, any slight discontentment and disgust was enough to spoil life for Homer.

Here we see that Nietzsche's contest transcends Homeric ideals. For Nietzsche, an adverse circumstance – great or small – presents an opportunity for the individual to overcome themselves. As long as the ability to develop a refined, sublime and even exquisite experience in suffering allows the sufferer to discover new possibilities for flourishing, it is desirable. But if this refined appreciation for the experience of suffering leads you to avoid it, it becomes a problem. Nietzsche sees a failure in the Homeric ethos here: ultimately this refined experience of suffering led Homer to avoid it.

We can develop this further by briefly sketching Bernard Reginster's account of Nietzsche's concept of the will to power.[8] Reginster contrasts Nietzsche's understanding of the will to power with Schopenhauer's understanding of the will to life. He argues that Nietzsche replaces Schopenhauer's pessimistic idea of the will to life with his optimistic notion of will as the exercise of power. On this reading, Nietzsche conceives the will to power as both the desire to obtain a particular outcome and the desire to overcome resistance in order to obtain it. For Reginster, the Nietzschean person must not only want the object of their desire, they must also want to overcome resistance in order to obtain it.[9] An apt metaphor might be that of an elite athlete: not only does an elite runner want to achieve results (victories or personal best times), he or she also desires the physical discomfort of the regimen that is required to get there.

This idea of the capacity to desire adversity is useful for understanding Nietzsche's concept of higher friendship. It implies that great individuals will court adversity in their social relationships and especially in their intimate lives. Given Nietzsche's view that adverse conditions are generally desirable for human flourishing, and that our social relationships are one of the most significant components of the environment in which we exist, it is easy to see the importance of integrating aversive emotional affects and adversarial behaviours into Nietzsche's ethics.

Higher friendship provides Nietzsche with this mechanism: it is designed to include these possibilities and to reject foundations for ethics such as love and compassion. The result is that higher friendship emerges as an extraordinarily productive form of social relationship because it is able, at least in theory, to incorporate every imaginable human experience. This captures the extraordinary productivity of an entire culture – that of ancient Greece – within the context of an intimate relationship. In Nietzsche's understanding of higher friendship, *agape* and compassionate love are possible, but they are subsumed within great love, which also licenses their opposites. In this ethics, a person's flourishing is enhanced by overcoming resistance. The greater the resistance, the greater the achievement in overcoming it, and the greater the result in terms of individual flourishing.

In higher friendship this ethic is put into practice. Friends have an interest in one another's flourishing, and therefore they may actively produce adverse conditions for one another. This is not done from a position of need or of deficit; it does not arise from a desire to destroy the other or to instrumentalize the other for self-fulfilment. We have seen in Chapter 6 that the great individual, the person capable of higher friendship, has a degree of self-sufficiency and personal autonomy that eliminates or minimizes these motivations. Rather, friendship arises from personal abundance and respects the otherness of the friend. On the basis of this kind of intimate distance, in higher friendship we see the deliberate production of adverse conditions as part of an overall process whereby the old is overthrown and new excellences established. This kind of interest in each other's personal development sits at the heart of Nietzsche's ethics of contest.

I propose this interpretation of Nietzsche's ethics as an intriguing possibility for an account of sociability that problematizes some of the usual requirements: love, compassion, mutual concern and reciprocity. The seemingly contradictory desires of the friend as contestant – both to oppose and to sustain their adversaries – can be understood as a shared commitment to the value of the contest itself. This is the essence of agonistic equilibrium in its social dimensions: friends both push against each other and pull towards each other. If this is done with sufficient regard to the specific characteristics of the person in question, the fragile, and therefore rare, state of a long-term, mutually supportive but agonistic partnership becomes possible. Applying Reginster's insight, we see that Nietzsche's great individual might not only endure adversaries and aversive emotions but they may even actively seek them out in her friends. A great individual involved in higher friendships sees that, win or lose, the contest provides a pathway to self-overcoming that is otherwise unavailable to them.

There is, then, a combination of self-interest and other-concern in friendship based on striving towards agonistic equilibrium between the parties. In higher friendship the parties seek to best each other, not to annihilate or to destroy:

> A larger commitment to agonism—or an agonistic ethos—may ensure that any reigning performance in the agon maintains its superiority or mastery only by virtue of and so long as it sustains challenge or opposition.[10]

The result is a fragile ecosystem of contesting parties who discover from one another new possibilities for human behaviour and achievement.

In what follows I will unpack Nietzsche's understanding of this relationship and the contribution that friendship-as-contest makes to each person's self-overcoming. Further, I show that this kind of relationship can only be entered into on the basis of intimate personal knowledge. One friend comprehends the other's specificity, namely, they comprehend the internal network of drives that constitute their friend, and they intuitively grasp how they might promote desirable drives and stultify undesirable ones. We will also consider two other forms of social relationship to help us better understand the dynamics of friendship, namely, neighbourliness and enmity. We will see that in friendship each party maintains hope for the other's benefit, even though their actual intention might be to secure victory by any means necessary. In neighbourliness the hope for another's flourishing is ambiguous and in enmity it is denied. Thus, friendship emerges as a stable but fragile agonistic equilibrium with productive benefits for both parties.

Against shared goals, shared joy

Let's begin this analysis by first understanding the significance of friendship as a theme for Nietzsche.[11] In developing this theme, he places himself within a tradition of philosophical reflection that begins with Plato and Aristotle[12] and continues into contemporary philosophy.[13] Understanding Nietzsche's debt to these sources has been the subject of significant academic endeavour and the importance of this theme for his own work has been extensively commented on.[14] One feature of this literature is the understanding that friendship holds a unique place in Nietzsche's ethics as the paradigm case of great individuals in a social context. It is widely recognized in this literature that this is due at least in part to Nietzsche's conception of friendship in terms of contest.[15] In particular, scholars have noted that Nietzschean higher friendship includes the possibility of enmity.[16]

What is not always clear in these discussions, however, is how to reconcile the conflicting impulses of friendship, for example, to support and to oppose. In my view, it is not sufficient to simply assert or assume the friend's intention to benefit the other. If both parties realize that beneficence underlies opposition that has been artificially manufactured, as it were, then the experience of adversity loses its power. To have the desired effect, enmity, for example, must be truly experienced as enmity.

One option discussed in the literature for integrating enmity into higher friendship is through the idea of purposes or goals, what might be called a teleological approach. Several scholars propose a variety of different goals for higher friendship. Robert Miner proposes that the goal of friendship is truth. While higher friendship avoids the pitfalls of pity, it embraces sympathy in the sense that both participants share in each other's commitment to truth, even if what they actually experience at the time is opposition.[17] Willow Verkerk proposes self-cultivation as a shared goal that brings enmity into higher friendship. Self-cultivation here includes self-overcoming, which can be expressed in shared joy, which ultimately leads to creative self-expression and the knowledge of the truth.[18] Common to both of these proposals is the idea that contest is important for achieving goals because it recognizes the role of adversity in doing so.

One key text for this approach is *GS* §14, 'The things people call love'. There Nietzsche describes different kinds of love, including neighbour-love and romantic love. It concludes with a definition of higher friendship as an evolution of these lower forms of love. He builds to this conclusion with the argument that many kinds of love, while often thought of as selfless, are better understood as greed. Given the importance of this text for understanding Nietzsche's view on love, enmity and friendship, I quote it here at length:

> Greed and love ... could be the same instinct, named twice ... Our love of our neighbours – is it not a craving for new *property*? And likewise our love of knowledge, of truth, and altogether any craving for what is new? ... When we see someone suffering, we like to use this opportunity to take possession of him; that is for example what those who become his benefactors and those who have compassion for him do, and they call the lust for new possessions that is awakened in them 'love', and their delight is like that aroused by the prospect of a new conquest. Sexual love, however, is what most clearly reveals itself as a craving for new property. The lover wants unconditional and sole possession of the longed-for person ... If one considers that this means *excluding* the whole

world from a precious good, from joy and enjoyment [and] that the lover aims at the impoverishment and deprivation of all the competitors ... as the most inconsiderate and selfish of all 'conquerors' [and] that to the lover himself the rest of the world appears indifferent, pale, and worthless and that he is prepared to make any sacrifice ... then one is indeed amazed that this wild greed and injustice of sexual love has furnished the concept of love as the opposite of egoism when it may in fact be the most candid expression of egoism ... Here and there on earth there is probably a kind of continuation of love in which this greedy desire of two people for each other gives way to a new desire and greed, a *shared* higher thirst [*einen gemeinsamen höheren Durste*] for an ideal above them [*nach einem über ihnen stehenden Ideale*]. But who knows such love? Who has experienced it? Its true name is *friendship*.

One of Nietzsche's claims here is that by transforming sexual love into friendship lovers might be able to deflect their passion away from each other and towards an ideal 'above' them. In this case, the lust to possess that characterizes sexual love could be transformed into something other than greed; it could be transformed into friendship, which pursues higher goals than mere possession. In the total context of this passage Nietzsche can be taken to include compassionate love and neighbour-love alongside sexual love as lower forms of love that might undergo this transformation into friendship. Importantly, to transform these into higher love a third element – an ideal that stands above them – is required. A teleological interpretation of this text, along the lines of Miner and Verkerk, is that this shared ideal – the goal – is higher friendship. The ideal stands 'above' them as that for which they strive, and which renders oppositional behaviours intelligible in their relationship. In supporting one other to strive for this shared goal, friends might express opposition and enmity, at least if it serves this purpose.

There are a number of issues that I see with this approach. The first is that the text indicates that what is shared between friends is not a shared ideal but rather a shared thirst (*gemeinsamen höheren Durste*). What Nietzsche emphasizes here is not sharing in a single goal but sharing in the thirst to achieve a goal.[19] Further, while it is true that the word ideal (*Ideale*) is here grammatically singular, in this context it could also be understood that the individuals may have quite different ideals based, as we have seen in earlier chapters, on their own unique composition as individuals. Thus, the preferred interpretation of this text, at least from my perspective, is that what friends share is the desire for each to achieve their own ideal.

Further, it is not obvious that the ideal that stands 'above' them does so as a goal in the sense of a purpose, a *telos*. Truth,[20] overcoming,[21] and self-overcoming[22] all feature in the literature as candidates for an overarching goal or purpose that might bind friends together and resolve some of these internal contradictions within higher friendship. However, even if we grant that here individuals support one another to pursue their own ideals, these ideals are not necessarily meant as goals. In my view, goal-orientation is problematic for Nietzsche in general. To claim a *telos* – a goal or a purpose – as the basis for higher friendship and even as the basis of Nietzsche's ethics ignores the way he problematizes goals and purposes (e.g. *D* §130; *GS* §1). Small, Siemens and Thiele are examples of scholars who convincingly attribute to Nietzsche a profoundly anti-teleological stance.[23]

In my view, it is best not to construe this text in terms of a shared goal or purpose but rather as a shared commitment to a process. In the context of this book, my claim is that this process is the emergent process of self-actualization. Friends have a shared passion for each person achieving their ideal version of themselves. In my view, it is more fitting to interpret the ideal that stands above friends as a standard of value – the value of becoming what you are – which acts as a foundation for the passionate life. On this interpretation, in this text the desire for one another that characterizes sexual love is redirected towards this higher standard. Instead of seeking to possess one another, each person seeks to further the other in their passionate desire to fashion themselves and their lives according to a personal aesthetic ideal. This is the foundation, the standard of value, by which the relationship is evaluated. It does not matter whether the ideal is attained, unattained or even unattainable; nor whether it gives their lives purpose. It is a commitment to live life within the constraints of this pursuit.

For these reasons I find the teleological approach to adversarial behaviours and aversive affects within higher friendship unconvincing. A different approach to this topic is to emphasize not shared goals but shared joy (*Mitfreude*). This idea, while noticed in passing by Miner,[24] has been extensively developed by Daniel Harris.[25] At the centre of Harris's approach is the combination of two texts: *GS* §14 and *GS* §338. We have seen above that *GS* §14 emphasizes shared thirst for higher ideals as the foundation for higher friendship. Harris amplifies this by incorporating the concept of shared joy from *GS* §338, where Nietzsche discusses the now-familiar problem of an unthinking commitment to compassion as the standard par excellence for ethical judgements.

In this text Nietzsche describes compassion as a mechanism for avoiding adversity and, in doing so, becoming distracted from one's own life task. Nietzsche concludes the text by describing an alternative form of help: help that promotes bravery rather than avoidance in the face of adversity. For Nietzsche this kind of help is not cruel because it is a purposeful response to the unique constitution of the sufferer. Here it is not a shared thirst for higher ideals that characterizes friendship, but rather a combination of shared suffering, shared hope and shared joy:

> You will also want to help – but only those whose distress you properly *understand* because they share with you one suffering and one hope – your *friends* – and only in the way you help yourself: I want to make them braver, more persevering, simpler, more full of gaiety. I want to teach them what is today understood by so few, least of all by these preachers of compassion [*Mitleiden*]: to share not pain, but *joy* [*Mitfreude*]!

Drawing from *GS* §14 the idea of shared desire and from this text the contrast between shared pain and shared joy, Harris argues that Nietzsche's concept of agonistic friendship centres on shared joy. The adversarial nature of higher friendship can be explained because of the shared joy that great individuals experience while striving together for excellence.[26]

Melanie Shepherd takes a similar approach to shared joy as a theme in Nietzsche's ethics.[27] She argues that in *TSZ* we see shared joy as a fundamental characteristic of what is means to be overhuman, an *Übermensch*. She convincingly shows that, at least in this text, the overhuman concept is not so much an ideal for each individual to attain on their own, but rather an ideal that has an ethical foundation in the relationships between people. To attain this ideal is to attain it specifically in how we relate to others. In this context, she argues that shared joy is Nietzsche's answer to shared suffering (compassion). Her analysis of shared joy as an important element in Nietzsche's attempt to break free from pessimistic interpretations of human experience is welcome, and her treatment of the theme in *TSZ* is compelling. However, it seems to me that neither joy nor suffering are in themselves either positive or negative for Nietzsche. Each may or may not be able to contribute to a person's life task. Nietzsche does not object to shared suffering per se, as Shepherd herself recognizes. He objects, rather, to the oral compulsion to avoid suffering in one's own life or to remove it from others' lives.

Further, our interpretation of *Mitfreude*, shared joy, depends first on how one understands *Freude*. The relatively straightforward translation of *Freude* as 'joy' can be misleading. The term has a wide range of uses and, more significantly, Nietzsche uses it as the opposite not of sadness but of pain and overwhelming passion.[28] Further, GS §338 describes several shared experiences including suffering (*Leid*), hope (*Hoffnung*) and joy (*Mitfreude*), and GS §14 emphasizes desire (*Begierde*). To single out the experience of joy as the most important feature of higher friendship lacks justification. Further still, while the idea of shared joy in striving for excellence through adversity may help to incorporate adversarial behaviour into higher friendship, it does not help us to understand how Nietzsche incorporates aversive emotional experiences. If the signature feature of higher friendship is this positive emotional experience of joy, emotions such as the feeling of enmity are difficult to explain.

These teleological and experiential explanations of higher friendship share one important feature. They seem to base higher friendship on concepts of mutuality and reciprocity. In order to develop a mechanism for reconciling adverse experiences created by friends with the desire of each for the other's flourishing, both approaches propose mutually held beliefs or desires which lead to reciprocal action between the parties. On this basis adversity finds its place within the relationship, licensed by underlying mutuality and reciprocity. In my view, if we are to focus on something that is mutual and reciprocal in higher friendship, it might be best to focus on hope. In the case where one friend causes adversity for the other through opposition or enmity, this can be incorporated into their friendship because the adversity arises out of a shared hope for one another's flourishing. While I do not accept the concept of purpose or a focus on shared emotional states (such as joy) as the signature features of higher friendship, I will return to this idea of hope for the other person's flourishing in my alternative account of higher friendship, which uses the themes of difference and abundance that have been developed throughout the book.

Friends, enemies and neighbours

Before developing my account of higher friendship, however, it will be useful to consider Nietzsche's approach to various social situations for the great individual. In particular, recurring themes in his texts include relations between friends, enemies and neighbours. In looking at these texts, I think we can see that Nietzsche's agonistic understanding of higher friendship goes much further than merely acknowledging that higher friendship can include enmity. I propose that, for Nietzsche, opposition and enmity as well as the supposedly antithetical experiences of fellow-feeling, cooperation and sympathy are *all* expressions of an underlying contest in the relationship. This contest is ultimately a direct consequence of both abundance and difference. It is the overflowing of each person's power so that both parties come up against one another, against an 'other'. In this Homeric-Nietzschean idea of difference neither party seeks to appropriate or to annihilate the other. Higher friendship is a contest that takes place between great individuals as each expresses their own power in order to advance their own life task, with the hope of also advancing the other's.

This begins with the idea that, for Nietzsche, higher friendship is structured to invite each party to express themselves as abundant natural beings. Whether this involves opposition and enmity or support and sympathy is not important. The commitment of one to the other is a commitment to a full expression of their individuality. They are able to engage with each other in the full range of behaviours and emotions that separately constitute each of them because both parties are abundant and therefore unafraid of sustaining an unrecoverable loss. The emphasis on 'separately' is deliberate: commitment to difference between one person and another, to the unique self-grounded personhood of each of them, and to the self-sufficiency of each as an abundant being, are features of higher friendship. Here there is no need to appropriate, ingest, consume, dominate or tyrannize others, as might be the case in other forms of social connection including 'lower' friendship.

Higher friendship

This description of friendship in the terms of contest provides a consistent interpretation of a variety of texts, including GS §338. We saw above that Harris relies on this text to interpret higher friendship through the lens of shared joy. While shared joy is an important idea in the text, there are other themes that modify how we are to understand it. For example, Nietzsche argues that a person should only help a friend in the same way that he or she is prepared to help themselves. In previous chapters we saw that Nietzsche's great individual helps themselves through adversity, through self-overcoming. It should be no surprise, then, that helping a friend might include foregoing compassion and even reinforcing their suffering, advancing that person's self-overcoming in the process.

Further, we see in GS §338 the importance of appreciating the particularity of each person, as described in Chapter 6. The adversarial element of friendship is not a sociopathic desire to inflict suffering on another human being under the guise of 'it'll be good for them', nor is it the result of self-interest or even of self-indulgence. Nietzsche argues instead that the decision to alleviate, prolong or even intensify a person's suffering can only be made on the basis of a detailed and personalized understanding of that person's constitution and their unique path to self-overcoming, and, therefore, to flourishing. Nietzsche argues this point in the negative, asserting that a benefactor's offer to alleviate suffering is often done in ignorance of that person's particular requirements, the 'economy' of their soul and 'the whole inner sequence and interconnection that spells misfortune for *me* or for *you*':

> What we most deeply and most personally suffer from is incomprehensible and inaccessible to nearly everyone else ... whenever we are *noticed* to be suffering, our suffering is superficially construed; it is the essence of the feeling of compassion that it *strips* the suffering of what is truly personal: our 'benefactors' diminish our worth more than our enemies do ... he knows nothing of the whole inner sequence and interconnection that spells misfortune for *me* or for *you*! The entire economy of my soul and the balance effected by 'misfortune' ... they want to *help* and have no thought that there is a personal necessity of misfortune ... that the path to one's own heaven always leads through the voluptuousness of one's own hell.

Here we see Nietzsche's interest in individual difference, expressed as an emphasis on the incommensurability of individuals' experiences. The sheer specificity of a person's experience makes it *almost* impossible for others to comprehend the dynamics and necessity of their suffering. Compassion, he argues, acts thoughtlessly towards others with a universalized understanding of suffering, and a corresponding compulsion to alleviate it. This obliterates the uniqueness of each person's experience. 'Vanilla' compassion diminishes the otherness of the friend, hindering their journey towards self-overcoming and flourishing. Better to have opposition that specifically fits the 'entire economy' of your soul than to have thoughtless, generic compassion foisted upon you.

This emphasis on personal specificity continues in the next sections of the text, where he turns from the perspective of the sufferer to the perspective of the benefactor, where vanilla compassion robs the benefactor of their uniqueness as well:

> I know, there are a hundred decent and praiseworthy ways of losing myself *from my path*, and, verily, highly 'moral' ways! Yes, the moral teacher of compassion even goes so far as to hold that precisely this and only this is moral – to lose *one's own way* like this in order to help a neighbour ... [and] take refuge in the conscience of the others and in the lovely temple of the 'religion of compassion.'

Nietzsche's solution to this problem of losing oneself through the feeling of compassion is twofold: protect yourself by keeping people at a distance and/or surround yourself with friends:

> I do not wish to keep quiet about my morality, which tells me: Live in seclusion so that you *are able* to live for yourself! ... You will also want to help – but only those whose distress you properly *understand* because they share with you one suffering and one hope – your *friends* – and only in the way you help yourself.

Nietzsche is not here recommending complete personal isolation in a quest to 'live for yourself'. Rather, he is discussing one remedy to the depersonalization of experience, namely, avoidance of others, in order to escape the seduction of compassion. His positive recommendation is to develop friendships where the specificity of each person is respected and the commitment of one to the other is incorporated into each person's unique path to flourishing, including adversity as necessary.

By surrounding themselves with people who 'properly *understand*', great individuals are able to help their friends but without the universalizing and depersonalizing compulsion of compassion. The standard by which friends' actions towards one another are evaluated is not the alleviation of suffering. It is whether or not the specific requirements of each person in the context of their own life task have been properly addressed.

Thus, using an agonistic lens for interpreting *GS* §338, we have come to quite a different conclusion to other scholars. The context for shared joy in higher friendship is respect for the otherness of a person and the uniqueness of their pathway through life. The structure of higher friendship is such that it maintains the differences between people and supports their individuality and specificity with bespoke responses. This seems to me to narrow the sense in which Nietzsche means for joy to be shared. I take it to mean that both parties experience the joy of overcoming adversity, even the adversity created by those you are most intimate with. This is the joy of 'becoming what you are'.

There is, however, a further complication to consider. One of the problems we are trying to solve in this picture of higher friendship is how adversarial behaviours and aversive emotions (such as enmity) might be incorporated into a concept of higher friendship without destroying the idea of friendship. The solution that I am proposing, namely, the backgrounding of mutuality and reciprocity and foregrounding instead abundance and difference, could be taken to imply another contradiction. That is, now it seems that great individuals engaged in higher friendship share a commitment to the notion that there is nothing shared in their experience. To deeply understand another person's experience, on the understanding that that experience is incommensurate with your own and inaccessible to you, suggests a tension between knowing and not-knowing, between really understanding another person and fully accepting their otherness.

The text 'On the Friend' in *TSZ* can be read as exploration of this problem. In this text Nietzsche uses a wide variety of metaphors and allusions to describe friendship. The sheer diversity of the text and the sudden appearance of new metaphors one after another can make it difficult to interpret. However, I think we can see in it some of the key themes of higher friendship: the possibility of intimate opposition (the friend is described as an enemy), the concept of shared striving towards an ideal (described as the 'overman')[29] and the issue of knowing and not-knowing (described through metaphors of masking/mirroring and dreaming/waking).

This text also adds to what we have already learnt about higher friendship from *GS* §§14 and 338 by showing Nietzsche's highly nuanced understanding of the dynamics of friendship and the problems it involves. It demonstrates Nietzsche's capacity to think about friendship while avoiding absolute and binary terms that we have become used to him using, namely, terms such as 'great' versus 'decadent' or 'higher' versus 'lower'. Here, through the voice of Zarathustra, Nietzsche demonstrates that the problems and possibilities of higher friendship can be understood as a matter of degree, construed in the relative terms of each person's progress towards their own ideals.

Nietzsche begins with a meditation on solitude and friendship, in which the friend appears as an interlocutor between 'I' and 'me', a kind of circuit-breaker for an internal dialogue, and then he turns to consider friendship and enmity directly:

> 'At least be my enemy!' – Thus speaks true respect that does not dare to ask for friendship. If one wants a friend, then one must also want to wage war for him: and in order to wage war, one must *be able* to be an enemy. One should honor the enemy even in one's friend. Can you step up to your friend without stepping over to him? In one's friend one should have one's best enemy. You should be closest to him in heart when you resist him.

Here a true friend is willing also to be an enemy, to express opposition and resistance. Respect for the other means rejecting lower aspirations for friendship, the longing for which he has described in the immediately preceding passages as self-betrayal. Rather, respect requires a different kind of friend who acts as the mediator in an internal conversation of self-discovery, and who is willing to 'wage war' in doing so. A friend not only steps 'up' to the other but they also step 'over to him'. Here at least their experiences do not seem totally incommensurate.

Zarathustra goes on to develop metaphors of nakedness and dreaming to describe the intimate opposition that takes place within the semi-commensurable experiences of higher friendship. These metaphors emphasize the contradiction between knowing and not-knowing in friendship, where artifice (as opposed the current fashionable emphasis on authenticity) is taken as essential to intimacy:

> You want to wear no garb before your friend? Is it supposed to be to your friend's honor that you give yourself to him as you are? But for that he curses you to the devil! Whoever makes no secret of himself outrages others; so much reason do you have to fear nakedness! ... For your friend you cannot groom yourself beautifully enough, for you should be his arrow and longing for the overman.

Here Nietzsche describes a great individual as someone who aspires towards the overhuman, to 'become what they are'. However, they have not as yet attained this beatified state and so they disguise themselves with careful 'grooming' for the sake of their friends. Through masking and pretence they foreshadow their future state, they imaginatively project themselves into what they are becoming, and so inspire the other on their own journey to self-overcoming. By presenting themselves in this way, friends hope to point the other towards their own superhumanity. By appearing beautiful to one another, even if this in some sense a deception, higher friends inspire one another in their ambition for self-overcoming and self-development. There is an interplay here between openness and pretence, or authenticity and masking, in a person's intimate relationships. Given each person's shortcomings with respect to their own ideals, artful self-presentation is required. Thus, intimate knowledge of another person, a condition seemingly necessary for higher friendship, is once again problematized. If your friends are presenting to you not what they are, but what they wish to become, then what kind of intimate knowledge of does each really have of the other?

This problem is further explored with the metaphor of wakefulness and dreaming:

> Have you ever seen your friend sleeping – so that you discover how he really looks? What after all is the face of your friend? It is your own face, in a rough and imperfect mirror ... Weren't you startled that your friend looks as he does? Oh my friend, human being is something that must be overcome. The friend should be a master of guessing and keeping silent: you must not want to see everything. Your dream should reveal to you what your friend does while waking. Let your compassion be a guessing, so that you might first know

whether your friend wants compassion. Perhaps what he loves in you is your unbroken eye and the look of eternity.

This is a complex text, the interpretation I venture here is tentative and somewhat speculative. I think we can see several issues addressed here in a poetically oblique kind of way. The first issue is that of subjectivity. In seeking to know a friend, even when they are asleep and their artifice of self-presentation is for once dropped, one can only see oneself, and imperfectly at that. The second issue is that of certitude. Friends do not have direct access to knowledge of each other. They are asked instead to alternate between guesswork and silence. Here guessing and dreaming are almost synonyms – instead of 'seeing' a friend directly and authentically, a person relies on creative guesswork and imaginative reconstruction, a state of mind not dissimilar to dreams or dream-like states. Not only does your friend present to you who they imagine themselves to be in process of becoming, when you comprehend your friend, you also do so imaginatively. The artifice works both ways. There are also other familiar ideas here: the friend won't always express compassion but will first 'guess' at their friends' real needs. Thus, each action between friends entails imagination: both in projecting oneself into the situation and in guessing at the other person's real needs.

One way to formulate this is through the idea of experiment. Each action is an attempt to discover something, both about oneself and about the friend. Perhaps here we see that the true foundation for action between friends is uncompromising commitment to the experiment itself. A true friend has 'an unbroken eye and the look of eternity'. Hardness towards one another is an essential component of the relationship, it provides the basis for any number of experiments through which the parties come to know more.

Taken together, these texts from *GS* and *TSZ* offer complementary perspectives. The texts from *TSZ* express a more nuanced understanding of abundance and difference than those from *GS*. In *TSZ* the great individuals engaged in higher friendship have not yet attained the ideal, the overhuman. This explains, in part, why they desire higher friendships. If the individuals involved were already overhuman, they would have no need or desire for one another. One of the underlying foundations for higher friendship is to continue a virtuous circle of self-development, to go from one level of abundance to the next, not only to transform oneself but also in order to flow outwards towards others. Thus, while in *GS* the abundance of the individual seems to be absolute and given, in *TSZ* we see it as a continuum and a development, a process that unfolds over time.

Higher friendship, then, can be understood as a desire for another person that includes a desire for contest. This is both self-directed and other-directed. It is self-directed in the sense that contest produces personal flourishing through self-overcoming. It is other-directed in that each individual is committed to developing a specific understanding of the other in order to support their flourishing, even if the mechanism for this is imagination and guesswork. On the basis of this understanding of another person's unique constitution and the mechanisms of their flourishing, a friend is able to contribute to that person's flourishing in any way necessary.

Thus, for Nietzsche, higher friendship is a form of social relationship structured around his adaptation of ancient Greek contest that has a particular ethics associated with it. As a form of contest, higher friendship is premised on personal abundance and difference between individuals. It is based on his understanding of the great individual's internal contest, their own self-overcoming, and so avoids excessive or abusive self-interest. Because the great individual's life task is self-mastery, attained through the process of self-overcoming, and because they have developed personal abundance through this process, they do not engage with others to make up for a deficit within themselves or because they have lost control of themselves. Instead, they engage with others in a self-reinforcing agonistic exchange directed at mutual flourishing.

Higher enmity

We can get further insight into this concept of higher friendship by considering how it compares with other relationships that Nietzsche analyses. Perhaps disconcertingly, one relationship that Nietzsche sometimes describes positively is enmity. For some, it would be difficult to describe a relationship between enemies as a form of sociability, and certainly not as an ethical form of social relationship. Nietzsche, however, can at times valorize the enemy relation, particularly when it takes place between great individuals.

We have seen above that enmity plays a role in higher friendship. In that analysis higher friendship is defined by intimate personal knowledge of a friend's personal requirements for their self-overcoming and, ultimately, their flourishing. Using this knowledge, we saw that a great individual might act towards his or her friend with enmity, in the hope that this would turn out to support their flourishing. We also saw that individuals' knowledge of one another is limited, meaning that friends are bound together in an experimental exchange of imaginative guesswork. Sometimes supportive, at other times adversarial, friends discover the best way to propel one another along their own unique path.

We can learn more about higher friendship by considering the differences between enmity between friends and enmity between enemies. Surprisingly little has been written on Nietzsche's philosophy of enmity and enemies: William Desmond, for example, simply notes that, in contrast with the significant tradition in the philosophy of friendship, Nietzsche and Schmitt are rare exceptions that approach the topic.[30] His approach to Nietzsche, however, is religious and metaphysical in character and yields little for this analysis. Debra Bergoffen's political analysis of the concept of the enemy in Nietzsche suggests a concept of higher enmity in which a worthy enemy offers an affirming experience in which reciprocity is at work.[31] She does not, however, distinguish the enmity that works within higher friendship with the enmity between straight-out enemies.

One way to approach this topic is to understand Nietzsche's concept of the enemy through the lens of warrior-ethics, another theme borrowed to some degree from Homer. Consider, for example, *D* §135:

> To see an enemy suffer, on the other hand, whom one recognises as one's equal in pride and who does not relinquish his pride under torture, and in general any creature who refuses to cry out for pity – cry out that is, for the most shameful and profoundest humiliation – this is an enjoyment of enjoyments, and beholding it the soul of the savage is elevated to *admiration*: in the end he kills such a valiant creature, if he has him in his power, and thus accords this *indomitable enemy* his last *honour*...

This text imagines a situation where an enemy is held captive by a victor, who causes them to suffer through deliberate cruelty. A kind of warrior ethics is applied to this situation, an ethics where admiration, pride and honour are the primary values. The desire of each to retain their honour requires, for both, the refusal of pity: the captor won't offer it and the captive won't ask for it. The distressing result is death: the only way for the captor to retain the honour of his captive – something he is bound to do by this warrior ethic – is to kill him.

The warrior archetype is also described in *TSZ* 'On War and Warriors'. In this text Nietzsche also writes positively of enmity within the warrior-relation, including aversive emotional experiences such as hatred and envy:

> We do not want to be spared by our best enemies, nor by those whom we love thoroughly ... My brothers in war! I love you thoroughly ... And I am also your best enemy ... I know of the hate and envy of your heart. You are not great enough to not know hate and envy. So at least be great enough to not be

ashamed of them! ... You should seek your enemy, wage your war and for your thoughts! ... War and courage have done more great things than love of one's neighbour. ... You may have only those enemies whom you can hate, but not enemies to despise. You must be proud of your enemy: then the successes of your enemy are your successes too ... I spare you not, I love you thoroughly, my brothers in war!

One clue to the interpretation of this dense and obscure text is that it is structured by a mirrored *inclusio* that combines kinship and war: 'My brothers in war! I love you thoroughly' and 'I love you thoroughly, my brothers in war!' This suggests an overarching theme: the enemy against whom the warrior fights is also their brother: 'I love you thoroughly ... I am also your best enemy.' Thus, the term 'brothers in war' here does not mean what it ordinarily means – fellow soldiers fighting together – but rather opposing soldiers, enemies, whose thorough and brotherly love for one another is expressed in enmity, hatred and envy. This does not, however, permit them to despise one another. This is because there is higher enmity at work here. By selecting enemies that are our equals, by selecting a brotherhood of enemies, we can instead be proud of our enemies. Even to lose to such an enemy – a valiant, strong and brave enemy – can be considered a success.

Here we see a different type of contest (*Kampf*) to that of friendship, it is here expressed as extreme enmity. Importantly, we see here that, with the enemy relation as with the friend relation, the contest is sublimated into psychological and intellectual 'warfare': 'wage your war and for your thoughts!' This kind of warfare, and the aversive emotional experiences that go with it, are such a positive feature of the enemy relation that Zarathustra encourages his listeners to actively seek them out. By attracting worthy enemies, even if defeated, the great individual stands to benefit.

This passage recalls the spirit of Greek warrior-ethics[32] and transposes it into a Nietzschean contest of self-overcoming in intellectual and psychological terms.[33] While discussing hatred, envy and warfare in positive terms may be confronting, there are elements here that help to shed light on higher friendship and the function of enmity within it. Higher enmity seems to have similar features to higher friendship, features that arise because both are forms of contest. Higher enmity, as with higher friendship, depends on the personal abundance of the individuals concerned. This minimizes the possibility of a harmful result such as annihilation. As with higher friendship, higher enmity emphasizes difference. It is not good enough simply to have worthy enemies. These enemies are chosen as '*your* enemies'. Good enemies are personally specific, chosen for their unique features. A great individual selects his or her enemies to meet the requirements of his or her own flourishing. Further, along with higher friendship, higher enmity includes a higher value standard that allows the participants to combine otherwise contradictory impulses. This value standard, described here in terms of honour, is characterized by self-overcoming, expressed here as the warrior's capacity for obedience.

While it is difficult to be categorical about the interpretation of this passage, it seems to me that the choice to engage an enemy is conceived by Nietzsche not as a destructive impulse but as an agonistic pursuit of the 'highest hope for life'. This can be connected to the process of self-overcoming. Having an enemy is not simply a violent lashing out, or a nihilistic impulse for chaos, or a desire for vengeance. It is obedience with respect to this highest hope. This is a reapplication of Nietzsche's understanding of personal relationships as the desire to discover what a person *could* be, or what they are becoming. If having enemies allows someone to 'become what they are', then enemies are desirable.

The difference between enmity and friendship is that in friendship this operates for the benefit of both, whereas in enmity the contestants seek only to benefit themselves. A person develops higher friendships in order to achieve their own unique life task, and also to support their friends in their own separate and distinct life task. Enmity within higher friendship is one method for achieving this, deployed selectively based on the specific needs of the moment. Higher enmity as a relation in itself does not include a hope that the other will benefit and flourish. It does not inherently desire either their destruction or their improvement, although either one may result. The important feature of higher enmity that distinguishes it from higher friendship is that it is a means only to enhancing one's own possibilities. Indeed, the concept of enmity would collapse if it did. This is the case even when one wants to strengthen the enemy: the purpose of this is simply to heighten the satisfaction derived from victory and, in so doing secure the victor against the inevitability of future defeat through the confidence they gain in their own abundance (see *GS* §163). The intention of enmity as an agonistic engagement is simple: to defeat the other and gain victory for oneself (*D* §571). Higher enmity recognizes the pride and strength of the other and accords it such respect as it commands. Higher friendship, however, hopes for the flourishing of the other.

Higher love of neighbour

A different type of social relationship that Nietzsche describes, which also sheds some light on higher friendship, is the relationship between neighbours, what might be called neighbour-love. We have seen in Chapter 2 that Nietzsche is critical of *agapic* love. We have also seen that higher friendship includes what he calls 'great love'. Nietzsche's response to the idea of neighbour-love, as with his rejection of *agapic* love, is shaped by the Christian tradition. Neighbour-love is an important feature of Christian ethics, to the point where the so-called 'golden rule' of Christian morality is often referred to as the injunction 'to love your neighbour as yourself'.[34] In neighbour-love people who do not know one another personally are brought into a relationship by sociocultural or geographical proximity. It is a relationship between strangers who nevertheless form a community.

As a social relationship between strangers, neighbour-love is unlike higher friendship or higher enmity in which a detailed personal knowledge of the other is required. Here the parties are unknown to each other and, in view of this, represent to each other the possibilities of either friendship or of enmity.[35] In the context of this ambiguity the neighbour-relation, at least as Nietzsche describes it, has both a higher and a lower form. In its lower form, neighbour-love is expressed as flight from oneself and self-dissolution, something we have seen Nietzsche strongly criticize in his critique of compassion. In *D* §516, for example, Nietzsche writes:

> *Do not let the devil enter into your neighbour!* ... benevolence and beneficence are constituents of the good man; only let us add: 'presupposing he is benevolently and beneficently disposed *towards himself*!' For *without this* – if he flees himself, hates himself, does harm to himself – he is certainly not a good man. For in this case all he is doing is rescuing himself from himself *in others...*

If we include the title of the text in its interpretation, we can see here both types of neighbour-love. Nietzsche here indicates that love for one's neighbour can avoid the pitfalls of compassion, but it could also fall into self-desertion.[36]

The problem of neighbour-love is further described in the section 'On Love of the Neighbour [*Von der Nächstenliebe*]' of *TSZ*. We can see in this text that lower neighbour-love has elements in common with *agapic* love and that higher neighbour-love shares some of the features of higher friendship. In this text higher neighbour-love is similar to higher friendship in that it involves shared striving for something that lies beyond both parties. As we have seen throughout this chapter, higher friendship includes great love for another individual that strives with that person so that they can 'become what they are'. It is love for their superhumanity; love, in a sense, for their future, even at the expense of their present.[37] For Nietzsche, neighbour-love shares this feature, described by the wordplay between neighbour/near [*Nächsten*] and future/far [*Fernsten*]:

Do I recommend love of the neighbour [*Nächstenliebe*] to you? I prefer instead to recommend flight from the neighbour [*Nächsten-Flucht*] and love of the farthest [*Fernsten-Liebe*]! Higher than love of the neighbour is love of the farthest [*Fernsten*] and the future ... One person goes to his neighbour because he seeks himself, and the other because he would like to lose himself ... my brothers, I do not recommend love of the neighbour [*Nächstenliebe*] to you: I recommend love of the farthest [*Fernsten-Liebe*] to you.

On the surface this text seems to reject neighbour-love in favour of higher friendship. In my view, however, we can distinguish between higher and lower forms of neighbour-love and understand this text as a comment on the lower form, which is characterized by flight from oneself, based on the subterfuge of the morality of selflessness.[38] This is premised on 'bad love' of oneself and a mistaken desire to find oneself in others. The play on words between nearest [*nächsten*], neighbour [*Nächsten*] and furthest [*Fernsten*] demonstrates that lower neighbour-love diminishes the possibilities for self-overcoming and self-development by loving the near and the present at the expense of the distant and the future.

We can see a clearer picture of the higher form of neighbour-love in *D* §146 'Out beyond our neighbour too' and *D* §471 'A different form of neighbour-love'. Together these texts describe Nietzsche's antidote to the problems of lower neighbour-love. Unsurprisingly, in higher neighbour-love the themes of abundance and difference are prominent, as they were for higher friendship and higher enmity.

D §146 can be read as an extended meditation on the Christian injunctions to 'love your neighbour as yourself' and 'to do to others as you would have them do to you'.[39] Given that the great individual's life task includes self-overcoming, the first of these can be taken to include self-overcoming. That is, if you love you neighbour, you will promote their self-overcoming just as you do your own. And, just as with higher friendship, this may require adversarial behaviour. To love your neighbour as yourself means to apply the same ruthless attitude to self-overcoming to them as to yourself. Thus, the question of sacrificing either oneself or one's neighbour is presented in *D* §146 as a question of the enhancement of power and happiness, not as a question of benefit or harm:

> *Out beyond our neighbour* [Nächsten] *too.* – What? Is the nature of the truly moral to lie in our keeping in view the most immediate and direct [*die nächsten*] consequences to others of our actions ... a higher and freer viewpoint ... is to *look beyond* these immediate [*diese nächsten*] consequences to others and under certain circumstances to pursue more distant [*entferntere*] goals *even at the cost of the suffering of others* ... May we not at least treat our neighbour as ourselves?

... Supposing we acted in the sense of self-sacrifice, what would forbid us from sacrificing our neighbour as well? ... Finally: we at the same time communicate to our neighbour the point of view from which he can *feel himself to be a sacrifice*, we persuade him to the task for which we employ him ... We, on the other hand, would, through sacrifice – in which *we and our neighbour* are both included – strengthen and raise higher the general feeling of human *power* ... a positive enhancement of *happiness*...

Nietzsche again uses the wordplay of immediate/nearest (*nächsten*), neighbour [*Nächsten*] and furthest [*entferntere*] to develop the contrast between lower and higher forms of neighbour-love. To be too concerned with harm or benefit for the neighbour is to lose sight of a higher standard. In the higher form of neighbour-love individuals stand together underneath the compelling force of something that is distant from them. They are prepared to sacrifice both themselves and their neighbours in pursuit of it. In the pursuit of this higher standard the neighbour is not a victim but a convinced participant: 'we persuade him to the task'.

In *D* §471 Nietzsche emphasizes the importance of difference for this type of agonistic neighbourliness. Here he describes both higher and lower neighbour-love, stemming from two types of passion, the 'excitable' form that contrasts with the 'great' form. Both can be expressed as neighbour-love. The lower form results from an excitable passion that is 'sociable and anxious to please'. The higher form results from great passion that is 'a gentle, reflective, relaxed friendliness'.[40] The association with friendliness (*Freundlichkeit*) describes this cold disposition as a nevertheless benevolent disposition. This disposition is premised on difference: the great neighbour is separated from the other in a kind of existential 'castle', both their 'fortress' and their 'prison'. From this viewpoint, the great individual appreciates the sheer otherness of their neighbours. They gaze down from their windows onto 'what is strange and free, into *what is different*'. It is this radical sense of difference between neighbours that here seems to function as the basis for higher neighbour-love realizing its benefits: '[this] does them so much good!'[41]

For Nietzsche, then, higher neighbour-love has features in common with higher friendship. It emphasizes difference, that interest in maintaining and enhancing an otherness that benefits both individuals. It contrasts with higher friendship in one crucial respect: difference between neighbours is premised on ignorance of the other person's intimate life, of the constitution of their drives and, consequently, of their pathway to self-overcoming. It therefore retains a certain ambivalence: neither person approaches the relationship with the hope to benefit the other, at least in part because neither person knows how to produce such a benefit for the other.

Conclusions

Thus, we can see that Nietzsche's presentations of friendship, enmity and neighbourliness share common features. The higher forms of these relationships take place between individuals who act towards one another out of personal abundance and who respect the differences between themselves. They see these social relations within the context of a higher standard of value, which valorizes self-overcoming in the context of each individual pursuing a unique life task. The higher standard of value is uniquely and personally developed by and for each participant. Given that each person is uniquely constituted as a set of internally contesting drives, the conditions for their personal self-overcoming and ultimate flourishing are also uniquely determined. Thus, in the higher forms of these social relationships, an agonistic ethos is evident.

However, not all of these higher forms of social relationship have equal merit for the great individual. Of those that we have considered, friendship emerges as the most desirable and productive. In friendship the participants hope not only for their own benefit but also for the benefit of the other. As Nietzsche seeks to internalize and personalize the ancient Greek societal practice of *agon*, it is friendship that emerges is its interpersonal analogue. In friendship a fragile but stable equilibrium is attained so that productive benefits can be realized through agonistic engagement over an extended period of time, with no particular end or conclusion in sight. Friendship becomes, like the ancient Greek social practice, a self-moderating system in which the contestants don't seek to annihilate but to sustain one another, and, further, they operate out of a respect for the social structures that make their engagement possible.[42]

This is why I have described, in higher friendship, the hope that each party has for the other. For a contest to be a genuine contest, each party must aim only to win. Beyond that intention, however, each also hopes that the other will experience benefits, win or lose. They hold this hope because they are intimately familiar with the other and can construct their agonistic engagements to maximize the possibility of benefit without compromising the integrity of the contest as contest. This is not true of either enemies or of neighbours. A person can seek out enemies whose particular strengths are valuable for advancing their own life task, making it a relatively more productive relationship than that of the neighbour. Neighbour-love, while perhaps not as desirable as higher enmity because of its inherent ambiguity and lack of specificity, still might offer the occasional opportunity for self-overcoming, for mutual or individual benefit.

The difference between these is perhaps best captured through the idea of the overhuman, that is, the process of becoming what one is, partly at least through social interaction. In higher friendship, friends can love not only who that person is in the present, but they are also able to love what each is capable of becoming, and act in order to bring that about. The capacity to love this future person is specific to friendship, it is excluded from other kinds of interactions such as enmity and neighbourliness.

The great love of higher friendship is hope for another person's flourishing, through love or enmity, support or opposition, distance or intimacy, authenticity or masking, honesty or deception. The capacity that friends have to incorporate this wide array of emotions and behaviours into the relationship is what makes higher friendship stand out as a central motif for Nietzsche's ethics of contest. It is great love.

8

Conclusion

The argument that I have developed in this book rests on the idea that the agonistic ethos of Greek antiquity was deeply influential in shaping Nietzsche's ethics. In Chapters 2 and 3 I showed that Nietzsche arrived at this understanding by a circuitous path. Born and raised in a Lutheran household and devoutly Christian in his early years, Nietzsche ultimately took a stand against Christianity. In particular, he rejected its claim that *agape* (or self-sacrificing) love defines moral behaviour in our social relationships. When he abandoned Christianity, Nietzsche embraced Schopenhauer's metaphysical pessimism. Yet, after a brief period of passionate engagement with that philosophy, Nietzsche came to reject Schopenhauer's claim that there is only one moral form of action, namely, alleviating the suffering of others. Thus, we find that in the early stages of his philosophical career, Nietzsche took a stand against what are arguably two of the most important features of contemporary morality: love and compassion.

When he moved on from these approaches, Nietzsche seems to have taken a decisive turn where, instead of basing morality on metaphysical ideas, he turned to the natural sciences. We saw in Chapter 4 how he developed a naturalistic account of social relationships and ethical norms. In that chapter I argued that Nietzsche's engagement with evolutionary biology led to an ambivalent stance. Positively, he appreciated the proposal within evolutionary science that species develop over long periods of time based on random variations and that in the struggle for existence these changes can either improve or diminish their capacities for survival and reproduction. Negatively, he saw the idea of the survival of the fittest as a problem. Nietzsche suggests that despite the claim to scientific objectivity, nineteenth-century evolutionary biologists interpreted nature through the lens of the weakest members of the species, those who aim at mere survival. For him, this fails to capture the ascendant multiplicity that he saw in human life, particularly in cultural and artistic endeavour. He then went on to draw a radical opposition between this pseudo-scientific approach to human experience and his own approach, which focuses not on minimalist survival but on maximalist expression, captured in his focus on human and natural abundance.

As we have seen throughout this book, classical agonism, which has its roots in Homeric epic poetry, provides some of Nietzsche's most important themes as he develops his ethics. Nietzsche saw in the agonistic competition that defined ancient Greek society an approach to social relationships that centred on humanity's greater capacities. In that cultural context, as Nietzsche understood it, human beings could develop themselves towards greatness by testing themselves against others. That is, growth, development and excellence was achieved through contest. Admittedly, Nietzsche recognized that the full realization of this might be limited to only a few individuals. However, by understanding the social dynamics and ethical principles that made it possible for those few, Nietzsche also identified the general principles that drive this ethics of greatness and excellence. In Chapter 5 we saw that these key principles include the touchstone ideas of personal abundance and difference. In agonistic contest, as Nietzsche conceived it, contestants bring their personal vitality to bear on each other without attempting to appropriate or tyrannize the other. For Nietzsche, the contest is a process for establishing new values and standards of excellence. Thus, any prevailing moral or social order is always susceptible to being overthrown and redefined by the outcomes of contest. I call this Nietzsche's new Homerism.

We saw in Chapter 6 that, in order to develop this approach into an ethics, Nietzsche had to transform the classical concept of contest so that it developed from performative or externalized contests – warfare, competitive games and rhetorical sparring – towards an internalized and personalized arena. To do so, he develops his understanding that the individual is constituted by an internal contest between their drives. Drawing on other ancient influences, such as the Stoics and the Epicureans, he uses the idea of self-cultivation to propose that the development of the great individual, based on this contest of drives, is achieved through self-overcoming. In Nietzsche's approach, this self-overcoming involves creating an environment in which desirable drives flourish and undesirable drives falter. Through this process the great individual brings about an internal agonistic equilibrium. This allows the great individual to organize and coordinate their internal world so that the contest of drives does not diminish their personal resources, but rather develops them. Thus, on Nietzsche's account, the internal contest of drives provides the personal abundance that characterizes his idealized great individual.

Nietzsche turns this understanding of great individuals outwards and examines its implications for their social relationships in Chapter 7. There we saw how Nietzsche captures this agonistic ethics in his idea of higher friendship. Nietzsche develops his idea of higher friendship thinking through the dynamics of the dyadic engagements between great individuals, whose internal drives have been brought into the kind of agonistic equilibrium described in Chapter 6. Nietzsche describes several different types of social relationships that might result, including friendship, enmity and neighbourliness. Amongst these, it is higher friendship in which the participants enter into a self-sustaining and productive equilibrium that is able to endure over time, in which each participant hopes for one another's self-overcoming. Nietzsche argues that in the contest that defines higher friendship individuals require and develop a profoundly personal understanding of each other, of the particular drives that define them and the environment that best promotes each person's pathway to self-overcoming and flourishing. Thus, in higher friendship, they express great love, which loves not only the person as they presently are, but also who they might become.

Nietzsche's concept of higher friendship includes the possibility that friends might oppose one another. He incorporates a wide array of adversarial behaviours and aversive emotions into higher friendship precisely because it values the contest that contributes to self-overcoming. Nietzsche argues that adversity, even within intimate relationships, provides important opportunities for individuals to flourish. Based on a deep understanding of what each person needs in order to flourish, friends may be called upon to provide adverse conditions for each other. While this may also be true of enemies and neighbours, ultimately these relations fall short of the aspirations and possibilities of friendship. Crucially, they are not able to sustain an equilibrium state, and instead they tend to collapse into victory for one and defeat for the other. In these relationships each party has no investment in, or hope for, the other's continued flourishing. It is only higher friendship that provides this positive possibility to activate in each other the process of becoming what they are.

Nietzsche's development of his ethics in this way has both strengths and weaknesses. Perhaps most significantly, Nietzsche's understanding of higher friendship provides an ethical alternative to love and compassion as the touchstone for our intimate relationships. He shows us that adversarial engagement can be desirable or even necessary for human flourishing in the context of their social relationships. In this way Nietzsche incorporates a positive appreciation of adversity into human social relationships, which in turn provides us with a critical lens for evaluating those social relationships that avoid, minimize or remove that difficulty.

Nietzsche's ethics, however, also leaves us with some unresolved issues for further investigation. Some of these I have discussed earlier. For example, in Chapter 6 I examined Nietzsche's psychology as one in which the individual is decomposed into their underlying drives. I alluded there to a problem inherent in this decompositional approach. That is, at times Nietzsche relies on the idea of a directing intelligence, an 'ego' that expresses some intention towards the drives – to stimulate some and stultify others. And yet he also claims that this is a fiction – the intelligence or 'ego' is merely an expression of another underlying drive vying for supremacy. I have proposed a materialist solution to this problem: perhaps we can see the body itself as a kind of non-cognitive presence that directs and limits the integration of drives. I think that this is an area for further investigation, perhaps by drawing on contemporary psychological or cognitive science.

Another issue that Nietzsche does not resolve relates to his emphasis on abundance. It seems that, for Nietzsche, it is only possible to enter into the ethical ideal of higher friendship on the basis of personal abundance, and yet higher friendship is necessary for developing this abundance. It might be possible to further develop this approach so that we can consider abundance and higher friendship as incrementally reinforcing one another in a kind of virtuous circle. One avenue for further research, as with the issue above, would be to consider this in the context of contemporary psychology or cognitive science.[1] Another avenue might be to consider social exchange theory, an approach that draws on economics and behavioural psychology to understand social interactions in which individuals do not diminish themselves when they enter into an exchange with others.[2]

Finally, it seems to me that more can be done to develop the idea of agonistic self-moderation by looking at agonistic equilibrium not only on the basis of dyadic interpersonal relationships, but also in complex social and institutional contexts. Christa Davis Acampora has recently made a significant contribution to begin this kind of analysis.[3] It seems to me that this could be a productive way forward for further developing Nietzsche's idea of higher friendship, where the concept of agonistic moderation can be fleshed out further in terms of the kinds of self-moderating practices and behaviours that place the individual into a mutually self-reinforcing relationship with their social institutions.

By way of conclusion, I offer a final thought about how we might understand Nietzsche's agonistic approach to social relations as an inspiration to social engagement, and not as an abrasive reality check or an excessively cynical understanding of sociability. It seems to me that Nietzsche's overhuman – the great superabundant individual engaged in contest relations of friendship, enmity, neighbourliness, amongst others – finds their fulfilment in the concepts of mastery and play. Nietzsche encourages us to take ourselves less seriously, to laugh and to dance through life in its ethical dimensions, and to experience the feeling of mastery in our relationships. He allows us to question the belief that everything is at stake in our intimate relationships and in our ethics, and that mistakes in this area are dire or even lethal. For him, these are the beliefs of someone not yet superabundant, who cannot yet afford to lose anything in the ethics of their intimate lives.

There is a compelling alternative here, the alternative of the great health (*GS* §382) where, overflowing with power and abundance, individuals are able to play at life:

> Another ideal runs before us, a peculiar, seductive, dangerous ideal to which we wouldn't want to persuade anyone, since we don't readily concede *the right to it* to anyone: the ideal of a spirit that plays naively, i.e. not deliberately but from overflowing abundance and power, with everything that was hitherto called holy, good, untouchable, divine … the ideal of a human, superhuman well-being and benevolence that will often enough appear *inhuman* – for example, when it places itself next to all earthly seriousness heretofore, all forms of solemnity in gesture, word, tone, look, morality, and task as if it were their most incarnate and involuntary parody – and in spite of all this, it is perhaps only with it that *the great seriousness* really emerges; that the real question mark is posed for the first time; that the destiny of the soul changes; the hand of the clock moves forward; the tragedy begins.

Nietzsche's great individuals are to see themselves as free in one important sense: free to experiment with their lives. This great experiment provides new information, new understandings of behaviours and their consequences, and allows them to attain a certain degree of mastery over themselves and over their relationships. And with mastery, you become free to experience these things – things previously experienced only with the greatest serious – with playfulness and virtuosity.

I finish with a poetic text that gives us an image of the ways that these abundant, playful and experimental individuals relate to one another. *D* §314 is the first in a series of prose poems (together with *D* §575 and *GS* §124) that centre on nautical imagery and the metaphor of seabirds. These texts capture the spirit of the Nietzschean 'we', an idealized community of great individuals involved with one another:

From the company of thinkers. – In the midst of the ocean of becoming we awake on a little island no bigger than a boat, we adventurers and birds of passage, and look around us for a few moments: as sharply and as inquisitively as possible, for how soon may a wind not blow us away or a wave not sweep across the little island, so that nothing more is left of us! But here, on this little space, we find other birds of passage and hear of others still who have been here before – and thus we live a precarious minute of knowing and divining, amid joyful beating of wings and chirping with one another, and in spirit we adventure out over the ocean, no less proud than the ocean itself.

Notes

Texts and translations

1. Arthur C. Danto, *Nietzsche as Philosopher* (New York, NY: Macmillan, 1964); Peter Poellner, *Nietzsche and Metaphysics* (Oxford, UK: Clarendon Press, 1995).
2. As a philologist myself, one notable shortcoming of this book is my limited facility with German. I have not been able to offer my own translations of key texts or analyse grammatical and/or literary devices. I have, however, been able to reflect at several points on lexical choices where appropriate.
3. With the added complexity that Book 5 of *The Gay Science* was a late addition, resulting in a second edition published in 1887.
4. This may seem to Nietzsche scholars an unusual grouping of texts, with two of his so-called 'free-spirit' works and *Thus Spoke Zarathustra*. For more on the relationship between *Daybreak*, *The Gay Science* and *Thus Spoke Zarathustra*, see Matthew Meyer, *Nietzsche's Free Spirit Works: A Dialectical Reading* (Cambridge, UK: Cambridge University Press, 2019).
5. Ruth Abbey, *Nietzsche's Middle Period* (Oxford, UK: Oxford University Press, 2000).
6. Friedrich Wilhelm Nietzsche, *The Portable Nietzsche*, trans. Walter Kaufmann (London, UK: Penguin Books, 1954); *Thus Spoke Zarathustra*, trans. R. J. Hollingdale, Penguin Classics (London, UK: Penguin Books, 1961; repr. 1969); *The Will to Power*, trans. Walter Kaufmann and R. J. Hollingdale, Vintage Books (New York, NY: Random House, 1968); *Beyond Good and Evil*, trans. Walter Kaufmann, Vintage Books (New York, NY: Random House, 1966); *On the Genealogy of Morals and Ecce Homo*, trans. R. J. Hollingdale and Walter Kaufmann (New York, NY: Random House, 1967); *Twilight of the Idols and The Anti-Christ*, trans. R. J. Hollingdale, Penguin Classics (London, UK: Penguin Books, 1968; repr. 2003); *Beyond Good and Evil*, trans. R. J. Hollingdale, Penguin Classics (London, UK: Penguin Books, 1973; repr. 2003); *The Gay Science*, trans. Walter Kaufmann, Vintage Books (New York, NY: Random House, 1974); *A Nietzsche Reader*, trans. R. J. Hollingdale, Penguin Classics (London, UK: Penguin Books, 1977); *Ecce Homo*, trans. R. J. Hollingdale, Penguin Classics (London, UK: Penguin Books, 1979; repr. 2004).
7. *Human, All Too Human*, ed. Karl Ameriks and Desmond Clarke, trans. R. J. Hollingdale, 2nd edn, Cambridge Texts in the History of Philosophy (Cambridge, UK: Cambridge University Press, 1996); *Daybreak*, ed. Karl Ameriks and

Desmond Clarke, trans. R. J. Hollingdale, 1st edn, Cambridge Texts in the History of Philosophy (Cambridge, UK: Cambridge University Press, 1997); *Untimely Meditations*; *The Birth of Tragedy and Other Writings*, ed. Karl Ameriks and Desmond Clarke, trans. Ronald Speirs, 1st edn, Cambridge Texts in the History of Philosophy (Cambridge, UK: Cambridge University Press, 1999); *The Gay Science*, ed. Karl Ameriks and Desmond Clarke, trans. Josefine Nauckhoff and Adrian Del Caro, 1st edn, Cambridge Texts in the History of Philosophy (Cambridge, UK: Cambridge University Press, 2001); *Beyond Good and Evil*, ed. Karl Ameriks and Desmond Clarke, trans. Judith Norman, 1st edn, Cambridge Texts in the History of Philosophy (Cambridge, UK: Cambridge University Press, 2002; repr. corrected edn); *Writings from the Late Notebooks*, ed. Karl Ameriks and Desmond Clarke, trans. Kate Sturge, 1st edn, Cambridge Texts in the History of Philosophy (Cambridge, UK: Cambridge University Press, 2003); *Thus Spoke Zarathustra*, ed. Karl Ameriks and Desmond Clarke, trans. Adrian Del Caro, 1st edn, Cambridge Texts in the History of Philosophy (Cambridge, UK: Cambridge University Press, 2006; repr. corrected edn); *Writings from the Early Notebooks*, ed. Karl Ameriks and Desmond Clarke, trans. Ladislaus Löb, 1st edn, Cambridge Texts in the History of Philosophy (Cambridge, UK: Cambridge University Press, 2009).
8 *On the Genealogy of Morals*, trans. Douglas Smith, Oxford World's Classics (Oxford, UK: Oxford University Press, 1996).
9 Kurt Aland et al., eds, *The Greek New Testament*, 3rd, corrected, edn (Stuttgart, Germany: United Bible Societies, 1983).

Chapter 1

1 E.g. Matthew Meyer, *Reading Nietzsche through the Ancients: An Analysis of Becoming, Perspectivism, and the Principle of Non-Contradiction*, Monographien Und Texte Zur Nietzsche-Forschung (Berlin, Germany: De Gruyter, 2014).
2 E.g. Christa Davis Acampora, 'Nietzsche Contra Homer, Socrates, and Paul', *Journal of Nietzsche Studies* 24, no. 1 (2002); Herman Siemens, 'Agonal Writing: Towards an Agonal Model for Critical Transvaluation', *Logoi.ph* (2015).
3 Paul E. Kirkland, 'Dissonance and Child's Play: Nietzsche, Tragedy, and Heraclitean Metaphor', *The Review of Metaphysics* 75, no. 2 (2021).
4 Jessica N. Berry, 'Nietzsche and Democritus: The Origins of Ethical Eudaimonism', in *Nietzsche and Antiquity: His Reaction and Response to the Classical Tradition*, ed. Paul Bishop, Studies in German Literature, Linguistics and Culture (Rochester, NY: Camden House, 2004); Paul A. Swift, *Becoming Nietzsche: Early Reflections on Democritus, Schopenhauer, and Kant* (Lanham, MD: Lexington Books, 2005).
5 Jessica N. Berry, *Nietzsche and the Ancient Skeptical Tradition* (Oxford, UK: Oxford University Press, 2011).

6   E.g. Dwight David Allman, 'Ancient Friends, Modern Enemies', *South Atlantic Quarterly* 97, no. 1 (1998); Robert Sinnerbrink, '"We Hyperboreans": Platonism and Politics in Heidegger and Nietzsche', *Contretemps*, no. 3 (2002).

7   E.g. Daniel I. Harris, 'Nietzsche and Aristotle on Friendship and Self-Knowledge', *Journal of Nietzsche Studies* 48, no. 2 (2017); Robert R. Williams, 'Aristotle, Hegel, and Nietzsche on Friendship', in *Tragedy, Recognition, and the Death of God: Studies in Hegel and Nietzsche* (Oxford, UK: Oxford University Press, 2012).

8   E.g. Vinod Acharya and Ryan J. Johnson, eds, *Nietzsche and Epicurus: Nature, Health and Ethics* (London, UK: Bloomsbury, 2020); Keith Ansell-Pearson, 'Heroic-Idyllic Philosophizing: Nietzsche and the Epicurean Tradition', *Royal Institute of Philosophy Supplement* 74 (2014); Fredrick Appel, *Nietzsche Contra Democracy* (Ithaca, NY: Cornell University Press, 1999); Berry, *Nietzsche and the Ancient Skeptical Tradition* (Oxford, UK: Oxford University Press, 2011); Michael Ure, 'Nietzsche's Free Spirit Trilogy and Stoic Therapy', *Journal of Nietzsche Studies* 38 (2009).

9   David E. Cartwright, 'Kant, Schopenhauer, and Nietzsche on the Morality of Pity', *Journal of the History of Ideas* 45, no. 1 (1984); Tsarina Doyle, 'The Kantian Background to Nietzsche's Views on Causality', *Journal of Nietzsche Studies* 43, no. 1 (2012); Michael Ure and Keith Ansell-Pearson, 'Contra Kant: Experimental Ethics in Guyau and Nietzsche', in *Nietzsche's Engagements with Kant and the Kantian Legacy: Nietzsche and Kantian Ethics*, ed. Joao Constancio and Tom Bailey (London, UK: Bloomsbury, 2017); Paulvan Tongeren, 'Kant, Nietzsche and the Idealization of Friendship into Nihilism', *Kriterion* 54, no. 128 (2013).

10 Cartwright, 'Kant, Schopenhauer, and Nietzsche on the Morality of Pity'; 'Schopenhauer's Compassion and Nietzsche's Pity', *Schopenhauer Jahrbuch* 69 (1988); Michael Ure, 'The Irony of Pity: Nietzsche Contra Schopenhauer and Rousseau', *Journal of Nietzsche Studies* 32 (2006); Julian Young, 'Schopenhauer, Nietzsche, Death and Salvation', *European Journal of Philosophy* 16, no. 2 (2008).

11 George J. Stack, *Lange and Nietzsche* (Berlin, Germany: De Gruyter, 1983).

12 Patrick Forber, 'Nietzsche Was No Darwinian', *Philosophy and Phenomenological Research* 75, no. 2 (2007); Dirk Robert Johnson, *Nietzsche's Anti-Darwinism* (Cambridge, UK: Cambridge University Press, 2010); John Richardson, *Nietzsche's New Darwinism* (Oxford, UK: Oxford University Press, 2004).

13 Arthur W. H. Adkins, *Merit and Responsibility: A Study in Greek Values* (Oxford, UK: Clarendon Press, 1970).

14 Acampora, 'Nietzsche Contra Homer, Socrates, and Paul'; 'Contesting Nietzsche', *Journal of Nietzsche Studies* 24, no. 1 (2002); *Contesting Nietzsche* (Chicago: University of Chicago Press, 2013); Lawrence J. Hatab, 'Prospects for a Democratic Agon: Why We Can Still Be Nietzscheans', *Journal of Nietzsche Studies* 24, no. 1 (2002); *Nietzsche's Life Sentence: Coming to Terms with Eternal Recurrence* (Abingdon, UK: Routledge, 2005); James Pearson, 'Nietzsche on the Sources

of Agonal Moderation', *Journal of Nietzsche Studies* 49, no. 1 (2018); Herman Siemens, 'Nietzsche's Agon with Ressentiment: Towards a Therapeutic Reading of Critical Transvaluation', *Continental Philosophy Review* 34, no. 1 (2001); 'Agonal Communities of Taste: Law and Community in Nietzsche's Philosophy of Transvaluation', *Journal of Nietzsche Studies*, no. 24 (2002); 'Agonal Writing: Towards an Agonal Model for Critical Transvaluation'; 'Nietzsche's Agon', in *The Nietzschean Mind*, ed. Paul Katsafanas (London, UK: Routledge, 2018).

15 It is noted here that several scholars have analysed this in terms of Nietzsche's response to Hegel: Stephen Houlgate, *Hegel, Nietzsche, and the Criticism of Metaphysics* (Cambridge, UK: Cambridge University Press, 1986); Elliot L. Jurist, *Beyond Hegel and Nietzsche, Philosophy, Culture, and Agency* (Cambridge, MA: MIT Press, 2000); Williams, 'Aristotle, Hegel, and Nietzsche on Friendship'.

16 Keith Ansell-Pearson and Rebecca Bamford, *Nietzsche's Dawn: Philosophy, Ethics, and the Passion of Knowledge* (Hoboken, NJ: Wiley-Blackwell, 2021); Maudemarie Clark, 'Nietzsche's Attack on Morality' (Doctoral Dissertation, University of Wisconsin-Madison, 1977); Brian Leiter, 'Nietzsche and the Critique of Morality: Philosophical Naturalism in Nietzsche's Theory of Value' (Doctoral Thesis, University of Michigan, 1995); *Nietzsche on Morality*, Routledge Philosophy Guidebooks (Abingdon, UK: Routledge, 2002).

17 Paul E. Kirkland, 'Nietzsche, Agonistic Politics, and Spiritual Enmity', *Political Research Quarterly* 73, no. 1 (2020); Siemens, 'Nietzsche's Agon'.

18 Pearson, 'Nietzsche on the Sources of Agonal Moderation'; Siemens, 'Nietzsche's Agon'; Paul van Tongeren, 'Nietzsche's Greek Measure', *Journal of Nietzsche Studies* 24 (2002).

19 Peter Berkowitz, *Nietzsche: The Ethics of an Immoralist* (Cambridge, MA: Harvard University Press, 1996); Arthur C. Danto, *Nietzsche as Philosopher* (New York, NY: Macmillan, 1964); Houlgate, *Hegel, Nietzsche, and the Criticism of Metaphysics*; Paul Patton, ed. *Nietzsche: Feminism & Political Theory* (Abingdon, UK: Routledge, 1993); Ted Sadler, *Nietzsche: Truth and Redemption* (London, UK: Athlone Press, 1995); Max Scheler, 'Ressentiment', in *Nietzsche: A Collection of Critical Essays*, ed. Robert C. Solomon (Garden City, NY: Anchor Press, 1973; reprint, University of Notre Dame Press).

20 Peter Sloterdijk, *Nietzsche Apostle*, trans. Steven Corcoran, vol. 16, *Intervention* (Los Angeles, CA: Semiotext(e), 2013).

21 Hugo Drochon, *Nietzsche's Great Politics* (Princeton, NJ: Princeton University Press, 2016).

22 Jeffrey Church, 'Nietzsche's Early Perfectionism', *Journal of Nietzsche Studies* 46, no. 2 (2015); 'The Aesthetic Justification of Existence: Nietzsche on the Beauty of Exemplary Lives', *Journal of Nietzsche Studies* 46, no. 3 (2015); 'Nietzsche's Early Ethical Idealism', *Journal of Nietzsche Studies* 47, no. 1 (2016); Thomas

Hurka, 'Nietzsche: Perfectionist', in *Nietzsche and Morality*, ed. Brian Leiter and Neil Sinhababu (Oxford, UK: Oxford University Press, 2007); Simon Robertson, 'Nietzsche's Ethical Revaluation', *Journal of Nietzsche Studies* 37, no. 1 (2009).

23 Bernard Reginster, *The Affirmation of Life: Nietzsche on Overcoming Nihilism* (Cambridge, MA: Harvard University Press, 2006); Leslie Paul Thiele, *Friedrich Nietzsche and the Politics of the Soul: A Study of Heroic Individualism* (Princeton, NJ: Princeton University Press, 1990).

24 Michel Foucault, *The Care of the Self*, trans. Robert Hurley, 3 vols, vol. 3, *The History of Sexuality* (New York, NY: Random House, 1986).

25 Acharya and Johnson, *Nietzsche and Epicurus: Nature, Health and Ethics*; Ansell-Pearson, 'Heroic-Idyllic Philosophizing: Nietzsche and the Epicurean Tradition'; Thomas H. Brobjer, 'Nietzsche's Affirmative Morality: An Ethics of Virtue', *Journal of Nietzsche Studies* 26 (2003); Christine Daigle, 'Nietzsche: Virtue Ethics ... Virtue Politics?', *Journal of Nietzsche Studies* 32, no. 1 (2006); Matthew Dennis, 'Nietzschean Self-Cultivation', *Journal of Value Inquiry* 53, no. 1 (2019); Foucault, *The Care of the Self*, 3; Robert C. Solomon, *Living with Nietzsche: What the Great 'Immoralist' Has to Teach Us* (Oxford, UK: Oxford University Press, 2004); Christine Swanton, *The Virtue Ethics of Hume and Nietzsche* (Hoboken, NJ: Wiley, 2015); Ure, 'Nietzsche's Free Spirit Trilogy and Stoic Therapy'.

26 Acampora, *Contesting Nietzsche*; Hatab, 'Prospects for a Democratic Agon: Why We Can Still Be Nietzscheans'; *Nietzsche's Life Sentence: Coming to Terms with Eternal Recurrence*; Siemens, 'Nietzsche's Agon with Ressentiment: Towards a Therapeutic Reading of Critical Transvaluation'; 'Agonal Communities of Taste: Law and Community in Nietzsche's Philosophy of Transvaluation'; 'Agonal Writing: Towards an Agonal Model for Critical Transvaluation'.

27 Doyle, 'The Kantian Background to Nietzsche's Views on Causality'; 'Nietzsche, Value and Objectivity', *International Journal of Philosophical Studies* 21, no. 1 (2013); *Nietzsche's Metaphysics of the Will to Power: The Possibility of Value* (Cambridge, UK: Cambridge University Press, 2018); 'Nietzsche on Epistemology and Metaphysics' (Doctoral Dissertation, University of Warwick, 2002); Peter Poellner, *Nietzsche and Metaphysics* (Oxford, UK: Clarendon Press, 1995); Martin Heidegger, *Nietzsche*, trans. David Farrell Krell, 2 vols, vol. 1 (San Francisco, CA: Harper & Row, 1991); ibid., 2.

28 Church, 'Nietzsche's Early Ethical Idealism'.

29 Mario Brandhorst, 'Naturalism and the Genealogy of Moral Institutions', *Journal of Nietzsche Studies* 40 (2010); Houlgate, *Hegel, Nietzsche, and the Criticism of Metaphysics*; Christopher Janaway and Simon Robertson, eds, *Nietzsche, Naturalism, and Normativity* (Oxford, UK: Oxford University Press, 2012); Dirk R. Johnson, *Nietzsche's Anti-Darwinism*; 'One Hundred Twenty-Two Years Later: Reassessing the Nietzsche–Darwin Relationship', *Journal of Nietzsche Studies*

44, no. 2 (2013); Leiter, 'Nietzsche and the Critique of Morality: Philosophical Naturalism in Nietzsche's Theory of Value'; *Nietzsche on Morality*; 'Normativity for Naturalists', *Philosophical Issues* 25, no. 1 (2015); 'Nietzsche's Moral and Political Philosophy', in *Stanford Encyclopaedia of Philosophy*, ed. Edward N. Zalta (2015); Matthew Meyer, *Nietzsche's Free Spirit Works: A Dialectical Reading* (Cambridge, UK: Cambridge University Press, 2019); Richard Schacht, 'Nietzsche's Naturalism', *Journal of Nietzsche Studies* 43, no. 2 (2012); 'Nietzsche's Naturalism and Normativity', in *Nietzsche, Naturalism and Normativity*, ed. Christopher Janaway and Simon Robertson (Oxford, UK: Oxford University Press, 2012); Siemens, 'Nietzsche's Agon with Ressentiment: Towards a Therapeutic Reading of Critical Transvaluation'; 'Nietzsche's Agon'; Peter R. Sedgwick, 'Hyperbolic Naturalism: Nietzsche, Ethics, and Sovereign Power', *Journal of Nietzsche Studies* 47, no. 1 (2016); Michael Ure, 'Nietzsche's Schadenfreude', *Journal of Nietzsche Studies* 44 (2013).

30 Features of 'high culture' such as art, music and theatre might be considered such phenomena.

31 See Maudemarie Clark and David Dudrick, 'The Naturalisms of *Beyond Good and Evil*', in *A Companion to Nietzsche*, ed. Keith Ansell-Pearson (Malden, MA: Blackwell, 2006); Maudemarie Clark, *Nietzsche on Ethics and Politics* (Oxford, UK: Oxford University Press, 2015); Janaway and Robertson, *Nietzsche, Naturalism, and Normativity*; Leiter, 'Nietzsche and the Critique of Morality: Philosophical Naturalism in Nietzsche's Theory of Value'; 'Normativity for Naturalists'; Simon Robertson, 'Normativity for Nietzschean Free Spirits', *Inquiry* 54, no. 6 (2011); Schacht, 'Nietzsche's Naturalism and Normativity'; 'Nietzsche's Naturalism'.

32 I note that here the same term, *der Überfluss*, is translated as abundance (*GS* §349) and overflow (*GS* §55). Another term Nietzsche uses in this regard is *die Fülle* (e.g. *GS* §370).

33 Keith Ansell-Pearson, *Germinal Life: The Difference and Repetition of Deleuze* (Abingdon, UK: Routledge, 1999); Gilles Deleuze, *Nietzsche and Philosophy*, trans. Hugh Tomlinson (New York, NY: Columbia University Press, 1983); *Difference and Repetition*, trans. Paul Patton, Athlone Contemporary European Thinkers (New York, NY: Continuum, 1994); Gianni Vattimo, *The Adventure of Difference: Philosophy after Nietzsche and Heidegger*, trans. Cyprian Blamires and Thomas Harrison (Cambridge, UK: Polity Press, 1993).

34 Friedrich Nietzsche, *The Nietzsche Reader*, ed. Keith Ansell-Pearson and Duncan Large, Blackwell Readers (Malden, MA: Blackwell, 2006), 95–100.

35 His essay *The Greek State* is also significant in this regard, see Church, 'Nietzsche's Early Perfectionism'.

36 Acampora, *Contesting Nietzsche*; Hatab, 'Prospects for a Democratic Agon: Why We Can Still Be Nietzscheans'; *Nietzsche's Life Sentence: Coming to Terms with Eternal*

Recurrence; Daniel I. Harris, 'Friendship as Shared Joy in Nietzsche', *Symposium* 19, no. 1 (2015); Kirkland, 'Nietzsche, Agonistic Politics, and Spiritual Enmity'; Siemens, 'Agonal Communities of Taste: Law and Community in Nietzsche's Philosophy of Transvaluation'; 'Nietzsche's Agon'; Willow Verkerk, 'Nietzsche's Agonistic Ethics of Friendship', *Symposium* 20, no. 2 (2016).

37 Nietzsche, *The Nietzsche Reader*, 100.
38 Pearson, 'Nietzsche on the Sources of Agonal Moderation'; Siemens, 'Nietzsche's Agon with Ressentiment: Towards a Therapeutic Reading of Critical Transvaluation'; van Tongeren, 'Nietzsche's Greek Measure'.
39 Acampora, *Contesting Nietzsche*, 25.
40 Siemens, 'Nietzsche's Agon', 333.
41 Ruth Abbey, 'Circles, Ladders and Stars: Nietzsche on Friendship', *Critical Review of International Social and Political Philosophy* 2, no. 4 (1999); Allman, 'Ancient Friends, Modern Enemies'; John C. Coker, 'Spectres of Friends and Friendship', *Journal of Nietzsche Studies* 16 (1998); Jacques Derrida, *Politics of Friendship*, trans. George Collins, Phronesis (London, UK: Verso, 1997); Christine Daigle, 'The Ethical Ideal of the Free Spirit in *Human All Too Human*', in *Nietzsche's Free Spirit Philosophy* (London, UK: Rowman and Littlefield, 2015); Dana Freibach-Heifetz, 'Pure Air and Solitude and Bread and Medicine: Nietzsche's Conception of Friendship', *Philosophy Today* 49, no. 3 (2005); Jean Gauthier, 'In Honour of Friendship' (Masters Thesis, Trent University, 1998); Daniel I. Harris, 'Friendship as Shared Joy in Nietzsche' (Doctoral Dissertation, University of Guelph, 2013); 'Friendship as Shared Joy in Nietzsche'; 'Nietzsche and Aristotle on Friendship and Self-Knowledge'; Horst Hutter, 'The Virtue of Solitude and the Vicissitudes of Friendship', *Critical Review of International Social and Political Philosophy* 2, no. 4 (1999); Robert C. Miner, 'Nietzsche on Friendship', *Journal of Nietzsche Studies* 40 (2010); Paul van Tongeren, 'Politics, Friendship and Solitude in Nietzsche (Confronting Derrida's Reading of Nietzsche in "Politics of Friendship")', *South African Journal of Philosophy* 19, no. 3 (2000); 'On Friends in Nietzsche's Zarathustra', *New Nietzsche Studies*, no. 5 (2003); 'Kant, Nietzsche and the Idealization of Friendship into Nihilism'; Willow Verkerk, 'Nietzsche's Goal of Friendship', *Journal of Nietzsche Studies* 45, no. 3 (2014); 'Nietzsche's Agonistic Ethics of Friendship'; *Nietzsche and Friendship*, Bloomsbury Studies in Continental Philosophy (New York, NY: Bloomsbury, 2019); John von Heyking, *The Form of Politics: Aristotle and Plato on Friendship* (Montreal, Canada: McGill-Queen's University Press, 2016); Williams, 'Aristotle, Hegel, and Nietzsche on Friendship'; Benedetta Zavatta, 'Nietzsche and Emerson on Friendship and Its Ethical-Political Implications', in *Nietzsche, Power and Politics: Rethinking Nietzsche's Legacy for Political Thought*, ed. Herman Siemens and Vasti Roodt (Berlin, Germany: De Gruyter, 2008).

42 Nietzsche, *The Nietzsche Reader*, 98.
43 Sophia Aneziri, 'Agon', ed. R.S. Bagnall et al., *The Encyclopedia of Ancient History* (2021), https://doi-org.simsrad.net.ocs.mq.edu.au/10.1002/9781444338386.wbeah09014.pub2; Elton T. E. Barker, *Entering the Agon: Dissent and Authority in Homer, Historiography, and Tragedy* (Oxford, UK: Oxford University Press, 2009); Paul Christesen and Donald G. Kyle, *A Companion to Sport and Spectacle in Greek and Roman Antiquity*, 1st edn, Blackwell Companions to the Ancient World (Somerset: John Wiley & Sons, Incorporated, 2014); Wang Daqing, 'On the Ancient Greek Αγων', *Procedia, Social and Behavioral Sciences* 2, no. 5 (2010); Evgeny Y. Rezhabek and Marina A. Bogdanova, 'Agon as an Immanent Characteristic Feature of Ancient Greek Culture', *Advanced Engineering Research* 11, no. 6 (2011); M. I. Finley and H. W. Pleket, *The Olympic Games: The First Thousand Years* (London, UK: Chatto and Windus, 1976); Jennifer Marie Gagnon, 'Agonistic Politics, Contest, and the "Oresteia"' (ProQuest Dissertations Publishing, 2012); Stephe Harrop, 'Greek Tragedy, Agonistic Space, and Contemporary Performance', *New Theatre Quarterly* 34, no. 2 (2018); Debra Hawhee, 'Agonism and Aretê', *Philosophy & Rhetoric* 35, no. 3 (2002); Kevin Hawthorne, 'The Chorus as Rhetorical Audience: A Sophoklean Agōn Pattern', *American Journal of Philology* 130, no. 1 (2009); Gunther Martin, 'Nothing but Rhetoric? Rhetoric, Pragmatics and Myth-Making in the Agōn of Euripides' Alcestis', *Classical Quarterly* 71, no. 2 (2021); David M. Pritchard, 'Sport, War and Democracy in Classical Athens', *International Journal of the History of Sport* 26, no. 2 (2009); *War, Democracy, and Culture in Classical Athens* (Cambridge, UK: Cambridge University Press, 2010); *Sport, Democracy and War in Classical Athens* (Cambridge, UK: Cambridge University Press, 2013); Boris Shoshitaishvili, 'Homer's World at War: Cosmic Agonism in the Iliad' (ProQuest Dissertations Publishing, 2019).
44 E.g. Finley and Pleket, *The Olympic Games: The First Thousand Years*.
45 Giuseppe Ballacci, 'Deliberative Agonism and Agonistic Deliberation in Hannah Arendt', *Theoria (Pietermaritzburg)* 66, no. 161 (2019); Bonnie Honig, *Political Theory and the Displacement of Politics*, Contestations (Ithaca, NY: Cornell University Press, 1993); 'Between Decision and Deliberation: Political Paradox in Democratic Theory', *The American Political Science Review* 101, no. 1 (2007); Chantal Mouffe, 'Deliberative Democracy or Agonistic Pluralism?', *Social Research* 66, no. 3 (1999).
46 Ansell-Pearson and Bamford, *Nietzsche's Dawn: Philosophy, Ethics, and the Passion of Knowledge*; Daigle, 'The Ethical Ideal of the Free Spirit in Human All Too Human'; Paul Katsafanas, *Agency and the Foundations of Ethics: Nietzschean Constitutivism* (Oxford, UK: Oxford University Press, 2013); 'Nietzsche on the Nature of the Unconscious', *Inquiry* 58, no. 3 (2014); *The Nietzschean Self: Moral Psychology, Agency, and the Unconscious* (Oxford, UK: Oxford University Press, 2016); Graham Parkes, *Composing the Soul: Reaches of Nietzsche's Psychology*

(Chicago, IL: University of Chicago Press, 1994); John Richardson, *Nietzsche's Values* (New York, NY: Oxford University Press, 2020); Thiele, *Friedrich Nietzsche and the Politics of the Soul: A Study of Heroic Individualism*.

47 Graham Parkes describes this using the metaphor of musical composition, Leslie Paul Thiele uses the analogy of the city state. See Parkes, *Composing the Soul: Reaches of Nietzsche's Psychology*; Solomon, *Living with Nietzsche: What the Great 'Immoralist' Has to Teach Us*; Thiele, *Friedrich Nietzsche and the Politics of the Soul: A Study of Heroic Individualism*.

48 Acharya and Johnson, *Nietzsche and Epicurus: Nature, Health and Ethics*; Ansell-Pearson, 'Heroic-Idyllic Philosophizing: Nietzsche and the Epicurean Tradition'; Rebecca Bamford, 'Health and Self-Cultivation in Dawn', in *Nietzsche's Free Spirit Philosophy*, ed. Rebecca Bamford (London, UK: Rowman and Littlefield, 2015); Dennis, 'Nietzschean Self-Cultivation'; Michael Ure, *Nietzsche's Therapy: Self-Cultivation in the Middle Works* (Lanham, MD: Lexington Books, 2008); 'Nietzsche's Free Spirit Trilogy and Stoic Therapy'.

49 Ansell-Pearson and Bamford, *Nietzsche's Dawn: Philosophy, Ethics, and the Passion of Knowledge*, 142ff; Bamford, 'Health and Self-Cultivation in *Dawn*', 91–2; Daigle, 'The Ethical Ideal of the Free Spirit in *Human All Too Human*', 35–9.

Chapter 2

1 Simon May, *Love: A History* (New Haven, CT: Yale University Press, 2011), 81.
2 Ibid., 4.
3 Ibid.
4 Ibid., 14.
5 Ibid., 25–6, 91–2.
6 Ibid., 21–2.
7 Ibid., 94.
8 Ibid., 6.
9 Ibid.
10 Ibid., 81–94.
11 Ibid., 188–98.
12 Ibid., 193–4.
13 See also Béatrice Han-Pile, 'Nietzsche and Amor Fati', *European Journal of Philosophy* 19, no. 2 (2011).
14 Christa Davis Acampora, 'Agonistic Communities: Love, War and Spheres of Activity', in *Conflict and Contest in Nietzsche's Philosophy*, ed. Herman Siemens and James Pearson (London, UK: Bloomsbury, 2019); Lawrence J. Hatab, '*Amor Agonis*: Conflict and Love in Nietzsche and Homer', in ibid.
15 Hatab, '*Amor Agonis*: Conflict and Love in Nietzsche and Homer', 110.

16 Ibid., 117–18.
17 Acampora, 'Agonistic Communities: Love, War and Spheres of Activity', 136–7.
18 Ibid., 127–30.
19 See also Daigle, 'The Ethical Ideal of the Free Spirit in *Human All Too Human*'.
20 Hatab, '*Amor Agonis*: Conflict and Love in Nietzsche and Homer', 105–6.
21 Acampora, 'Agonistic Communities: Love, War and Spheres of Activity', 136.
22 Dana Freibach-Heifetz, 'Pure Air and Solitude and Bread and Medicine: Nietzsche's Conception of Friendship', *Philosophy Today* 49, no. 3 (2005); Horst Hutter, 'The Virtue of Solitude and the Vicissitudes of Friendship', *Critical Review of International Social and Political Philosophy* 2, no. 4 (1999); van Tongeren, 'Politics, Friendship and Solitude in Nietzsche (Confronting Derrida's Reading of Nietzsche in "Politics of Friendship")', *South African Journal of Philosophy* 19, no. 3 (2000).
23 Anders Nygren, *Agape and Eros*, trans. Philip S. Watson (London, UK: SPCK, 1982), 75–81.
24 Karl Barth, *Evangelical Theology: An Introduction*, trans. Grover Foley (Grand Rapids, MI: Eerdmans, 1963), 201.
25 Ibid., 200–1. See also Wolfhart Pannenberg, *Systematic Theology*, trans. Geoffrey W. Bromiley, 3 vols, vol. 3 (Grand Rapids, MI: Eerdmans, 1998), vol. 3, 182ff.
26 Karl Barth, *The Doctrine of Reconciliation*, ed. Geoffrey W. Bromiley and Thomas F. Torrance, trans. Geoffrey W. Bromiley, 1st paperpack edn, vol. IV.2, Church Dogmatics (London, UK: T&T Clark International, 2004).
27 Pannenberg, *Systematic Theology*, vol. 1, 482.
28 Thomas F. Torrance, *The Trinitarian Faith: The Evangelical Theology of the Ancient Catholic Church* (Edinburgh, UK: T&T Clark, 1995); *The Christian Doctrine of God: One Being Three Persons* (Edinburgh, UK: T&T Clark, 1996).
29 James Stevenson, *A New Eusebius: Documents Illustrating the History of the Church to AD 337*, rev. edn, SPCK Church History (London, UK: SPCK, 1987), 338–55.
30 James Stevenson, *Creeds, Councils and Controversies: Documents Illustrating the History of the Church, AD 337–461*, rev. edn, SPCK Church History (London, UK: SPCK, 1989), 111–41.
31 Ibid., 332–68.
32 Torrance, *The Trinitarian Faith: The Evangelical Theology of the Ancient Catholic Church*, 125–45.
33 Ibid., 310–25.
34 Torrance, *The Christian Doctrine of God: One Being Three Persons*, 168–202.
35 Ibid., 102–3.
36 Torrance, *The Trinitarian Faith: The Evangelical Theology of the Ancient Catholic Church*, 91–2, 181–90.
37 Torrance, *The Christian Doctrine of God: One Being Three Persons*, 254.
38 See *GS* §§108, 125, 343 and in *TSZ* §2 of the *Prologue, Of the Compassionate, Retired from Service* and *Of the Higher Man*.

39 Julian Young, *The Death of God and the Meaning of Life* (Abingdon, UK: Routledge, 2003), 83.
40 Karl Jaspers, *Nietzsche and Christianity*, trans. E. B. Ashton, Gateway Edition (Chicago, IL: H. Regnery Co, 1967).
41 Julian Young, *Friedrich Nietzsche: A Philosophical Biography* (Cambridge, UK: Cambridge University Press, 2010).
42 Leiter, for example, omits Christianity entirely when describing Nietzsche's intellectual development. See Brian Leiter, *Nietzsche on Morality*, ed. Tim Crane and Jonathan Woolf (Abingdon, UK: Routledge, 2002), 31–72. On the complex relationship between Nietzsche's thought and Christian thought, see Andre J. Groenewald, 'Interpreting the Theology of Barth in Light of Nietzsche's Dictum "God Is Dead"', *HTS Teologiese Studies/Theological Studies* 63, no. 4 (2007); John Hennig, 'Nietzsche, Jaspers and Christianity', *Blackfriars* 29, no. 343 (1948); Craig Hovey, *Nietzsche and Theology*, Philosophy and Theology (London, UK: T&T Clark, 2008); Jaspers, *Nietzsche and Christianity*; Walter Kaufmann, *Nietzsche: Philosopher, Psychologist, Antichrist*, 4th edn (Princeton, NJ: Princeton University Press, 1974); *Critique of Religion and Philosophy* (Princeton, NJ: Princeton University Press, 1978); Gregory Moore, 'Nietzsche, Degeneration, and the Critique of Christianity', *Journal of Nietzsche Studies* 19, nos 1–18 (2000); Richard Rorty, *The Future of Religion*, ed. Gianni Vattimo and Santiago Zabala (New York, NY: Columbia University Press, 2005); Gianni Vattimo, *After Christianity*, Italian Academy Lectures (New York, NY: Columbia University Press, 2002); 'Nihilism as Emancipation', *Cosmos and History: The Journal of Natural and Social Philosophy* 5, no. 1 (2009); Craig Wiley, 'I Was Dead and Behold, I Am Alive Forevermore: Responses to Nietzsche in 20th Century Christian Theology', *intersections* 10, no. 1 (2009); Stephen N. Williams, *The Shadow of the Antichrist: Nietzsche's Critique of Christianity* (Grand Rapids, MI: Baker Academic, 2006).
43 For an insightful analysis of Homeric divinities and their ethical implications, see Hatab, '*Amor Agonis*: Conflict and Love in Nietzsche and Homer'.
44 I say 'loosely' described because Nietzsche's attitude to science is not overwhelmingly positive. However, the proposals in these two texts seem to be consistent with the overall approach to his naturalism that I discuss will in later chapters.
45 Nietzsche, *The Nietzsche Reader*.
46 Herman Siemens, 'Nietzsche on Productive Resistance', in *Conflict and Contest in Nietzsche's Philosophy*, ed. Herman Siemens and James Pearson (London, UK: Bloomsbury, 2019).
47 Nietzsche, *The Nietzsche Reader*, 98. Nietzsche's concept of contest explored in this essay will be more fully addressed in Chapter 5.
48 *Sittlichkeit der Sitte* and cognate forms, found in *HAH* §II.89; *D* §§9, 10, 14, 18, 19, 33, 101; *GS* §§ 43, 46, 143, 149, 296; *GM* Preface.4, II.2, III.9. See Keith

Ansell-Pearson and Rebecca Bamford, *Nietzsche's Dawn: Philosophy, Ethics, and the Passion of Knowledge* (Hoboken, NJ: Wiley-Blackwell, 2021), 1–13; Rebecca Bamford, 'Health and Self-Cultivation in Dawn', in *Nietzsche's Free Spirit Philosophy* (London, UK: Rowman and Littlefield, 2015); 'The Ethos of Inquiry: Nietzsche on Experience, Naturalism, and Experimentalism', *Journal of Nietzsche Studies* 47, no. 1 (2016); Maudemarie Clark and Brian Leiter, 'Introduction', in *Daybreak*, Cambridge Texts in the History of Philosophy (Cambridge, UK: Cambridge University Press, 1997).

49 'Ecstatic' meaning *ex-stasis,* in which the being of each person is found not within the person but outside of themselves in others. See Pannenberg, *Systematic Theology*, 1, 482.
50 Remembering that Jesus Christ is thought to be the second person of the trinity in human form.
51 I return to theme of neighbour-love in Chapter 7.

Chapter 3

1 Julian Young, 'Schopenhauer, Nietzsche, Death and Salvation', *European Journal of Philosophy* 16, no. 2 (2008); *Friedrich Nietzsche: A Philosophical Biography* (Cambridge, UK: Cambridge University Press, 2010), 81–5.
2 E.g. *D* §§148, 167; *GS* §§13, 99, 118; *TSZ* 'Of the Compassionate' and 'Of the Love of One's Neighbour'.
3 E.g. *D* §§99, 113
4 David E. Cartwright, 'Schopenhauer's Compassion and Nietzsche's Pity', *Schopenhauer Jahrbuch* 69 (1988).
5 Ibid., 561.
6 David E. Cartwright, 'Compassion and Solidarity with Sufferers: The Metaphysics of Mitleid', *European Journal of Philosophy* 16, no. 2 (2008); 'Schopenhauer on the Value of Compassion', in *A Companion to Schopenhauer*, ed. Bart Vandenabeele (Hoboken, NJ: Wiley, 2012).
7 Cartwright, 'Compassion and Solidarity with Sufferers', 294–7.
8 Cartwright, 'Schopenhauer on the Value of Compassion', 255.
9 Cartwright, 'Compassion and Solidarity with Sufferers', 301–2.
10 Wolfgang Schirmacher, ed., *The Essential Schopenhauer: Key Selections from The World as Will and Representation and Other Writings* (New York, NY: HarperCollins, 2010), 223.
11 Ibid., 224.
12 Ibid., 225.
13 Ibid., 213.

14 Cartwright, 'Compassion and Solidarity with Sufferers', 301–2; 'Schopenhauer on the Value of Compassion', 263.
15 Schirmacher, *The Essential Schopenhauer*, 199.
16 Ibid., 201.
17 Ibid., 200.
18 Young, 'Schopenhauer, Nietzsche, Death and Salvation', 317.
19 David E. Cartwright, 'The Last Temptation of Zarathustra', *Journal of the History of Philosophy* 31, no. 1 (1993): 54.
20 Bernard Reginster, 'Knowledge and Selflessness: Schopenhauer and the Paradox of Reflection', *European Journal of Philosophy* 16, no. 2 (2008).
21 Ibid., 255.
22 Ibid., 261.
23 Ibid., 266–8.
24 Schirmacher, *The Essential Schopenhauer*, 239.
25 Cartwright, 'Schopenhauer on the Value of Compassion'.
26 Schirmacher, *The Essential Schopenhauer*, 239.
27 Cartwright, 'Schopenhauer's Compassion and Nietzsche's Pity', 564.
28 Nietzsche, *Writings from the Early Notebooks*, trans. Ladislaus Löb, ed. Karl Ameriks and Desmond Clarke (Cambridge, UK: Cambridge University Press, 2009), 4. See also Christopher Janaway, 'Schopenhauer as Nietzsche's Educator', in *Willing and Nothingness: Schopenhauer as Nietzsche's Educator*, ed. Christopher Janaway (Oxford, UK: Clarendon Press, 1998); Julian Young, *Friedrich Nietzsche: A Philosophical Biography* (Cambridge, UK: Cambridge University Press, 2010), 90–5.
29 See Nuno Nabais, 'The Individual and Individuality in Nietzsche', in *A Companion to Nietzsche*, ed. Keith Ansell-Pearson, Blackwell Companions to Philosophy (Malden, MA: Blackwell, 2006).
30 The classical composer and cultural figure Richard Wagner was an important influence on Nietzsche in his early years, being both a mentor and an inspiration. See Young, *Friedrich Nietzsche: A Philosophical Biography*.
31 E.g. *GS* §371 and *TSZ* §18, 'Of the Tree on the Mountainside'.
32 See also *D* §§ 532 and 549 on Nietzsche's rejection of self-dissolution.
33 I prefer a less literal translation of *Von den Hinterweltern*, Kaufmann's translation has it as 'Of The Afterworldly' and Hollingdale as 'Of the Afterworldsmen', both of which are preferable. However, for consistency, I provide Del Caro's translation from the Cambridge University Press series. See Nietzsche, *Thus Spoke Zarathustra*, 58; *Thus Spoke Zarathustra*, trans. Walter Kaufmann (London, UK: Penguin Books, 1966), 30; *Thus Spoke Zarathustra*, 20.
34 It is a commonplace in several traditions within academic philosophy to distinguish between the world of appearance (the phenomenal world), to which human

beings have access, and the thing-in-itself (the noumenal world), to which human beings do not have direct access. See Immanuel Kant, *Prolegomena to Any Future Metaphysics* (Raleigh, NC: Generic NL Freebook Publisher, 1998).

Chapter 4

1. Martin Heidegger, *Nietzsche*, trans. David Farrell Krell, vol. 1 (San Francisco: Harper & Row, 1991), 199–208; ibid., vol. 2: 200–10.
2. Arthur C. Danto, *Nietzsche as Philosopher* (New York, NY: Macmillan, 1964); Peter Poellner, *Nietzsche and Metaphysics* (Oxford, UK: Clarendon Press, 1995).
3. Tsarina Doyle, *Nietzsche's Metaphysics of the Will to Power: The Possibility of Value* (Cambridge, UK: Cambridge University Press, 2018).
4. Jeffrey Church, 'Nietzsche's Early Perfectionism', *Journal of Nietzsche Studies* 46, no. 2 (2015); Nietzsche's Early Ethical Idealism', *Journal of Nietzsche Studies* 47, no. 1 (2016).
5. Church, 'Nietzsche's Early Ethical Idealism', 12.
6. Maudemarie Clark, 'Nietzsche's Attack on Morality' (Doctoral Dissertation, University of Wisconsin-Madison, 1977); *Nietzsche on Truth and Philosophy* (Cambridge, UK: Cambridge University Press, 1990); Brian Leiter, 'Nietzsche and the Critique of Morality: Philosophical Naturalism in Nietzsche's Theory of Value' (Doctoral Thesis, University of Michigan, 1995); *Nietzsche on Morality* (Abingdon, UK: Routledge, 2002); Nietzsche, *Daybreak*, vii–xxxiv, Introduction by Maudemarie Clark and Brian Leiter (Cambridge, UK: Cambridge University Press, 1997); Richard Schacht, *Nietzsche* (Abingdon, UK: Routledge, 1985); 'Nietzsche's Naturalism', *Journal of Nietzsche Studies* 43, no. 2 (2012).
7. The relationship between Nietzsche's understanding of the will to power and his naturalist conception of human existence is a complex topic that has divided scholars. It might be useful in future research to connect the idea of contest, the drives of an individual naturalistically conceived and social relationships of contest together under the rubric of a naturalist conception of the will to power.
8. It is not clear that Darwin's approach warrants this criticism. For the purposes of this book it is enough that Nietzsche perceived this to be a weakness in the Darwinian schema.
9. Matthew Meyer's dialectical reading of the free spirit works, as a journey from scientific positivism in *HAH* ending in an appreciation of the tragedy of existence, is particularly instructive. See Matthew Meyer, *Nietzsche's Free Spirit Works: A Dialectical Reading* (Cambridge, UK: Cambridge University Press, 2019).
10. See also Arthur W. H. Adkins, *Merit and Responsibility: A Study in Greek Values* (Oxford, UK: Clarendon Press, 1970); Terence Irwin, *Classical Thought* (Oxford, UK: Oxford University Press, 1989).

11 Irwin, *Classical Thought*.
12 Ibid., 39.
13 Ibid., 113–17.
14 Ibid., 130–2. In a similar vein, Dodds demonstrates that otherwise-naturalistic explanations of phenomena that defied the rationality of the classical mind were often explained using metaphysical devices. See E. R. Dodds, *The Greeks and the Irrational* (Berkeley, CA: University of California Press, 1951).
15 Michael N. Forster, Kristin Gjesdal and Kurt Bayertz, *Materialism*, 1st edn (Oxford, UK: Oxford University Press, 2015).
16 Keith Ansell-Pearson, *Nietzsche and Modern German Thought* (Abingdon, UK: Routledge, 1991); Katia Hay and Leonel Ribeiro Dos Santos, eds, *Nietzsche, German Idealism and Its Critics* (Berlin, Germany: De Gruyter, 2015); George J. Stack, *Lange and Nietzsche* (Berlin, Germany: De Gruyter, 1983); Paul A. Swift, *Becoming Nietzsche: Early Reflections on Democritus, Schopenhauer, and Kant* (Lanham, MD: Lexington Books, 2005).
17 The influence of Burckhardt in relation to struggle and contest is also important. See Enrico Müller, 'Competitive Ethos and Cultural Dynamic. The Principle of Agonism in Jacob Burckhardt and Friedrich Nietzsche', in *Conflict and Contest in Nietzsche's Philosophy*, ed. Herman Siemens and James Pearson (London, UK: Bloomsbury, 2019).
18 Lukas Soderstrom, 'Nietzsche as a Reader of Wilhelm Roux, or the Physiology of History', *Symposium* 13, no. 2 (2009).
19 Also Feuerbach, Lange, Burckhardt, and Darwinism through Spencer.
20 Leiter, 'Nietzsche and the Critique of Morality'; *Nietzsche on Morality*; 'Nietzsche's Moral and Political Philosophy', in *Stanford Encyclopaedia of Philosophy*, ed. Edward N. Zalta (2015); 'Normativity for Naturalists', *Philosophical Issues* 25, no. 1 (2015).
21 E.g. Leiter, *Nietzsche on Morality*, 3–11.
22 Leiter, 'Normativity for Naturalists'.
23 Leiter, *Nietzsche on Morality*.
24 Leiter, 'Normativity for Naturalists'.
25 E.g. *GS* §§37, 57, 111, 112, 427.
26 These texts come from a later period of Nietzsche's writing, originally published as Book 5 of *The Gay Science* in 1887. However, in my view they are consistent with themes less clearly expressed in earlier writings. Matthew Meyer has argued that the free spirit works have been composed to show the trajectory of the free spirit from scientific positivism to the tragic-comic outlook. See Meyer, *Nietzsche's Free Spirit Works: A Dialectical Reading*.
27 Other writers who address these issues include Christoph Cox, *Nietzsche: Naturalism and Interpretation* (Berkeley, CA: University of California Press, 1999); Christopher Janaway, *Beyond Selflessness: Reading Nietzsche's Genealogy* (Oxford,

UK: Oxford University Press, 2007); 'Beyond Selflessness in Ethics and Inquiry', *Journal of Nietzsche Studies* 35, no. 1 (2008); Christopher Janaway and Simon Robertson, eds, *Nietzsche, Naturalism, and Normativity* (Oxford, UK: Oxford University Press, 2012).
28 'Nietzsche's Naturalism and Normativity', in *Nietzsche, Naturalism and Normativity*, ed. Christopher Janaway and Simon Robertson (Oxford, UK: Oxford University Press, 2012), 208.
29 Ibid., 193–4.
30 Ibid., 2.
31 See also *GS* §335, *Long live physics*, where Nietzsche writes that 'we must become the best learners and discoverers of everything that is lawful and necessary in the world, we must become physicists'. It is clear from the context that he is applying the title of 'physicist' to ethics: he is calling for an as-yet undeveloped science of society, morality and personality.
32 Patrick Forber, 'Nietzsche Was No Darwinian', *Philosophy and Phenomenological Research* 75, no. 2 (2007); Dirk Robert Johnson, 'Nietzsche's Darwin, and the Spirit of the Agon' (Doctoral Dissertation, Indiana University, 2000); 'Nietzsche's Early Darwinism: The "David Strauss" Essay of 1873', *Nietzsche-Studien* 30 (2001); 'On the Way to the "Anti-Darwin": Nietzsche's Darwinian Meditations in the Middle Period', *Tijdschrift voor Filosofie* 65, no. 4 (2003); *Nietzsche's Anti-Darwinism* (Cambridge, UK: Cambridge University Press, 2010); 'Dirk R. Johnson, *Nietzsche's Anti-Darwinism*; 'One Hundred Twenty-Two Years Later: Reassessing the Nietzsche–Darwin Relationship', *Journal of Nietzsche Studies* 44, no. 2 (2013); John Richardson, 'Nietzsche Contra Darwin', *Philosophy and Phenomenological Research* 65, no. 3 (2002); *Nietzsche's New Darwinism* (Oxford, UK: Oxford University Press, 2004).
33 Richardson, 'Nietzsche Contra Darwin'; *Nietzsche's New Darwinism*; 'On Richard Schacht's Nietzsche', *Journal of Nietzsche Studies* 46, no. 2 (2015).
34 E.g. Doyle, *Nietzsche's Metaphysics of the Will to Power: The Possibility of Value*; Heidegger, *Nietzsche*, 1.
35 Richardson, 'Nietzsche Contra Darwin', 537.
36 Richardson, *Nietzsche's New Darwinism*, 26–35.
37 Ibid., 52–9.
38 The supposed centrality of this thought, at least in my view, has been significantly bolstered as an historical artefact of his sister's cynical compilation of aphorisms, published as *The Will to Power*.
39 Richardson, *Nietzsche's New Darwinism*, 78.
40 Ibid., 120.
41 Ibid., 121.
42 Ibid., 123.
43 Ibid.
44 Ibid., 103.

Chapter 5

1. Important contributions on the topic of Nietzsche and contest include Christa Davis Acampora, 'Nietzsche Contra Homer, Socrates, and Paul', *Journal of Nietzsche Studies* 24, no. 1 (2002); 'Contesting Nietzsche', *Journal of Nietzsche Studies* 24, no. 1 (2002); *Contesting Nietzsche* (Chicago, IL: University of Chicago Press, 2013); 'Agonistic Communities: Love, War and Spheres of Activity', in *Conflict and Contest in Nietzsche's Philosophy*, ed. Herman Siemens and James Pearson (London, UK: Bloomsbury, 2019); Lawrence J. Hatab, 'Prospects for a Democratic Agon: Why We Can Still Be Nietzscheans', *Journal of Nietzsche Studies* 24, no. 1 (2002); *Nietzsche's Life Sentence: Coming to Terms with Eternal Recurrence* (Abingdon, UK: Routledge, 2005); '*Amor Agonis*: Conflict and Love in Nietzsche and Homer' in *Conflict and Contest in Nietzsche's Philosophy*, ed. Herman Siemens and James Pearson (London, UK: Bloomsbury, 2019); Enrico Müller, 'Competitive Ethos and Cultural Dynamic. The Principle of Agonism in Jacob Burckhardt and Friedrich Nietzsche', in *Conflict and Contest in Nietzsche's Philosophy*, ed. Herman Siemens and James Pearson (London, UK: Bloomsbury, 2019); Herman Siemens, 'Nietzsche's Agon with Ressentiment: Towards a Therapeutic Reading of Critical Transvaluation', *Continental Philosophy Review* 34, no. 1 (2001); 'Agonal Communities of Taste: Law and Community in Nietzsche's Philosophy of Transvaluation', *Journal of Nietzsche Studies*, no. 24 (2002); 'Agonal Writing: Towards an Agonal Model for Critical Transvaluation'; 'Nietzsche's Agon', in *The Nietzschean Mind*, ed. Paul Katsafanas (London, UK: Routledge, 2018); 'Nietzsche on Productive Resistance' in *Conflict and Contest in Nietzsche's Philosophy*, ed. Herman Siemens and James Pearson (London, UK: Bloomsbury, 2019).
2. See Arthur C. Danto, *Nietzsche as Philosopher* (New York, NY: Macmillan, 1964); John Richardson, *Nietzsche's System* (Oxford, UK: Oxford University Press, 1996).
3. General introductions to the background in antiquity can be found in Arthur W. H. Adkins, *Merit and Responsibility: A Study in Greek Values* (Oxford, UK: Clarendon Press, 1970); E. R. Dodds, *The Greeks and the Irrational* (Berkeley, CA: University of California Press, 1951); Terence Irwin, *Classical Thought* (Oxford, UK: Oxford University Press, 1989).
4. On the importance of difference for Nietzschean contest, see Paul E. Kirkland, 'Nietzsche, Agonistic Politics, and Spiritual Enmity', *Political Research Quarterly* 73, no. 1 (2020), 6; James Pearson, 'Nietzsche on the Sources of Agonal Moderation', *Journal of Nietzsche Studies* 49, no. 1 (2018); Siemens, 'Nietzsche's Agon with Ressentiment', 333.
5. Brendan Donnellan, 'Friedrich Nietzsche and Paul Rée: Cooperation and Conflict', *Journal of the History of Ideas* 43, no. 4 (1982); Robin Small, *Nietzsche and Rée: A Star Friendship* (Oxford, UK: Oxford University Press, 2005).

6 Acampora, *Contesting Nietzsche*, 50.
7 Ibid., 17.
8 Acampora, 'Agonistic Communities: Love, War and Spheres of Activity'.
9 Ibid., 136–7.
10 Ibid., 133–4.
11 Ibid., 128.
12 Acampora, *Contesting Nietzsche*, 56–64.
13 Ibid., 25, 36–7.
14 Ibid., 193.
15 Hatab, 'Prospects for a Democratic Agon: Why We Can Still Be Nietzscheans', 134–5.
16 Hatab, '*Amor Agonis*: Conflict and Love in Nietzsche and Homer', 106. Original emphasis.
17 Siemens, 'Nietzsche's Agon', 333.
18 Siemens, 'Nietzsche's Agon with Ressentiment', 9–12.
19 Siemens, 'Nietzsche on Productive Resistance', 23.
20 Ibid., 33.
21 Ibid., 27.
22 Fredrick Appel, *Nietzsche Contra Democracy* (Ithaca, NY: Cornell University Press, 1999); Dana Freibach-Heifetz, 'Pure Air and Solitude and Bread and Medicine: Nietzsche's Conception of Friendship', *Philosophy Today* 49, no. 3 (2005); Horst Hutter, 'The Virtue of Solitude and the Vicissitudes of Friendship', *Critical Review of International Social and Political Philosophy* 2, no. 4 (1999); Paul van Tongeren, 'Politics, Friendship and Solitude in Nietzsche (Confronting Derrida's Reading of Nietzsche in "Politics of Friendship")', *South African Journal of Philosophy* 19, no. 3 (2000).
23 Acampora, *Contesting Nietzsche*, 42–3.
24 Siemens, 'Nietzsche's Agon with Ressentiment', 10.
25 Nietzsche, *The Birth of Tragedy and Other Writings*, trans. Ronald Speirs, ed. Karl Ameriks and Desmond Clarke (Cambridge, UK: Cambridge University Press, 1999), 127.
26 Ibid., 133.
27 Ibid., 25.
28 Ibid., 39.
29 Ibid., 24.
30 Ibid., 22.
31 For an in-depth (and sometimes contrary) treatment of this theme, see Béatrice Han-Pile, 'Nietzsche's Metaphysics in the Birth of Tragedy', *European Journal of Philosophy* 14, no. 3 (2006).
32 Friedrich Nietzsche, *The Nietzsche Reader*, ed. Keith Ansell-Pearson and Duncan Large, Blackwell Readers (Malden, MA: Blackwell, 2006), 96.

33 Ibid., 96–7.
34 Ibid., 97.
35 Ibid., 98.
36 Ibid.
37 Ibid., 99.
38 Especially *The Greek State* and *Philosophy in the Tragic Age of the Greeks* (ibid., 88–94, 101–13.)
39 See Nietzsche, *Daybreak*, vii–xxxiv, Introduction by Maudemarie Clark and Brian Leiter, Cambridge Texts in the History of Philosophy (Cambridge, UK: Cambridge University Press, 1997).
40 For example, Yunus Tuncel, 'The Principle of Agon in Nietzsche's Thought' (Doctoral Thesis, The New School, 2000).
41 This is perhaps intended to recall the garden of Epicurus.

Chapter 6

1 It should be remembered that when I use the term 'individual', I am referring to a particular person as constituted by their underlying drives – a 'social' structure of drives and affects. The term should not be taken to refer to an indivisible soul or a disembodied consciousness.
2 Graham Parkes, *Composing the Soul: Reaches of Nietzsche's Psychology* (Chicago, IL: University of Chicago Press, 1994); Leslie Paul Thiele, *Friedrich Nietzsche and the Politics of the Soul: A Study of Heroic Individualism* (Princeton, NJ: Princeton University Press, 1990), 196.
3 Parkes, *Composing the Soul*, 320.
4 Ibid., 35, 262–66.
5 Ibid., 252, 312.
6 Ibid., 159–73.
7 Whether Parkes is right to attribute this stance to Nietzsche is questionable. The question for Nietzsche seems to be one of the passions either being inflamed and out of control (something he associates with Christianity, see *D* §§58, 192), or being moderated through self-cultivation. In either case, the passion for self-distinction and pre-eminence – a Homeric passion – seems at the same time to him inimical to Christianity and central to personal flourishing.
8 Parkes, *Composing the Soul*, 309.
9 Ibid., 354.
10 Ibid., 357–8.
11 Ibid., 280–2.
12 Ibid., 124–6.

13 Ibid., 164.
14 KSA 9:11 [197], 1881.
15 I argued in chapter 2 that Acampora, Siemens and Hatab also (erroneously) make this claim. See also Christine Daigle, 'The Ethical Ideal of the Free Spirit in *Human All Too Human*', in *Nietzsche's Free Spirit Philosophy* (London, UK: Rowman and Littlefield, 2015), 35–8.
16 Parkes, *Composing the Soul*, 360.
17 Ibid., 289–90.
18 Ibid., 359.
19 Ibid., 153.
20 Ibid., 159.
21 Thiele, *Friedrich Nietzsche and the Politics of the Soul*.
22 Ibid., 66–7.
23 Ibid., 42–4, 51, 106–8.
24 Ibid., 99–100, 86, 200–1.
25 Ibid., 30–6.
26 Ibid., 37–40.
27 Ibid., 180.
28 Ibid., 44–7.
29 Ibid., 172–4.
30 Ibid., 220–4.
31 Ibid., 20–1.
32 Ibid., 204.
33 Ibid., 204–5.
34 Ibid., 211.
35 Ibid., 207–8.
36 Parkes, *Composing the Soul*, 250.
37 Thiele, *Friedrich Nietzsche and the Politics of the Soul*, 57.
38 Daigle, 'The Ethical Ideal of the Free Spirit in *Human All Too Human*'.
39 Ibid., 33.
40 Ibid., 36.
41 Ibid., 38.
42 See also Keith Ansell-Pearson and Rebecca Bamford, *Nietzsche's Dawn: Philosophy, Ethics, and the Passion of Knowledge* (Hoboken, NJ: Wiley-Blackwell, 2021), 158–9.
43 Acampora, *Contesting Nietzsche*, 151ff.
44 Ibid., 154.
45 Ibid., 168.
46 Ibid., 158.
47 Nietzsche presents an individual human being as constituted in such a way as to discharge its drives (*der Trieb*), to express its passions (*die Leidenschaft, die*

Begierde) and to act on its instincts (*der Instinkt*). This vocabulary presents a naturalistic interpretation of human behaviour.

48 Noting that this decision is itself the outcome of another, different underlying contest between drives.
49 *Kampf*, usually translated as 'struggle' and related to *Wettkampf*, 'contest', is here translated as 'battle'.
50 For extensive discussion of Nietzsche's use of garden imagery, its origins and application to these questions, see Babette Babich, 'Epicurean Gardens and Nietzsche's White Seas', in *Nietzsche and Epicurus*, ed. Vinod Acharya and Ryan J. Johnson (London, UK: Bloomsbury, 2020); Rebecca Bamford, 'Health and Self-Cultivation in Dawn', in *Nietzsche's Free Spirit Philosophy* (London, UK: Rowman and Littlefield, 2015).
51 Ansell-Pearson and Bamford, *Nietzsche's Dawn*, 142.
52 Ibid., 158–9. See also Daigle, 'The Ethical Ideal of the Free Spirit in *Human All Too Human*'.
53 This text is presented twice in Nietzsche's work: the first time as the final text of book four of *The Gay Science* (1882 edition) and also as the first text of *Thus Spoke Zarathustra*, published in 1883.

Chapter 7

1 For an excellent description of Nietzschean individuality that focuses on the passions, see Matthew Dennis, 'Passionate Individuation: Epicurean Self-Cultivation in Mill and Nietzsche', in *Nietzsche and Epicurus*, ed. Vinod Acharya and Ryan J. Johnson (London, UK: Bloomsbury, 2020); *Cultivating Our Passionate Attachments*, Routledge Studies in Ethics and Moral Theory (New York, NY: Routledge, 2021).
2 Siemens proposes the provocative but underdeveloped notion of 'hostile love' as a signature feature of Nietzsche's ethics. See Siemens, 'Nietzsche on Productive Resistance', in *Conflict and Contest in Nietzsche's Philosophy*, ed. Herman Siemens and James Pearson (London, UK: Bloomsbury, 2019), 23, 41.
3 'Decadent' is here used in its Nietzschean sense: decadent in the sense of decay.
4 Ruth Abbey, *Nietzsche's Middle Period* (Oxford, UK: Oxford University Press, 2000); Paul Franco, *Nietzsche's Enlightenment: The Free-Spirit Trilogy of the Middle Period* (Chicago, IL: University of Chicago Press, 2011); Michael Ure, *Nietzsche's 'The Gay Science': An Introduction* (Cambridge, UK: Cambridge University Press, 2019).
5 This term was coined by Georg Brandes in 1887 and approved of by Nietzsche in personal correspondence. See Friedrich Wilhelm Nietzsche, *Selected Letters of Friedrich Nietzsche*, trans. Christopher Middleton (Chicago, IL: University of

Chicago Press, 1969), 279; see also Bruce Detwiler, *Nietzsche and the Politics of Aristocratic Radicalism* (Chicago, IL: University of Chicago Press, 1990).

6   Müller argues convincingly that, somewhat paradoxically, the inequality of competitive outcomes presupposes the equality of the contestants. See Enrico Müller, 'Competitive Ethos and Cultural Dynamic. The Principle of Agonism in Jacob Burckhardt and Friedrich Nietzsche', in *Conflict and Contest in Nietzsche's Philosophy*, ed. Herman Siemens and James Pearson (London, UK: Bloomsbury, 2019), 97.

7   See, for example, *D* §§172, 460, 477, 542; *GS* §§1, 19, 23, 26, 48, 106, 119, 120, 159, 268, 283, 297, 302, 371.

8   Bernard Reginster, *The Affirmation of Life: Nietzsche on Overcoming Nihilism* (Cambridge, MA: Harvard University Press, 2006).

9   Ibid., 134. The importance of overcoming resistance as a key to flourishing has been discussed extensively by Herman Siemens. See Siemens, 'Nietzsche on Productive Resistance'.

10 Christa Davis Acampora, 'Agonistic Communities: Love, War and Spheres of Activity', in *Conflict and Contest in Nietzsche's Philosophy*, ed. Herman Siemens and James Pearson (London, UK: Bloomsbury, 2019), 128.

11 Substantive references to 'friend' [*Freund*] and 'friendship' [*Freundschaft*] and related forms can be found in *D* §§69, 102, 174, 287, 313, 369, 437, 485, 489, 503, 566; *GS* §§7, 14, 16, 30, 61, 98, 168, 279; *TSZ* 'On the Friend', 'On the Thousand and One Goals', 'On Love of the Neighbour', 'On the Bestowing Virtue'.3, 'Before Sunrise'; and *BGE* §§27, 40, 217.

12 Julia Annas, 'Plato and Aristotle on Friendship and Altruism', *Mind* 86, no. 344 (1977); Philip Bashor, 'Plato and Aristotle on Friendship', *Journal of Value Inquiry* 2, no. 4 (1968); Lorraine Smith Pangle, *Aristotle and the Philosophy of Friendship* (Cambridge, UK: Cambridge University Press, 2002); A. W. Price, *Love and Friendship in Plato and Aristotle* (Oxford, UK: Clarendon, 1989); Andra Striowski, 'Plato and Aristotle on Philia' (Master's Thesis, Dalhousie University, 2008); John von Heyking, *The Form of Politics: Aristotle and Plato on Friendship* (Montreal, Canada: McGill-Queen's University Press, 2016).

13 E.g. Jacques Derrida, *Politics of Friendship*, trans. George Collins (London, UK: Verso, 1997); A. C. Grayling, *Friendship. Vices and Virtues*, ed. Richard G. Newhauser and John Jeffries Martin (London, UK: Yale University Press, 2013); Horst Hutter, 'The Virtue of Solitude and the Vicissitudes of Friendship', *Critical Review of International Social and Political Philosophy* 2, no. 4 (1999); Mark Vernon, *The Philosophy of Friendship* (Abingdon, UK: Palgrave Macmillan, 2005); David Webb, 'On Friendship: Derrida, Foucault, and the Practice of Becoming', *Research in Phenomenology* 33, no. 1 (2003).

14 Ruth Abbey, 'Circles, Ladders and Stars: Nietzsche on Friendship', *Critical Review of International Social and Political Philosophy* 2, no. 4 (1999); Dwight

David Allman, 'Ancient Friends, Modern Enemies', *South Atlantic Quarterly* 97, no. 1 (1998); Fredrick Appel, *Nietzsche Contra Democracy* (Ithaca, NY: Cornell University Press, 1999); John C. Coker, 'Spectres of Friends and Friendship', *Journal of Nietzsche Studies*, no. 16 (1998); Christine Daigle, 'The Ethical Ideal of the Free Spirit in *Human All Too Human*', in *Nietzsche's Free Spirit Philosophy* (London, UK: Rowman and Littlefield, 2015); Dana Freibach-Heifetz, 'Pure Air and Solitude and Bread and Medicine: Nietzsche's Conception of Friendship', *Philosophy Today* 49, no. 3 (2005); Jean Gauthier, 'In Honour of Friendship' (Master's Thesis, Trent University, 1998); Daniel I. Harris, 'Friendship as Shared Joy in Nietzsche' (Doctoral Dissertation, University of Guelph, 2013). 'Nietzsche and Aristotle on Friendship and Self-Knowledge', *Journal of Nietzsche Studies* 48, no. 2 (2017); Hutter, 'The Virtue of Solitude and the Vicissitudes of Friendship'; Walter Kaufmann, *Nietzsche: Philosopher, Psychologist, Antichrist* (Princeton, NJ: Princeton University Press, 1974); Robert C. Miner, 'Nietzsche on Friendship', *Journal of Nietzsche Studies* 40 (2010); Robin Small, *Nietzsche and Rée: A Star Friendship* (Oxford, UK: Oxford University Press, 2005); Paul van Tongeren, 'Politics, Friendship and Solitude in Nietzsche (Confronting Derrida's Reading of Nietzsche in "Politics of Friendship")', *South African Journal of Philosophy* 19, no. 3 (2000); 'Kant, Nietzsche and the Idealization of Friendship into Nihilism', *Kriterion* 54, no. 128 (2013); Willow Verkerk, 'Nietzsche's Goal of Friendship', *Journal of Nietzsche Studies* 45, no. 3 (2014); 'Nietzsche's Agonistic Ethics of Friendship', *Symposium* 20, no. 2 (2016); 'On Love, Women, and Friendship: Reading Nietzsche with Irigaray', *Nietzsche-Studien* 46, no. 1 (2017); *Nietzsche and Friendship* (New York, NY: Bloomsbury, 2019); Robert R. Williams, 'Aristotle, Hegel, and Nietzsche on Friendship', in *Tragedy, Recognition, and the Death of God: Studies in Hegel and Nietzsche* (Oxford, UK: Oxford University Press, 2012); Benedetta Zavatta, 'Nietzsche and Emerson on Friendship and Its Ethical-Political Implications', in *Nietzsche, Power and Politics: Rethinking Nietzsche's Legacy for Political Thought*, ed. Herman Siemens and Vasti Roodt (Berlin, Germany: De Gruyter, 2008).
15 Daniel I. Harris, 'Nietzsche and Virtue', *Journal of Value Inquiry* 49, no. 3 (2015): 216; Willow Verkerk, 'Nietzsche's Agonistic Ethics of Friendship', *Symposium* 20, no. 2 (2016), 24.
16 Miner, 'Nietzsche on Friendship', 64–5; Verkerk, 'Nietzsche's Agonistic Ethics of Friendship', 281.
17 Miner, 'Nietzsche on Friendship'.
18 Verkerk, 'Nietzsche's Goal of Friendship'; 'Nietzsche's Agonistic Ethics of Friendship'.
19 See also Gauthier, 'In Honour of Friendship', 42.
20 Miner, 'Nietzsche on Friendship'.
21 Verkerk, 'Nietzsche's Goal of Friendship'.

22 Freibach-Heifetz, 'Pure Air and Solitude and Bread and Medicine: Nietzsche's Conception of Friendship'.
23 Herman Siemens, 'Nietzsche's Agon with Ressentiment: Towards a Therapeutic Reading of Critical Transvaluation', *Continental Philosophy Review* 34, no. 1 (2001); Small, *Nietzsche and Rée*; Leslie Paul Thiele, *Friedrich Nietzsche and the Politics of the Soul: A Study of Heroic Individualism* (Princeton, NJ: Princeton University Press, 1990).
24 Miner, 'Nietzsche on Friendship', 47.
25 Harris, 'Friendship as Shared Joy in Nietzsche'; 'Nietzsche and Virtue'; 'Compassion and Affirmation in Nietzsche', *Journal of Nietzsche Studies* 48, no. 1 (2017); 'Nietzsche and Aristotle on Friendship and Self-Knowledge'; Michael Ure, *Nietzsche's Therapy: Self-Cultivation in the Middle Works* (Lanham, MD: Lexington Books, 2008).
26 Harris, 'Friendship as Shared Joy in Nietzsche', 9.
27 Melanie Shepherd, 'Nietzsche's *Übermensch*: From Shared Suffering to Shared Joy', in *Joy and Laughter in Nietzsche's Philosophy*, eds. Paul E. Kirkland and Michael J McNeal (London, UK: Bloomsbury, 2022).
28 The term and its cognates appear throughout the middle period in a number of different contexts. *GS* §12, e.g. describes in its first half how science causes people to experience either pleasure (*Lust*) or displeasure (*Unlust*). The text transitions to a discussion of the 'refined pleasures and joys' (*gekosteten Lüsten und Freude*) and concludes by contrasting 'pain' (*Schmerz*) with 'joy' (*Freude*). In *GS* §3 it is used to refer to the irrational pleasure a noble person takes in displaying magnanimity, and in *GS* §49 it is rendered as the 'delight' a magnanimous person takes in their own generosity. In *TSZ* Book 1, 'On the Passions of Pleasure and Pain', *Freudenschaften* ('passions of pleasure') are opposed to passions *simpliciter* (*Leidenschaften*), which having once been regarded as 'evil' (*Böse*) have flowered into virtues (*Tugenden*), which in turn have ultimately become pleasures.
29 See also Shepherd, 'Nietzsche's *ÜBermensch*: From Shared Suffering to Shared Joy'.
30 William Desmond, *Is There a Sabbath for Thought?: Between Religion and Philosophy*, ed. John D. Caputo (New York, NY: Fordham University Press, 2005), 289ff.
31 Debra Bergoffen, 'On Nietzsche and the Enemy: Nietzsche's New Politics', in *Nietzsche, Power and Politics: Rethinking Nietzsche's Legacy for Political Thought*, ed. Herman Siemens and Vasti Roodt (Berlin, Germany: De Gruyter, 2008).
32 Joseph M. Bryant, *Moral Codes and Social Structure in Ancient Greece: A Sociology of Greek Ethics from Homer to the Epicureans and Stoics* (Albany, NY: State University of New York Press, 1996).
33 See also Bradley C. S. Watson, 'The Western Ethical Tradition and the Morality of the Warrior', *Armed Forces & Society* 26, no. 1 (1999).
34 Mark 12:30–31, Matthew 22:39.

35 Coker, 'Spectres of Friends and Friendship', 12.
36 See also *GS* §§21, 338 on the destructive possibilities of neighbour-love.
37 It is interesting that here it seems Nietzsche has failed to escape the eschatological orientation of his Christian heritage.
38 See *D* §516; *GS* §§21, 338.
39 Matthew 22:37–40: 'Jesus replied, "Love the Lord your God with all your soul and with all your mind." This is the first and greatest commandment. And the second is like it: "Love your neighbour as yourself." All the Law and the Prophets hang on these two commandments.'; Matthew 7:12: 'So in everything, do to others what you would have them do to you, for this sums up the Law and the Prophets' (NIV).
40 See also Coker, 'Spectres of Friends and Friendship'.
41 See also Nietzsche's discussion of hospitality towards strangers in *D* §174.
42 On self-moderating agonism, see Acampora, 'Agonistic Communities: Love, War and Spheres of Activity'; Paul E. Kirkland, 'Nietzsche, Agonistic Politics, and Spiritual Enmity', *Political Research Quarterly* 73, no. 1 (2020); Müller, 'Competitive Ethos and Cultural Dynamic. The Principle of Agonism in Jacob Burckhardt and Friedrich Nietzsche'; James Pearson, 'Nietzsche on the Sources of Agonal Moderation', *Journal of Nietzsche Studies* 49, no. 1 (2018); Siemens, 'Nietzsche's Agon with Ressentiment: Towards a Therapeutic Reading of Critical Transvaluation'; 'Nietzsche's Agon', in *The Nietzschean Mind*, ed. Paul Katsafanas (London, UK: Routledge, 2018).

Conclusion

1 See, for example, Rex Welshon, *Nietzsche's Dynamic Metapsychology: This Uncanny Animal* (Abingdon, UK: Palgrave Macmillan, 2014).
2 Ronald M. Sabatelli, 'Social Exchange Theory', in *Encyclopedia of Human Relationships*, ed. Harry T. Reis and Susan Sprecher (New York, NY: SAGE, 2009).
3 Christa Davis Acampora, 'Agonistic Communities: Love, War and Spheres of Activity', in *Conflict and Contest in Nietzsche's Philosophy*, ed. Herman Siemens and James Pearson (London, UK: Bloomsbury, 2019).

Bibliography

Abbey, Ruth. 'Circles, Ladders and Stars: Nietzsche on Friendship'. *Critical Review of International Social and Political Philosophy* 2, no. 4 (1999): 50–73.
Abbey, Ruth. *Nietzsche's Middle Period*. Oxford, UK: Oxford University Press, 2000.
Acampora, Christa Davis. 'Contesting Nietzsche'. *Journal of Nietzsche Studies* 24, no. 1 (2002): 1–4.
Acampora, Christa Davis. 'Nietzsche Contra Homer, Socrates, and Paul'. *Journal of Nietzsche Studies* 24, no. 1 (2002): 25–53.
Acampora, Christa Davis. *Contesting Nietzsche*. Chicago, IL: University of Chicago Press, 2013.
Acampora, Christa Davis. 'Agonistic Communities: Love, War and Spheres of Activity'. In *Conflict and Contest in Nietzsche's Philosophy*, edited by Herman Siemens and James Pearson, 122–44. London, UK: Bloomsbury, 2019.
Acharya, Vinod, and Ryan J. Johnson, eds. *Nietzsche and Epicurus: Nature, Health and Ethics*. London, UK: Bloomsbury, 2020.
Adkins, Arthur W. H. *Merit and Responsibility: A Study in Greek Values*. Oxford, UK: Clarendon Press, 1970.
Allman, Dwight David. 'Ancient Friends, Modern Enemies'. *South Atlantic Quarterly* 97, no. 1 (1998): 113–35.
Annas, Julia. 'Plato and Aristotle on Friendship and Altruism'. *Mind* 86, no. 344 (1977): 532–54.
Aneziri, Sophia. 'Agon'. In *The Encyclopedia of Ancient History*, edited by R. S. Bagnall, K. Brodersen, C. B. Champion, A. Erskine and S. R. Huebner, 2021. https://doi-org.simsrad.net.ocs.mq.edu.au/10.1002/9781444338386.wbeah09014.pub2.
Ansell-Pearson, Keith. *Nietzsche and Modern German Thought*. Abingdon, UK: Routledge, 1991.
Ansell-Pearson, Keith. *Germinal Life: The Difference and Repetition of Deleuze*. Abingdon, UK: Routledge, 1999.
Ansell-Pearson, Keith. 'Heroic-Idyllic Philosophizing: Nietzsche and the Epicurean Tradition'. *Royal Institute of Philosophy Supplement* 74 (2014): 237–63.
Ansell-Pearson, Keith, and Rebecca Bamford. *Nietzsche's Dawn: Philosophy, Ethics, and the Passion of Knowledge*. Hoboken, NJ: Wiley-Blackwell, 2021.
Appel, Fredrick. *Nietzsche Contra Democracy*. Ithaca, NY: Cornell University Press, 1999.
Babich, Babette. 'Epicurean Gardens and Nietzsche's White Seas'. In *Nietzsche and Epicurus*, edited by Vinod Acharya and Ryan J. Johnson, 52–67. London, UK: Bloomsbury, 2020.

Ballacci, Giuseppe. 'Deliberative Agonism and Agonistic Deliberation in Hannah Arendt'. *Theoria (Pietermaritzburg)* 66, no. 161 (2019): 1–24.

Bamford, Rebecca. 'Health and Self-Cultivation in Dawn'. In *Nietzsche's Free Spirit Philosophy*, edited by Rebecca Bamford, 85–110. London, UK: Rowman and Littlefield, 2015.

Bamford, Rebecca. 'The Ethos of Inquiry: Nietzsche on Experience, Naturalism, and Experimentalism'. *Journal of Nietzsche Studies* 47, no. 1 (2016): 9–29.

Barker, Elton T. E. *Entering the Agon: Dissent and Authority in Homer, Historiography, and Tragedy*. Oxford, UK: Oxford University Press, 2009.

Barth, Karl. *Evangelical Theology: An Introduction*. Translated by Grover Foley. Grand Rapids, MI: Eerdmans, 1963. *Einführung in die evangelische Theologie*, 1962.

Barth, Karl. *The Doctrine of Reconciliation*. Translated by Geoffrey W. Bromiley. Church Dogmatics, edited by Geoffrey W. Bromiley and Thomas F. Torrance. 1st paperpack edn. Vol. IV.2, London, UK: T&T Clark International, 2004. *Die Kirckliche Dogmatik IV: Die Lehre von der Versohnung* 2, 1955.

Bashor, Philip. 'Plato and Aristotle on Friendship'. *Journal of Value Inquiry* 2, no. 4 (1968): 269–80.

Bergoffen, Debra. 'On Nietzsche and the Enemy: Nietzsche's New Politics'. In *Nietzsche, Power and Politics: Rethinking Nietzsche's Legacy for Political Thought*, edited by Herman Siemens and Vasti Roodt, 491–510. Berlin, Germany: De Gruyter, 2008.

Berkowitz, Peter. *Nietzsche: The Ethics of an Immoralist*. Cambridge, MA: Harvard University Press, 1996.

Berry, Jessica N. 'Nietzsche and Democritus: The Origins of Ethical Eudaimonism'. In *Nietzsche and Antiquity: His Reaction and Response to the Classical Tradition*, edited by Paul Bishop. Studies in German Literature, Linguistics and Culture, 98–113. Rochester, NY: Boydell and Brewer, 2004.

Berry, Jessica N. *Nietzsche and the Ancient Skeptical Tradition*. Oxford, UK: Oxford University Press, 2011.

Brandhorst, Mario. 'Naturalism and the Genealogy of Moral Institutions'. *Journal of Nietzsche Studies* 40 (2010): 5–28.

Brobjer, Thomas H. 'Nietzsche's Affirmative Morality: An Ethics of Virtue'. *Journal of Nietzsche Studies*, no. 26 (2003): 64–78.

Bryant, Joseph M. *Moral Codes and Social Structure in Ancient Greece: A Sociology of Greek Ethics from Homer to the Epicureans and Stoics*. Albany, NY: State University of New York Press, 1996.

Cartwright, David E. 'Kant, Schopenhauer, and Nietzsche on the Morality of Pity'. *Journal of the History of Ideas* 45, no. 1 (1984): 83–98.

Cartwright, David E. 'Schopenhauer's Compassion and Nietzsche's Pity'. *Schopenhauer Jahrbuch* 69 (1988): 557–67.

Cartwright, David E. 'The Last Temptation of Zarathustra'. *Journal of the History of Philosophy* 31, no. 1 (1993): 49–69.

Cartwright, David E. 'Compassion and Solidarity with Sufferers: The Metaphysics of Mitleid'. *European Journal of Philosophy* 16, no. 2 (2008): 292–310.

Cartwright, David E. 'Schopenhauer on the Value of Compassion'. In *A Companion to Schopenhauer*, edited by Bart Vandenabeele, 249–63. Hoboken, NJ: Wiley, 2012.

Christesen, Paul, and Donald G. Kyle. *A Companion to Sport and Spectacle in Greek and Roman Antiquity*. Blackwell Companions to the Ancient World. 1st edn. Somerset, UK: John Wiley & Sons, 2014.

Church, Jeffrey. 'The Aesthetic Justification of Existence: Nietzsche on the Beauty of Exemplary Lives'. *Journal of Nietzsche Studies* 46, no. 3 (2015): 289–307.

Church, Jeffrey. 'Nietzsche's Early Perfectionism'. *Journal of Nietzsche Studies* 46, no. 2 (2015): 248–60.

Church, Jeffrey. 'Nietzsche's Early Ethical Idealism'. *Journal of Nietzsche Studies* 47, no. 1 (2016): 81–100.

Clark, Maudemarie. 'Nietzsche's Attack on Morality'. Doctoral Dissertation, University of Wisconsin-Madison, 1977.

Clark, Maudemarie. *Nietzsche on Truth and Philosophy*. Cambridge, UK: Cambridge University Press, 1990.

Clark, Maudemarie. *Nietzsche on Ethics and Politics*. Oxford, UK: Oxford University Press, 2015.

Clark, Maudemarie, and David Dudrick. 'The Naturalisms of *Beyond Good and Evil*'. In *A Companion to Nietzsche*, edited by Keith Ansell-Pearson, Chap. 9, 146–67. Malden, MA: Blackwell, 2006.

Clark, Maudemarie, and Brian Leiter. 'Introduction'. In *Daybreak*. Cambridge Texts in the History of Philosophy, vii–xxxiv. Cambridge, UK: Cambridge University Press, 1997.

Coker, John C. 'Spectres of Friends and Friendship'. *Journal of Nietzsche Studies*, no. 16 (1998): 1–32.

Cox, Christoph. *Nietzsche: Naturalism and Interpretation*. Berkeley, CA: University of California Press, 1999.

Daigle, Christine. 'Nietzsche: Virtue Ethics ... Virtue Politics?'. *Journal of Nietzsche Studies* 32, no. 1 (2006): 1–21.

Daigle, Christine. 'The Ethical Ideal of the Free Spirit in *Human All Too Human*'. In *Nietzsche's Free Spirit Philosophy*, 33–48. London, UK: Rowman and Littlefield, 2015.

Danto, Arthur C. *Nietzsche as Philosopher*. New York, NY: Macmillan, 1964.

Daqing, Wang. 'On the Ancient Greek αγων'. *Procedia, Social and Behavioral Sciences* 2, no. 5 (2010): 6805–12.

Deleuze, Gilles. *Nietzsche and Philosophy*. Translated by Hugh Tomlinson. New York, NY: Columbia University Press, 1983. *Nietzsche et la philosophie*, 1962.

Deleuze, Gilles. *Difference and Repetition*. Translated by Paul Patton. Athlone Contemporary European Thinkers. New York, NY: Continuum, 1994. *Différence et Répétition*, 1969.

Dennis, Matthew. 'Nietzschean Self-Cultivation'. *Journal of Value Inquiry* 53, no. 1 (2019): 55–73.

Dennis, Matthew. 'Passionate Individuation: Epicurean Self-Cultivation in Mill and Nietzsche'. In *Nietzsche and Epicurus*, edited by Vinod Acharya and Ryan J. Johnson, 125–42. London, UK: Bloomsbury, 2020.

Dennis, Matthew. *Cultivating Our Passionate Attachments*. Routledge Studies in Ethics and Moral Theory. New York, NY: Routledge, 2021.

Derrida, Jacques. *Politics of Friendship*. Translated by George Collins. Phronesis. London, UK: Verso, 1997. *Politiques de l'amitié*, 1994.

Desmond, William. *Is There a Sabbath for Thought?: Between Religion and Philosophy*, edited by John D. Caputo. New York, NY: Fordham University Press, 2005.

Detwiler, Bruce. *Nietzsche and the Politics of Aristocratic Radicalism*. Chicago, IL: University of Chicago Press, 1990.

Dodds, E. R. *The Greeks and the Irrational*. Berkeley, CA: University of California Press, 1951.

Donnellan, Brendan. 'Friedrich Nietzsche and Paul Rée: Cooperation and Conflict'. *Journal of the History of Ideas* 43, no. 4 (1982): 595–612.

Doyle, Tsarina. 'Nietzsche on Epistemology and Metaphysics'. Doctoral Dissertation, University of Warwick, 2002.

Doyle, Tsarina. 'The Kantian Background to Nietzsche's Views on Causality'. *Journal of Nietzsche Studies* 43, no. 1 (2012): 44–56.

Doyle, Tsarina. 'Nietzsche, Value and Objectivity'. *International Journal of Philosophical Studies* 21, no. 1 (2013): 41–63.

Doyle, Tsarina. *Nietzsche's Metaphysics of the Will to Power: The Possibility of Value*. Cambridge, UK: Cambridge University Press, 2018.

Drochon, Hugo. *Nietzsche's Great Politics*. Princeton, NJ: Princeton University Press, 2016.

Finley, M. I., and H. W. Pleket. *The Olympic Games: The First Thousand Years*. London, UK: Chatto and Windus, 1976.

Forber, Patrick. 'Nietzsche Was No Darwinian'. *Philosophy and Phenomenological Research* 75, no. 2 (2007): 369–82.

Forster, Michael N., Kristin Gjesdal and Kurt Bayertz. *Materialism*. 1st edn. Oxford, UK: Oxford University Press, 2015.

Foucault, Michel. *The Care of the Self*. Translated by Robert Hurley. The History of Sexuality. 3 vols. Vol. 3, New York, NY: Random House, 1986. *Le Souci de Soi*, 1984.

Franco, Paul. *Nietzsche's Enlightenment: The Free-Spirit Trilogy of the Middle Period*. Chicago, IL: University of Chicago Press, 2011.

Freibach-Heifetz, Dana. 'Pure Air and Solitude and Bread and Medicine: Nietzsche's Conception of Friendship'. *Philosophy Today* 49, no. 3 (2005): 245–55.

Gagnon, Jennifer Marie. 'Agonistic Politics, Contest, and the "Oresteia"'. ProQuest Dissertations Publishing, 2012.

Gauthier, Jean. 'In Honour of Friendship'. Master's Thesis, Trent University, 1998.

Grayling, A. C. *Friendship. Vices and Virtues*. Edited by Richard G. Newhauser and John Jeffries Martin. London, UK: Yale University Press, 2013.

Groenewald, Andre J. 'Interpreting the Theology of Barth in Light of Nietzsche's Dictum "God Is Dead"'. *HTS Teologiese Studies/Theological Studies* 63, no. 4 (2007): 1429–45.

Han-Pile, Béatrice. 'Nietzsche's Metaphysics in the Birth of Tragedy'. *European Journal of Philosophy* 14, no. 3 (2006): 373–403.

Han-Pile, Béatrice. 'Nietzsche and Amor Fati'. *European Journal of Philosophy* 19, no. 2 (2011): 224–61.

Harris, Daniel I. 'Friendship as Shared Joy in Nietzsche'. Doctoral Dissertation, University of Guelph, 2013.

Harris, Daniel I. 'Friendship as Shared Joy in Nietzsche'. *Symposium* 19, no. 1 (2015): 199–221.

Harris, Daniel I. 'Nietzsche and Virtue'. *Journal of Value Inquiry* 49, no. 3 (2015): 325–8.

Harris, Daniel I. 'Compassion and Affirmation in Nietzsche'. *Journal of Nietzsche Studies* 48, no. 1 (2017): 17–28.

Harris, Daniel I. 'Nietzsche and Aristotle on Friendship and Self-Knowledge'. *Journal of Nietzsche Studies* 48, no. 2 (2017): 245–60.

Harrop, Stephe. 'Greek Tragedy, Agonistic Space, and Contemporary Performance'. *New Theatre Quarterly* 34, no. 2 (2018): 99–114.

Hatab, Lawrence J. 'Prospects for a Democratic Agon: Why We Can Still Be Nietzscheans'. *Journal of Nietzsche Studies* 24, no. 1 (2002): 132–47.

Hatab, Lawrence J. *Nietzsche's Life Sentence: Coming to Terms with Eternal Recurrence*. Abingdon, UK: Routledge, 2005.

Hatab, Lawrence J. '*Amor Agonis*: Conflict and Love in Nietzsche and Homer'. In *Conflict and Contest in Nietzsche's Philosophy*, edited by Herman Siemens and James Pearson, 105–21. London, UK: Bloomsbury, 2019.

Hawhee, Debra. 'Agonism and Aretê'. *Philosophy & Rhetoric* 35, no. 3 (2002): 185–207.

Hawthorne, Kevin. 'The Chorus as Rhetorical Audience: A Sophoklean Agōn Pattern'. *American Journal of Philology* 130, no. 1 (2009): 25–46.

Hay, Katia, and Leonel Ribeiro Dos Santos, eds. *Nietzsche, German Idealism and Its Critics*. Berlin, Germany: De Gruyter, 2015.

Heidegger, Martin. *Nietzsche*. Translated by David Farrell Krell. 2 vols. Vol. 1, San Francisco, CA: Harper & Row, 1991. *Nietzsche*, 1961.

Heidegger, Martin. *Nietzsche*. Translated by David Farrell Krell. 2 vols. Vol. 2, San Francisco, CA: Harper & Row, 1991. *Nietzsche*, 1961.

Hennig, John. 'Nietzsche, Jaspers and Christianity'. *Blackfriars* 29, no. 343 (1948): 476–80.

Hill, Charles E. *The Johannine Corpus in the Early Church*. Oxford, UK: Oxford University Press, 2004.

Honig, Bonnie. *Political Theory and the Displacement of Politics*. Contestations. Ithaca, NY: Cornell University Press, 1993.

Honig, Bonnie. 'Between Decision and Deliberation: Political Paradox in Democratic Theory'. *The American Political Science Review* 101, no. 1 (2007): 1–17.

Houlgate, Stephen. *Hegel, Nietzsche, and the Criticism of Metaphysics*. Cambridge, UK: Cambridge University Press, 1986.

Hovey, Craig. *Nietzsche and Theology*. Philosophy and Theology. London, UK: T&T Clark, 2008.

Hurka, Thomas. 'Nietzsche: Perfectionist'. In *Nietzsche and Morality*, edited by Brian Leiter and Neil Sinhababu, Chap. 1, 9–31. Oxford, UK: Oxford University Press, 2007.

Hutter, Horst. 'The Virtue of Solitude and the Vicissitudes of Friendship'. *Critical Review of International Social and Political Philosophy* 2, no. 4 (1999): 131–48.

Irwin, Terence. *Classical Thought*. Oxford, UK: Oxford University Press, 1989.

Janaway, Christopher. 'Schopenhauer as Nietzsche's Educator'. In *Willing and Nothingness: Schopenhauer as Nietzsche's Educator*, edited by Christopher Janaway, 13–36. Oxford, UK: Clarendon Press, 1998.

Janaway, Christopher. *Beyond Selflessness: Reading Nietzsche's Genealogy*. Oxford, UK: Oxford University Press, 2007.

Janaway, Christopher. 'Beyond Selflessness in Ethics and Inquiry'. *Journal of Nietzsche Studies* 35, no. 1 (2008): 124–40.

Janaway, Christopher, and Simon Robertson, eds. *Nietzsche, Naturalism, and Normativity*. Oxford, UK: Oxford University Press, 2012.

Jaspers, Karl. *Nietzsche and Christianity*. Translated by E. B. Ashton. Gateway Edition. Chicago, IL: H. Regnery Co, 1967. *Nietzsche und das Christentum*, 1938.

Johnson, Dirk Robert. 'Nietzsche's Darwin, and the Spirit of the Agon'. Doctoral Dissertation, Indiana University, 2000.

Johnson, Dirk Robert. 'Nietzsche's Early Darwinism: The "David Strauss" Essay of 1873'. *Nietzsche-Studien* 30 (2001): 62–79.

Johnson, Dirk Robert. 'On the Way to the "Anti-Darwin": Nietzsche's Darwinian Meditations in the Middle Period'. *Tijdschrift voor Filosofie* 65, no. 4 (2003): 657–79.

Johnson, Dirk Robert. *Nietzsche's Anti-Darwinism*. Cambridge, UK: Cambridge University Press, 2010.

Johnson, Dirk Robert. 'One Hundred Twenty-Two Years Later: Reassessing the Nietzsche–Darwin Relationship'. *Journal of Nietzsche Studies* 44, no. 2 (2013): 342–53.

Jurist, Elliot L. *Beyond Hegel and Nietzsche*. Philosophy, Culture, and Agency. Cambridge, MA: MIT Press, 2000.

Kant, Immanuel. *Prolegomena to Any Future Metaphysics*. Raleigh, NC: Generic NL Freebook Publisher, 1998.

Katsafanas, Paul. *Agency and the Foundations of Ethics: Nietzschean Constitutivism*. Oxford, UK: Oxford University Press, 2013.

Katsafanas, Paul. 'Nietzsche on the Nature of the Unconscious'. *Inquiry* 58, no. 3 (2014): 1–26.

Katsafanas, Paul. *The Nietzschean Self: Moral Psychology, Agency, and the Unconscious*. Oxford, UK: Oxford University Press, 2016.

Kaufmann, Walter. *Nietzsche: Philosopher, Psychologist, Antichrist*. 4th edn. Princeton, NJ: Princeton University Press, 1974.

Kaufmann, Walter. *Critique of Religion and Philosophy*. Princeton, NJ: Princeton University Press, 1978.

Kirkland, Paul E. 'Dissonance and Child's Play: Nietzsche, Tragedy, and Heraclitean Metaphor'. *The Review of Metaphysics* 75, no. 2 (2021): 317–43.

Kirkland, Paul E. 'Nietzsche, Agonistic Politics, and Spiritual Enmity'. *Political Research Quarterly* 73, no. 1 (2020): 3–14.

Kirkland, Paul E. 'Dissonance and Child's Play: Nietzsche, Tragedy, and Heraclitean Metaphor'. *The Review of Metaphysics* 75, no. 2 (2021): 317–43.

Leiter, Brian. 'Nietzsche and the Critique of Morality: Philosophical Naturalism in Nietzsche's Theory of Value'. Doctoral Thesis, University of Michigan, 1995.

Leiter, Brian. *Nietzsche on Morality*. Routledge Philosophy Guidebooks. Edited by Tim Crane and Jonathan Woolf. Abingdon, UK: Routledge, 2002.

Leiter, Brian. 'Nietzsche's Moral and Political Philosophy'. In *Stanford Encyclopaedia of Philosophy*, edited by Edward N. Zalta, 2015. Summer 2021 edition. https://plato.stanford.edu/archives/sum2021/entries/nietzsche-moral-political/.

Leiter, Brian. 'Normativity for Naturalists'. *Philosophical Issues* 25, no. 1 (2015): 64–79.

Martin, Gunther. 'Nothing but Rhetoric? Rhetoric, Pragmatics and Myth-making in the Agōn of Euripides' Alcestis'. *Classical Quarterly* 71, no. 2 (2021): 538–52.

May, Simon. *Love: A History*. New Haven, CT: Yale University Press, 2011.

Meyer, Matthew. *Reading Nietzsche through the Ancients: An Analysis of Becoming, Perspectivism, and the Principle of Non-Contradiction*. Monographien Und Texte Zur Nietzsche-Forschung. Berlin, Germany: De Gruyter, 2014.

Meyer, Matthew. *Nietzsche's Free Spirit Works: A Dialectical Reading*. Cambridge, UK: Cambridge University Press, 2019.

Miner, Robert C. 'Nietzsche on Friendship'. *Journal of Nietzsche Studies* 40 (2010): 47–69.

Moore, Gregory. 'Nietzsche, Degeneration, and the Critique of Christianity'. *Journal of Nietzsche Studies*, no. 19 (2000): 1–18.

Mouffe, Chantal. 'Deliberative Democracy or Agonistic Pluralism?'. *Social Research* 66, no. 3 (1999): 745–58.

Müller, Enrico. 'Competitive Ethos and Cultural Dynamic. The Principle of Agonism in Jacob Burckhardt and Friedrich Nietzsche'. In *Conflict and Contest in Nietzsche's Philosophy*, edited by Herman Siemens and James Pearson, 89–104. London, UK: Bloomsbury, 2019.

Nabais, Nuno. 'The Individual and Individuality in Nietzsche'. In *A Companion to Nietzsche*, edited by Keith Ansell-Pearson. Blackwell Companions to Philosophy, Chap. 5, 76–94. Malden, MA: Blackwell, 2006.

Nietzsche, Friedrich. *The Portable Nietzsche*. Translated by Walter Kaufmann. London, UK: Penguin Books, 1954.

Nietzsche, Friedrich Wilhelm. *Thus Spoke Zarathustra* [Also Sprach Zarathustra]. Translated by R. J. Hollingdale. Penguin Classics. London, UK: Penguin Books, 1961. Reprinted 1969.

Nietzsche, Friedrich Wilhelm. *Beyond Good and Evil*. Translated by Walter Kaufmann. Vintage Books. New York, NY: Random House, 1966. *Jenseits von Gut und Böse*.

Nietzsche, Friedrich Wilhelm. *Thus Spoke Zarathustra*. Translated by Walter Kaufmann. London, UK: Penguin Books, 1966. *Also Sprach Zarathustra*.

Nietzsche, Friedrich Wilhelm. *On the Genealogy of Morals and Ecce Homo*. Translated by R. J. Hollingdale and Walter Kaufmann. New York, NY: Random House, 1967. *Zur Genealogie der Moral, Ecce Homo*.

Nietzsche, Friedrich Wilhelm. *Twilight of the Idols and The Anti-Christ*. Translated by R. J. Hollingdale. Penguin Classics. London, UK: Penguin Books, 1968. Reprinted 2003. *Götzen-Dämmerung, Der Antichrist*.

Nietzsche, Friedrich Wilhelm. *The Will to Power*. Translated by Walter Kaufmann and R. J. Hollingdale. Vintage Books. New York, NY: Random House, 1968. *Nachgelassene Werke: Der Wille zur Macht*, 1901; edited by Elisabeth Förster-Nietzsche.

Nietzsche, Friedrich Wilhelm. *Selected Letters of Friedrich Nietzsche*. Translated by Christopher Middleton. Chicago, IL: University of Chicago Press, 1969.

Nietzsche, Friedrich Wilhelm. *Beyond Good and Evil*. Translated by R. J. Hollingdale. Penguin Classics. London, UK: Penguin Books, 1973. Reprinted 2003. *Jenseits von Gut und Böse*.

Nietzsche, Friedrich Wilhelm. *The Gay Science*. Translated by Walter Kaufmann. Vintage Books. New York, NY: Random House, 1974. *Fröhliche Wissenschaft*.

Nietzsche, Friedrich Wilhelm. *A Nietzsche Reader*. Translated by R. J. Hollingdale. Penguin Classics. London, UK: Penguin Books, 1977.

Nietzsche, Friedrich Wilhelm. *Ecce Homo*. Translated by R. J. Hollingdale. Penguin Classics. London, UK: Penguin Books, 1979. Reprinted 2004.

Nietzsche, Friedrich Wilhelm. *Human, All Too Human*. Translated by R. J. Hollingdale. Cambridge Texts in the History of Philosophy. Edited by Karl Ameriks and Desmond Clarke. 2nd edn. Cambridge, UK: Cambridge University Press, 1996. *Menschliches, Alllzumenschliches*.

Nietzsche, Friedrich Wilhelm. *On the Genealogy of Morals*. Translated by Douglas Smith. Oxford World's Classics. Oxford, UK: Oxford University Press, 1996. *Zur Genealogie der Moral*.

Nietzsche, Friedrich Wilhelm. *Daybreak*. Translated by R. J. Hollingdale. Cambridge Texts in the History of Philosophy. Edited by Karl Ameriks and Desmond Clarke. 1st edn. Cambridge, UK: Cambridge University Press, 1997. *Morgenröthe*.

Nietzsche, Friedrich Wilhelm. *Untimely Meditations*. Translated by R. J. Hollingdale. Cambridge Texts in the History of Philosophy. Edited by Karl Ameriks and Desmond Clarke. 1st edn. Cambridge, UK: Cambridge University Press, 1997. *Unzeitgemässe, Betrachtungen*.

Nietzsche, Friedrich Wilhelm. *The Birth of Tragedy and Other Writings*. Translated by Ronald Speirs. Cambridge Texts in the History of Philosophy. Edited by Karl Ameriks and Desmond Clarke. 1st edn. Cambridge, UK: Cambridge University Press, 1999.

Nietzsche, Friedrich Wilhelm. *The Gay Science*. Translated by Josefine Nauckhoff and Adrian Del Caro. Cambridge Texts in the History of Philosophy. Edited by Karl Ameriks and Desmond Clarke. 1st edn. Cambridge, UK: Cambridge University Press, 2001. *Fröhliche Wissenschaft*.

Nietzsche, Friedrich Wilhelm. *Beyond Good and Evil*. Translated by Judith Norman. Cambridge Texts in the History of Philosophy. Edited by Karl Ameriks and Desmond Clarke. 1st edn. Cambridge, UK: Cambridge University Press, 2002. Corrected edition. *Jenseits von Gut und Böse*.

Nietzsche, Friedrich Wilhelm. *Writings from the Late Notebooks*. Translated by Kate Sturge. Cambridge Texts in the History of Philosophy. Edited by Karl Ameriks and Desmond Clarke. 1st edn. Cambridge, UK: Cambridge University Press, 2003.

Nietzsche, Friedrich Wilhelm. *The Nietzsche Reader*. Blackwell Readers. Edited by Keith Ansell-Pearson and Duncan Large. Malden, MA: Blackwell, 2006.

Nietzsche, Friedrich Wilhelm. *Thus Spoke Zarathustra*. Translated by Adrian Del Caro. Cambridge Texts in the History of Philosophy. Edited by Karl Ameriks and Desmond Clarke. 1st edn. Cambridge, UK: Cambridge University Press, 2006. Corrected edition. *Also Sprach Zarathustra*.

Nietzsche, Friedrich Wilhelm. *Writings from the Early Notebooks*. Translated by Ladislaus Löb. Cambridge Texts in the History of Philosophy. Edited by Karl Ameriks and Desmond Clarke. 1st edn. Cambridge, UK: Cambridge University Press, 2009.

Nygren, Anders. *Agape and Eros*. Translated by Philip S. Watson. London, UK: SPCK, 1982. *Eros och Agape*, 1930, 1936.

Pangle, Lorraine Smith. *Aristotle and the Philosophy of Friendship*. Cambridge, UK: Cambridge University Press, 2002.

Pannenberg, Wolfhart. *Systematic Theology*. Translated by Geoffrey W. Bromiley. 3 vols. Vol. 1, Grand Rapids, MI: Eerdmans, 1991. *Systematische Theologie*, 1988.

Pannenberg, Wolfhart. *Systematic Theology*. Translated by Geoffrey W. Bromiley. 3 vols. Vol. 3, Grand Rapids, MI: Eerdmans, 1998. *Systematische Theologie*, 1993.

Parkes, Graham. *Composing the Soul: Reaches of Nietzsche's Psychology*. Chicago, IL: University of Chicago Press, 1994.

Patton, Paul, ed. *Nietzsche: Feminism & Political Theory*. Abingdon, UK: Routledge, 1993.

Pearson, James. 'Nietzsche on the Sources of Agonal Moderation'. *Journal of Nietzsche Studies* 49, no. 1 (2018): 102–29.

Poellner, Peter. *Nietzsche and Metaphysics*. Oxford, UK: Clarendon Press, 1995.

Price, A. W. *Love and Friendship in Plato and Aristotle*. Oxford, UK: Clarendon, 1989.

Pritchard, David M. 'Sport, War and Democracy in Classical Athens'. *International Journal of the History of Sport* 26, no. 2 (2009): 212–45.

Pritchard, David M. *War, Democracy, and Culture in Classical Athens*. Cambridge, UK: Cambridge University Press, 2010.

Pritchard, David M. *Sport, Democracy and War in Classical Athens*. Cambridge, UK: Cambridge University Press, 2013.

Reginster, Bernard. *The Affirmation of Life: Nietzsche on Overcoming Nihilism*. Cambridge, MA: Harvard University Press, 2006.

Reginster, Bernard. 'Knowledge and Selflessness: Schopenhauer and the Paradox of Reflection'. *European Journal of Philosophy* 16, no. 2 (2008): 251–72.

Rezhabek, Evgeny Y., and Marina A. Bogdanova. 'Agon as an Immanent Characteristic Feature of Ancient Greek Culture'. *Advanced Engineering Research* 11, no. 6 (2011): 911–17.

Richardson, John. *Nietzsche's System*. Oxford, UK: Oxford University Press, 1996.

Richardson, John. 'Nietzsche Contra Darwin'. *Philosophy and Phenomenological Research* 65, no. 3 (2002): 537–75.

Richardson, John. *Nietzsche's New Darwinism*. Oxford, UK: Oxford University Press, 2004.

Richardson, John. 'On Richard Schacht's Nietzsche'. *Journal of Nietzsche Studies* 46, no. 2 (2015): 198–206.

Richardson, John. *Nietzsche's Values*. New York, NY: Oxford University Press, 2020.

Robertson, Simon. 'Nietzsche's Ethical Revaluation'. *Journal of Nietzsche Studies* 37, no. 1 (2009): 66–90.

Robertson, Simon. 'Normativity for Nietzschean Free Spirits'. *Inquiry* 54, no. 6 (2011): 591–613.

Rorty, Richard. *The Future of Religion*. Edited by Gianni Vattimo and Santiago Zabala. New York, NY: Columbia University Press, 2005.

Sabatelli, Ronald M. 'Social Exchange Theory'. In *Encyclopedia of Human Relationships*, edited by Harry T. Reis and Susan Sprecher, 1521–4. New York, NY: SAGE, 2009.

Sadler, Ted. *Nietzsche: Truth and Redemption*. London, UK: Athlone Press, 1995.

Schacht, Richard. *Nietzsche*. Abingdon, UK: Routledge, 1985.

Schacht, Richard. 'Nietzsche's Naturalism'. *Journal of Nietzsche Studies* 43, no. 2 (2012): 185–212.

Schacht, Richard. 'Nietzsche's Naturalism and Normativity'. In *Nietzsche, Naturalism and Normativity*, edited by Christopher Janaway and Simon Robertson, 236–57. Oxford, UK: Oxford University Press, 2012.

Scheler, Max. 'Ressentiment'. In *Nietzsche: A Collection of Critical Essays*, edited by Robert C. Solomon, 243–57. Garden City, NY: Anchor Press, 1973. Reprint, University of Notre Dame Press.

Schirmacher, Wolfgang, ed. *The Essential Schopenhauer: Key Selections from The World as Will and Representation and Other Writings*. New York, NY: HarperCollins, 2010.

Schopenhauer, Arthur. *The Basis of Morality*. Translated by Arthur Brodrick Bullock. London, UK: Allen & Unwin, 1915. Dover Philosophical Classics, Mineola, NY: Dover, 2005. *Beiden Grundprobleme der Ethik*, 1841.

Sedgwick, Peter R. 'Hyperbolic Naturalism: Nietzsche, Ethics, and Sovereign Power'. *Journal of Nietzsche Studies* 47, no. 1 (2016): 141–66.

Shepherd, Melanie. 'Nietzsche's Übermensch: From Shared Suffering to Shared Joy'. In *Joy and Laughter in Nietzsche's Philosophy*, edited by Paul E. Kirkland and Michael J McNeal 47–65. London, UK: Bloomsbury, 2022.

Shoshitaishvili, Boris. 'Homer's World at War: Cosmic Agonism in the Iliad'. ProQuest Dissertations Publishing, 2019.

Siemens, Herman. 'Nietzsche's Agon with Ressentiment: Towards a Therapeutic Reading of Critical Transvaluation'. *Continental Philosophy Review* 34, no. 1 (2001): 69–93.

Siemens, Herman. 'Agonal Communities of Taste: Law and Community in Nietzsche's Philosophy of Transvaluation'. *Journal of Nietzsche Studies*, no. 24 (2002): 83–112.

Siemens, Herman. 'Agonal Writing: Towards an Agonal Model for Critical Transvaluation'. *Logoi.ph* (2015): 10–29.

Siemens, Herman. 'Nietzsche's Agon'. In *The Nietzschean Mind*, edited by Paul Katsafanas, 314–33. London, UK: Routledge, 2018.

Siemens, Herman. 'Nietzsche on Productive Resistance'. In *Conflict and Contest in Nietzsche's Philosophy*, edited by Herman Siemens and James Pearson, 23–43. London, UK: Bloomsbury, 2019.

Sinnerbrink, Robert. '"We Hyperboreans": Platonism and Politics in Heidegger and Nietzsche'. *Contretemps*, no. 3 (2002): 161–74.

Sloterdijk, Peter. *Nietzsche Apostle*. Translated by Steven Corcoran. *Intervention*. Vol. 16. Los Angeles, CA: Semiotext(e), 2013.

Small, Robin. *Nietzsche and Rée: A Star Friendship*. Oxford, UK: Oxford University Press, 2005.

Soderstrom, Lukas. 'Nietzsche as a Reader of Wilhelm Roux, or the Physiology of History'. *Symposium* 13, no. 2 (2009): 55–67.

Solomon, Robert C. *Living with Nietzsche: What the Great 'Immoralist' Has to Teach Us*. Oxford, UK: Oxford University Press, 2004.

Stack, George J. *Lange and Nietzsche*. Berlin, Germany: De Gruyter, 1983.

Stevenson, J. *A New Eusebius: Documents Illustrating the History of the Church to AD 337*. SPCK Church History. Revised edn. London, UK: SPCK, 1987.

Stevenson, J. *Creeds, Councils and Controversies: Documents Illustrating the History of the Church, AD 337–461*. SPCK Church History. Revised edn. London, UK: SPCK, 1989.

Striowski, Andra. 'Plato and Aristotle on Philia'. Master's Thesis, Dalhousie University, 2008.

Swanton, Christine. *The Virtue Ethics of Hume and Nietzsche*. Hoboken, NJ: Wiley, 2015.

Swift, Paul A. *Becoming Nietzsche: Early Reflections on Democritus, Schopenhauer, and Kant*. Lanham, MD: Lexington Books, 2005.

Thiele, Leslie Paul. *Friedrich Nietzsche and the Politics of the Soul: A Study of Heroic Individualism*. Princeton, NJ: Princeton University Press, 1990.

Torrance, Thomas F. *The Trinitarian Faith: The Evangelical Theology of the Ancient Catholic Church*. Edinburgh, UK: T&T Clark, 1995.

Torrance, Thomas F. *The Christian Doctrine of God: One Being Three Persons*. Edinburgh, UK: T&T Clark, 1996.

Tuncel, Yunus. 'The Principle of Agon in Nietzsche's Thought'. Doctoral Thesis, The New School, 2000.

Ure, Michael. 'The Irony of Pity: Nietzsche Contra Schopenhauer and Rousseau'. *Journal of Nietzsche Studies*, no. 32 (2006): 68–91.

Ure, Michael. *Nietzsche's Therapy: Self-Cultivation in the Middle Works*. Lanham, MD: Lexington Books, 2008.

Ure, Michael. 'Nietzsche's Free Spirit Trilogy and Stoic Therapy'. *Journal of Nietzsche Studies*, no. 38 (2009): 60–84.

Ure, Michael. 'Nietzsche's Schadenfreude'. *Journal of Nietzsche Studies* 44, no. 1 (2013): 25–48.

Ure, Michael. *Nietzsche's 'The Gay Science': An Introduction*. Cambridge Introductions to Key Philosophical Texts. Cambridge, UK: Cambridge University Press, 2019.

Ure, Michael, and Keith Ansell-Pearson. 'Contra Kant: Experimental Ethics in Guyau and Nietzsche'. In *Nietzsche's Engagements with Kant and the Kantian Legacy: Nietzsche and Kantian Ethics*, edited by Joao Constancio and Tom Bailey, vol. 2, 257–89. London, UK: Bloomsbury, 2017.

van Tongeren, Paul. 'Politics, Friendship and Solitude in Nietzsche (Confronting Derrida's Reading of Nietzsche in "Politics of Friendship")'. *South African Journal of Philosophy* 19, no. 3 (2000): 209–22.

van Tongeren, Paul. 'Nietzsche's Greek Measure'. *Journal of Nietzsche Studies* 24 (2002): 5–24.

van Tongeren, Paul. 'On Friends in Nietzsche's Zarathustra'. *New Nietzsche Studies*, no. 5 (2003): 73–88.

van Tongeren, Paul. 'Kant, Nietzsche and the Idealization of Friendship into Nihilism'. *Kriterion* 54, no. 128 (2013): 401–17.

Vattimo, Gianni. *The Adventure of Difference: Philosophy after Nietzsche and Heidegger*. Translated by Cyprian Blamires and Thomas Harrison. Cambridge, UK: Polity Press, 1993.

Vattimo, Gianni. *After Christianity*. Italian Academy Lectures. New York, NY: Columbia University Press, 2002.

Vattimo, Gianni. 'Nihilism as Emancipation'. *Cosmos and History: The Journal of Natural and Social Philosophy* 5, no. 1 (2009): 20–3.

Verkerk, Willow. 'Nietzsche's Goal of Friendship'. *Journal of Nietzsche Studies* 45, no. 3 (2014): 279–91.

Verkerk, Willow. 'Nietzsche's Agonistic Ethics of Friendship'. *Symposium* 20, no. 2 (2016): 22–41.

Verkerk, Willow. 'On Love, Women, and Friendship: Reading Nietzsche with Irigaray'. *Nietzsche-Studien* 46, no. 1 (2017): 135–52.

Verkerk, Willow. *Nietzsche and Friendship*. Bloomsbury Studies in Continental Philosophy. New York, NY: Bloomsbury, 2019.

Vernon, Mark. *The Philosophy of Friendship*. Abingdon, UK: Palgrave Macmillan, 2005.

von Heyking, John. *The Form of Politics: Aristotle and Plato on Friendship*. Montreal, Canada: McGill-Queen's University Press, 2016.

Watson, Bradley C. S. 'The Western Ethical Tradition and the Morality of the Warrior'. *Armed Forces & Society* 26, no. 1 (1999): 55–72.

Webb, David. 'On Friendship: Derrida, Foucault, and the Practice of Becoming'. *Research in Phenomenology* 33, no. 1 (2003): 119–40.

Welshon, Rex. *Nietzsche's Dynamic Metapsychology: This Uncanny Animal*. Abingdon, UK: Palgrave Macmillan, 2014.

Wiley, Craig. 'I Was Dead and Behold, I Am Alive Forevermore: Responses to Nietzsche in 20th Century Christian Theology'. *intersections* 10, no. 1 (2009): 507–17.

Williams, Robert R. 'Aristotle, Hegel, and Nietzsche on Friendship'. In *Tragedy, Recognition, and the Death of God: Studies in Hegel and Nietzsche*, 54–85. Oxford, UK: Oxford University Press, 2012.

Williams, Stephen N. *The Shadow of the Antichrist: Nietzsche's Critique of Christianity*. Grand Rapids, MI: Baker Academic, 2006.

Young, Julian. *The Death of God and the Meaning of Life*. Abingdon, UK: Routledge, 2003.

Young, Julian. 'Schopenhauer, Nietzsche, Death and Salvation'. *European Journal of Philosophy* 16, no. 2 (2008): 311–24.

Young, Julian. *Friedrich Nietzsche: A Philosophical Biography*. Cambridge, UK: Cambridge University Press, 2010.

Zavatta, Benedetta. 'Nietzsche and Emerson on Friendship and Its Ethical-Political Implications'. In *Nietzsche, Power and Politics: Rethinking Nietzsche's Legacy for Political Thought*, edited by Herman Siemens and Vasti Roodt, 511–42. Berlin, Germany: De Gruyter, 2008.

Index

abundance 5–6, 9, 13, 84
  concept 8
  conflicting with *agape* (self-sacrificial) love 16–17
  and difference/individual differences 13, 14, 35, 100, 120
    Christian love 28–9
    Homerism/new Homerism 72–3, 80, 81
  and drives *see* drives
  personal
    Acampora on 100–101
    assumption of, at several levels 79
    and drives 126
    and individual differences 35, 72–3, 93, 95, 154
    and self-sufficiency 97
  and suffering 51
Acampora, Christa Davis 7, 10, 75–8, 81, 156, 178n15
  on Christian love 18–19, 20, 23
  Contesting Nietzsche 74
  and the individual 99, 100–101
adversity
  and contest 127–31
  and happiness 128–9
  and human flourishing 7, 8, 127, 128
  and social relationships 7, 129, 155
affirmative love 18
agape (self-sacrificial) love, Nietzsche's rejection of 3, 14, 28–33, 78, 92, 99, 101
  see also asceticism/ascetic self-denial; Christian love; love; self-abnegation/self-sacrifice
  based on a specific idea of personhood 20, 21
  and Christian concept of God 24
  Christian valorizing of 53
  conflicting with abundance 16–17
  crucifixion of Christ seen as supreme example 22
  distinguished from Nygren's view 20–1
  as erasure of the individual 20
  and *eros* 21
  and friendship/higher friendship 29–30
  great love contrasted with *agape* love 30, 31–3
  and individualism 20
  as pursuit of the beloved, 21
  seen as selflessness 17
  and self-abnegation 72
  as self-emptying 21–2
  as surrender of sovereignty of lover 21
agon (Greek concept of contest) *see* contest
agonism 1, 130
  see also agonistic ethics
  agonistic spirit of ancient Greece 9–10, 15, 154
  drives 10, 75
  engagement 2, 13, 19–20, 72, 85, 146, 150
  equilibrium *see* agonistic equilibrium
  ethos 76, 131, 150, 153
  exchange/contest 6, 7, 9–11, 20, 26, 67, 72, 75–7, 124, 143, 154
  friendship 2, 13, 14, 35, 68, 125, 135, 136
  'play of forces' 80
  self-moderating 183n42
  social relationships, agonistic interpretation 3, 14, 19–20, 33, 150, 154
agonistic equilibrium 75, 119, 126, 127, 130, 131, 156
  internal 112, 154
agonistic ethics 1, 10, 14–16, 28, 76, 77, 131, 150, 153, 155
  Homeric-agonistic interpretation of Nietzsche's ethics 4, 5, 74
  and naturalism 53, 55
  renewed 54

Index

altruism 1, 50
ancient Greece
   see also Aristotle; Homerism/new Homerism; Plato
   agape (self-sacrificial) love *see agape* (self-sacrificial) love
   agon see contest
   agonistic ethics of 14
   agonistic spirit of 9–10, 15, 154
   and contest 1, 9, 33, 36, 72, 74, 81, 125, 143, 150
      and naturalism 53, 64
   culture 6
   eros see eros (passionate love)
   philia (brotherly love) 16
   scope of 9
   self-cultivation concept 11, 12, 94, 102, 113, 116, 121
Ansell-Pearson, Keith 117
Arendt, Hannah 9
aristocratic radicalism 128
Aristotle 1, 17
   Aristotelian tradition 57
asceticism/ascetic self-denial 39, 43, 44
   see also agape (self-sacrificial) love, Nietzsche's rejection of; self-abnegation/self-sacrifice
   Nietzsche's rejection of 48–51
atheism 59

Bamford, Rebecca 117
Barth, Karl 20–1, 22
benevolence 38
Bergoffen, Debra 144
Brandes, Georg 179n5
Burckhardt, Jacob 173n17, 180n6

Cartwright, David E. 35–9, 41–3
Chalcedon, ecumenical council (425 ce) 22
chance, concept of 65, 115
character 2, 8, 14, 30, 37–9, 41, 78, 79, 104, 116, 121, 122
   bad 38, 39
   deceptive 40
   dual 85
   good 38
   implicit 88
   innate 38, 39
   types 37–8
   weak 122
Christian love 1, 14–34, 169n42
   see also agape (self-sacrificial) love, Nietzsche's rejection of; friendship; higher friendship
   Christian morality centring on the concept of 14, 16
   explaining 17–23
   and hatred 18
   higher friendship 29–33
   Judeo-Christian roots of 3, 18, 23
   and love for others 17
   and morality 14
   Nietzsche's rejection of *agape* love 3, 14, 16, 28–33
   Nietzsche's rejection of customary morality 27–8
   Nietzsche's rejection of monotheism 16, 24–7
   Nietzsche's rejection of tyranny of love 16, 23–8
   self-abnegation, perceived as 16, 17, 21, 23, 24, 31
Christianity
   see also Christian love; Jesus Christ
   Christian tradition 17, 18, *20–21*
   and human deficit 9
   Lutheran tradition 20–1
   metaphysics 5, 20, 35
   Nietzsche's enthusiasm for and later rejection of 24
   self-sacrifice ideal 31
   and social organization 80
   theology 20, 30
   Trinity doctrine 20, 22
Church, Jeffrey 54
city (*polis*) 75, 96
   city-state analogy (individual) 94, 167n47
compassion
   compassionate love 133
   ethics of 36
   and love 2
   morality of 14, 44
   Nietzsche's rejection of as foundation for ethics 3, 7, 35–52, 138, 147
   Schopenhauer on 3, 15, 36, 37, 42, 46, 53, 71, 128
   vanilla 138

competition 1
  contest as 77
  drives 12, 81, 98, 102, 117, 125
  negative form 89
  and pessimism 89
  positive form 89
  and struggle 68, 73, 89
consciousness 104–105, 109, 111
  conscious choice and agency 114
  conscious reflection 105
Constantinople, ecumenical council (381 CE) 22
contemplation 42, 43
contest 1, 2, 8, 11, 18–19, 172n7
  see also ancient Greece; Homerism/new Homerism; love
  and abundance 9, 13
  and adversity 127–31
  agonistic 6, 7, 9–11, 20, 26, 67, 72, 75–7, 124, 143, 154
  ancient Greek concept/Homerism 1, 9, 33, 36, 69, 125, 143, 150
    Homerism/new Homerism 72, 74, 81
    and naturalism 53, 64
  as competition 77
  concept of *agon* 3, 4, 6, 19, 74, 150
  as developmental and social process 75–6
  and difference/individual differences 8, 13, 26, 72, 93–124, 175n4
  drives and internal contest 102–122
  dyadic 19
  equality of contestants 180n6
  ethical 2, 53
  ethos see under Homerism/New Homerism
  and evolutionary biology 5, 7, 58
  extensions of 88–92
  friendship as 32, 125–51
  heroic 31, 52, 53, 58, 68, 72, 125
  Homeric see Homerism/new Homerism
  and human nature 73
  individual as 93–124
  internal 102–122, 126, 128
  Nietzsche's concept of 14, 26, 81–8
    and new Homerism 35, 93, 102, 108, 154
  performative notion 90
  power of individual contestants 19
  and psychological analysis 58, 68
  and self-cultivation 94
  and social relationships 5, 7, 74, 80, 100, 172n7
  and struggle 88, 89, 173n17, 179n49
corruption 89–90
courage 69, 120, 145
customary morality 2, 24
  see also ethics; morality
  and monotheism 28–9
  Nietzsche's rejection of 27–8, 117

Daigle, Christine 99–100
Darwin, Charles 53, 64, 73, 172n8
Darwinism 6, 55, 56, 64, 67, 85, 88, 89
death of God 23
decadence 179n3
deception 40, 41
democracy, and agonism 9
Desmond, William 144
determinism 113, 116
difference 6, 8, 13
  see also individualism/individuality
  and abundance 13, 14, 28–9, 35, 80, 81, 100, 120
    individual difference and personal abundance 35, 72–3, 95
  in agonistic equilibrium 119
  and contest 8, 13, 26, 72, 175n4
  difference-as-opposition 92
  and differentiation 6
  generative power of 15
  genetic variation 5, 6, 55, 64
  Homeric 47
  individual 26, 51–2
    and personal abundance 72–3
    and motivational pluralism 41
    Nietzsche's perspective on 25
    Schopenhauer on 45
Dionysian suffering 49, 83
Dodds, E. R. 173n14
Doyle, Tsarina 54
dreams/dream-states 105, 141–2
drives
  see also individualism/individuality
  and abundance 14
  agonistic 10, 75
  Apollonian 82, 83, 87
  arrangement of 95

and choice 103–112
competing 12, 81, 98, 102, 117, 125
composite of 91
and consciousness 104–105
differential and opposing 126
Dionysian 82, 83, 87
and friendship 12, 13, 32
harmonizing 94–5, 118
individual differences 13, 14, 74, 91, 97, 99, 118–22, 148, 150
  and choice 103–112
  and individuality 118–22
  and internal contest 102–122
  and self-development 118–22
  specific drives defining the individual 126
integration of 96, 101–102, 119, 156
and internal contest 102–122
multiplicity of 96
Nietzsche's understanding of 11
and self-development 112–18
and self-overcoming 10, 150, 154
and taste 67, 112, 119, 120

ego 96, 100, 104
  see also individualism/individuality; self
egoism, acts of 38, 39, 74
enmity/higher enmity 143–6
  extreme 145
  and friendship 146
Epicureanism 1, 11, 154
eros (passionate love) 16, 20, 21
  see also romantic love
error, in science 59
eternal return of the same 97–8
ethics
  agonistic *see* agonism
  classical 1
  contemporary, importance of love and compassion for 3
  ethical contest 2, 53
  and evolutionary biology 76
  heroic 121
  and metaphysics 38
  naturalistic 52
  and sociability 87
  and social relationships x, 1, 3, 14, 101, 153
  warrior-ethics 144, 145

evolutionary biology 153
  and contest 5, 7, 58
  and difference 6, 55
  and ethics 76
  as a natural science 5
  and natural selection *see* natural selection
  and naturalism 63–8
  nineteenth-century 5
  three levels of evolutionary analysis 66
existence/survival, struggle for 56, 57, 71, 73, 76, 85, 86, 89, 153
ex-statis (ecstatic), defining 21, 29, 82, 172n49

fate, love of 18, 19
Feuerbach, Ludwig Andreas von 57
Fichte, Johann 94
flourishing, individual 7, 8, 109, 127, 128, 143
free spirit 99, 172n9, 173n26
friendship
  and adversaries 8
  agonistic 2, 13, 14, 35, 68, 125, 135, 136
  and compassion 14
  as contest 32, 125–51
  and enmity 146
  friends, enemies and neighbours 136–49
  heroic 12, 47, 58
  higher *see* higher friendship
  and love/great love 3, 14, 17, 29–33, 34
  mutuality 136
  Nietzsche's concept of 1
  reciprocity 136
  and self-interest 131, 137, 143
  and self-overcoming 12, 13, 32, 148, 151

garden imagery, use of 11, 179n50
genetic variation/mutation 5, 6, 55, 64
goals, shared 131–6
God
  see also Christian love; Christianity; Jesus Christ; Trinity doctrine
  being of 22
  concept in formation of Western ethics 23–4
  death of 23, 30, 31
  as love 23

great love
  contrasted with *agape* love 30, 31–3
  and friendship 3, 17, 29–33, 34
guesswork 142, 143

happiness 128–9
Harris, Daniel 134
Hatab, Lawrence J. 18–19, 20, 23, 77, 78, 99, 178n15
health, Nietzsche's concept of 79–80
Heidegger, Martin 53–4
Hellenism 6, 85
heroism 8, 25–7, 46, 50, 56, 63
  contest 31, 52, 53, 58, 68, 72, 125
  courage 69
  and ethics 121
  friendship 12, 47, 58
  heroic ethics 121
  heroic experiment 68
  Homeric 57, 69, 97, 125
  of the individual 45, 51, 78, 96, 108
  of Nietzsche 50
  and pain 68
  and search for knowledge 68, 69, 90
  species-preserving/enhancing 68
  and struggle 97
  of Wagner 46, 47
higher enmity 143–6
higher friendship 3, 12, 13, 124, 130, 134, 137–43, 155
  see also friendship; higher enmity
  and *agape* love 29–30
  compared with other forms of interaction 126–7
  defining Nietzsche's ideal of 2, 3, 8, 13
  as great love 29–33
  intimacy and mutual inspiration within 14
  purpose 32
Hölderlin, Friedrich 94
Homer 19, 74, 144
  see also Homerism/new Homerism
  epic poetry 82, 125, 154
  Iliad 10
  Nietzsche on 6, 74
  The Odyssey 10
Homerism/new Homerism 9, 35, 53, 55, 71–92
  see also ancient Greece; contest
  art 83

difference 47
happiness 128–9
Homeric contest 2, 4, 26, 34–6, 44, 48, 53, 57, 84–6, 88, 89, 93, 97, 102, 108, 154
  ethos of 5, 7–10, 48, 77, 78, 91, 125–6, 129
  Homeric ideals 1, 36, 72–3
  individual difference and personal abundance 72–3
  and monism 44
  new Homerism of Nietzsche 7, 8, 10, 36, 44, 53, 71, 95
  and contest *see above under* Homeric contest
  reconceptualizing Homeric ideals 73–92
  themes 51–2, 55
  passion for self-distinction and pre-eminence 177n7
  recent interpretations 74–81
  themes 51–2
Honig, Bonnie 9
hostile love 179n2

idealism 4, 5, 16
individualism/individuality
  see also difference; personhood; psychological analysis; self
  city-state analogy 94, 167n47
  and community 97
  and contest 93–124
  and customary morality 28
  defining 177n1
  denial of 47
  dissolution of (Schopenhauer) 45, 46, 47, 83
  drives 14, 74, 91, 97, 99, 148, 150
    and choice 103–112
    and individuality 118–22
    and internal contest 102–122
    and self-development 118–22
  flourishing 7, 8, 109, 127, 128
  heroic 45, 51, 78, 96, 108
  individualization 76
  in love relations 23
  narcissistic *see* narcissism
  Nietzsche's interest in promoting 25–6, 45
  noble individual 120

psychological analysis 7, 12, 26, 45
reality of 45–8
Schopenhauer on 40–2, 45, 46, 47
and self-overcoming 14, 74, 97, 99
solipsistic *see* solipsism
superabundance of 100, 124
innocence 100
innovation, moral 109
integration 12, 94, 118, 123
  of drives 96, 101–102, 119, 156
internal contest, and drives 102–122
intimate relationships 3, 13–14, 141
  see also eros (passionate love); romantic love
Irwin, Terence 56–7

Jesus Christ 183n39
  see also Christian love
  death of/crucifixion 22, 23, 24, 30
  incarnation of 22, 23
  as Son of God and Holy Spirit *see* Trinity doctrine
Judeo-Christianity, and roots of love 3, 18, 23
  see also Christian love; Christianity

Kant, Immanuel 1, 4, 54
Kirkland, Paul E. 175n3
knowledge
  intuitive, of the ascetic 43
  of others 143
  rational 43
  search for, as heroic 68, 69, 90
  of the truth 109
  and will 42, 111–12

Lange, Friedrich 1
laxity 89–90
Leiter, Brian 58, 59, 60, 62, 67, 169n42
love
  see also contest; great love; higher friendship; *romantic love; sexual love*
  affirmative 18
  Christian *see* Christian love
  and compassion *see* compassion
  compassionate 133
  and contest 18–19
  eros (passionate love) 16, 20, 21
  as fatality 101

fetishization of 14
God as 23
hostile 179n2
Judeo-Christian roots 3, 18, 23
  as a moral ideal 16
neighbour-love *see* neighbour-love
Nietzsche's perspective on
  agape, rejection of 3, 14, 16, 28–33
  as a foundation for ethics, rejection of 3, 7
  higher friendship as great love 3, 29–33
  love and contest 18–19
  love of fate 18, 19
  self-love 17, 18
  tyranny of love, Nietzsche's rejection of 16, 23–8
philia (brotherly love) 16
self-sacrificial *see agape* (self-sacrificial) love, Nietzsche's rejection of

malice, acts of 38
materialism 5, 56, 57
May, Simon 14, 18, 19, 21
  see also ontological rootedness
  Love: A History 17
meaning-making 61
metaphysical monism 37–8, 40, 52, 125
metaphysical warrant 39
metaphysics 4, 26, 38, 39, 44, 54
  see also metaphysical monism; metaphysical warrant; Schopenhauer, Arthur
  anti-metaphysical pragmatism 5
  Christian 5, 20, 35
  intuitive knowledge of union 43
  monist 35–8, 40, 44, 45, 51, 52, 125
  and naturalism 5, 54, 173n14
  Schopenhauer on 5, 35, 36, 37–44, 45
    monist 35–8, 40, 44, 45, 51, 52, 125
    of will 36, 37–44, 84
  of will 35–6, 37–44, 83, 84
Meyer, Matthew 172n9, 173n26
Miner, Robert 132, 133, 134
monism
  and asceticism 48–51
  metaphysical *see* metaphysical monism
  Nietzsche's rejection of 36, 44–51
  and polytheism 24–5

reality of the individual 45–8
of Schopenhauer 36
monotheism
  and customary morality 28–9
  Nietzsche's rejection of 16, 24–7
  and polytheism 22, 24–5
  reductionistic 125
  seen as moral hegemony by Nietzsche 25, 26
morality
  see also ethics
  of compassion 14, 44
  conduct 40
  conscious reflection 105
  customary 2, 24
    Nietzsche's rejection of 27–8, 117
  monotheism seen as moral hegemony by Nietzsche 25, 26
  moral judgements 112
  of Schopenhauer 41
  taste 106, 119, 120
motivational pluralism 37–8, 41
Mouffe, Chantal 9
Müller, Enrico 180n6
music 61, 71, 73, 82, 167n47
  harmony 82, 83
  motif 94
  musical composition as a metaphor 167n47
  of Wagner 49

narcissism 4, 8, 13, 14, 18, 19, 121, 122, 126
natural selection 55, 58, 64–9, 72, 76, 108, 125
naturalism 4, 35, 36, 53–69, 76
  disagreement about shape of 5
  and evolutionary theory 4, 63–8
  and higher friendship 6
  and materialism 56, 57
  and metaphysics 5, 54, 173n14
  and naturalism in antiquity 57
  Nietzsche's extension of scientific methods to 59
  overflow and abundance 5–6
  and scientific naturalism/scientism 58–63
    hard science, naturalistic equivocations 60
    and natural science 55, 62
  and social relationships 67, 153

stochastic approach 65, 118, 126
and teleology 65
vulnerable forms 56
and will to power 172n7
necessity 100–101, 115–16
neighbour-love 31, 132, 150–1
  and friendship 136–49
  higher and lower forms 148
  higher love of 146–9
  selfless 32
  and self-overcoming 148, 149
  and self-sacrifice 32
Nicea, ecumenical council (325 CE) 22
Nietzsche, Friedrich Wilhelm
  see also drives
  anti-egalitarianism, alleged 19, 128
  on Christian love see Christian love
  on compassion see compassion
  earlier and later writings 173n26
  eschatological orientation of Christian heritage 183n37
  on 'eternal return of the same' 97–8
  on garden imagery, use of 11, 179n50
  Hegel, response to 162n15
  on Homer see Homer; Homerism/new Homerism
  on the individual see individualism/individuality
  on naturalism see naturalism
  rejection of love and compassion as foundations for ethics 3, 7
  scholars' views of Nietzsche's ethics 4
  and Schopenhauer 3, 34–6
    Cartwright on relationship between 44–5
    Nietzsche's rejection of philosophy 35, 43, 44, 51
  science, attitude to 25–6, 169n44, 174n31, 182n28
  self-perception as the anti-Christ 24
  on will to power see will to power
  writings see publications by Nietzsche
Nietzschean soul 94–102
nihilism 54
nobility 119, 120
Nygren, Anders 20

ontological rootedness 17, 19, 21
otherness 8, 21
  Schopenhauer on self and other 41–2

pain 69, 128, 182n28
  and pleasure 47, 68
  shared 135
  as a warning signal 68
  wisdom in 68
Pannenberg, Wolfhart 21
Parkes, Graham 94–6, 98–9, 167n47, 177n7
passions 11, 25–6, 59, 126, 177n7, 178n47, 179n1, 182n28
  see also eros (passionate love); great love; love
  awakening of 108
  harmful 107–108, 120
  and the individual 94, 107, 121, 122
  internal 11, 106
  private 11, 90, 106
perfectionism 4
personal abundance *see* abundance
personhood
  see also individualism/individuality; self
  Christian definition of 20, 21, 22, 23
  deceptive character of experienced reality 40
  'ecstatic' understanding 29
  emergent 121
pessimism
  about human existence 89
  and competition 89
  Darwinian 71
  Dionysian 49, 83
  metaphysical 72–3
  of Nietzsche 118
  of Reginster 42
  romantic 36
  of Schopenhauer 34, 44, 84, 129, 153
    and metaphysics of will 36–7, 41
    and monism, Nietzsche's rejection of 46, 48, 49
philia (brotherly love) 16
pity 30, 41, 46, 132, 144
Plato 1, 17, 54, 96
  Forms, concept of 57
polytheism
  and metaphysics 26
  and monotheism 22, 24–5
power
  see also will to power
  generative, of difference 15

pragmatism, anti-metaphysical 5
psyche, individual 10
psychological analysis 57, 87, 92–4, 117, 145
  see also drives; ego; individualism/individuality; self
  and contest 58, 68
  and Homerism 76
  and the individual 7, 12, 26, 45
  and Schopenhauer 41, 42, 44
  and science 59, 60
  and the will 37, 47
publications by Nietzsche
  The Anti-Christ (*AC*) xiii
  Beyond Good and Evil (*BGE*) 88
  The Birth of Tragedy and Other Writings (*BT*) 24, 82
  Daybreak (*D*) 11, 12, 27, 35, 60, 123
    and friendship 134, 144, 146, 148, 149, 157
    Homerism/new Homerism 81, 87, 88, 91
    and the individual 102, 104–106, 114–16
  The Dionysian World View (*DWV*) 82
  Dionysus against the Crucified 24
  Ecce Homo (*EH*) 24
  The Gay Science (*GS*) 6, 10–11, 16, 123–4, 157, 173n26, 179n53
    Aftereffects of the most ancient religiosity 47
    and Christian love 25, 33–4, 45–6
    and friendship 134, 137, 139, 140, 142, 146
    Homerism/new Homerism 87, 88
    and the individual 102, 106, 107–108, 113, 119, 123
    and naturalism 59–60, 63, 68
  On the Genealogy of Morals (*GM*) 30, 87, 127
  Homer's Contest (*HC*) 6, 8, 26, 82, 84, 87, 89
  Human, All Too Human (*HAH*) 27, 87
  Long live physics 174n31
  The Nietzsche Reader 164n34, 169n45, 176n32
  The Portable Nietzsche xii
  Selected Letters of Friedrich Nietzsche 179n5

Thus Spoke Zarathustra (*TSZ*) 30–3, 50–1, 88, 135, 140–1, 179n53
   'On the Friend' 140
   'On the Hinterworldly' 50
   'On Love of the Neighbour' 147
   'On the Pitying' 30–1
   Of the Tarantulas, Of Science 59
   'On War and Warriors' 144
Twilight of the Idols and The Anti-Christ (*TI*) xiii
Untimely Meditations (*UM*) xiii, 47
The Will to Power 174n38
Writings from the Early Notebooks xiii, 171n28
Writings from the Later Notebooks xiii

radical self-acceptance 18
rational knowledge 43
Realpolitic 4, 8, 74
reductionism 5, 53
Rée, Paul 73
reflection, paradox of 42–3
Reginster, Bernard 42–3, 44, 129, 130
Richardson, John 64–5, 66, 67
romantic love 3, 132
   see also eros (passionate love)
Romanticism 49, 51
Roux, Wilhelm 57

Schacht, Richard 61, 62, 63, 67
Schmitt 144
Schopenhauer, Arthur 1
   see also asceticism/ascetic self-denial
   asceticism of 49
   on compassion 3, 15, 36, 37, 42, 46, 53, 71, 128
   on difference 45
   and human deficit 9
   on incentives for action 37
   on the individual 40–2
      annihilation of 45, 46, 47
   on metaphysics
      monist 35–8, 40, 44, 45, 51, 52, 125
      of will 36, 37–44, 84
   morality of 41
   mysticism 43
   and Nietzsche 3, 34–6

   Cartwright on relationship between 44–5
   rejection of Schopenhauer's philosophy 35, 43, 44, 51
   pessimism of 34, 44, 84, 129, 153
   and metaphysics of will 36–7, 41
   and monism, Nietzsche's rejection of 46, 48, 49
   and psychological analysis 41, 42, 44
   on self and other 41–2
   theory of the self 42–3
   on will 47–8
   World as Will and Representation (*WWR*) 38, 40
science
   see also evolutionary biology; naturalism
   and error 59
   hard science, naturalistic equivocations 60
   incorporation of physical and natural 5
   Nietzsche's attitude to 25–6, 169n44, 174n31, 182n28
   and psychological analysis 59, 60
scientism, naturalism as 58–63
self
   see also difference; ego; individualism/individuality; self-abnegation/self-sacrifice; self-awareness; self-cultivation; self-emptying, *agape* love seen as an act of; self-interest; selfishness; self-love; self-mastery; self-overcoming; self-reflection; self-renunciation; self-selection
   composite 88, 94, 101–102
   deconstructed 100
   'ecstatic' idea of 21, 29, 33, 79, 99
   multiplicity of 94
   and other 41–2
   Schopenhauer's theory of 42–3
   and society 98
   and the world 42–3
self-abnegation/self-sacrifice 27, 29, 32, 71, 149
   see also agape (self-sacrificial) love, Nietzsche's rejection of
   Christian love perceived as 16, 17, 21, 23, 24, 31

and neighbour-love 32
self-sacrifice ideal, in Christianity 31
self-awareness 104–105
self-cultivation 11, 12, 94, 102, 113, 116, 121
self-emptying, *agape* love seen as an act of 21–2
self-interest
   and the contest 22
   eros seen as act of 21
   and friendship/higher friendship 131, 137, 143
selfishness 31, 46, 74
   innocent 101
self-love 17, 18
self-mastery 98
self-overcoming 28, 74, 93, 126
   and drives 10, 150, 154
   and friendship 12, 13, 32, 148, 151
   hierarchical 128
   and the individual 14, 74, 97, 99, 148, 150
   'lower' forms 127
   and neighbours 148, 149
   process of 99, 126, 143, 146
   and social relationships 126
self-reflection 43
self-renunciation 44
self-sacrifice *see* self-abnegation/self-sacrifice
self-selection 67
sexual love 133
shared goals and joy 131–6
Shepherd, Melanie 135
Siemens, Herman 7, 10, 74, 77–80, 81, 99, 134, 178n15, 179n2
singular value standard concept 119, 120
Skepticism 1
Small, Robin 134
social Darwinism 5, 8
social relationships
   and adversity 7, 129, 155
   and contest 5, 7, 74, 80, 100, 172n7
   and ethics x, 1, 3, 14, 101, 153
   hierarchical 128
   higher forms 150
   higher friendship *see* higher friendship
   and the individual 95–6, 100, 155
   naturalistic 67, 153
   Nietzsche's perspective on 5–7, 13, 58, 79, 80–1, 93, 99, 126

   agonistic interpretation 3, 14, 19–20, 33, 150, 154
   alternative vision 36
   and science/Darwinism 5–6
   and self-overcoming 13
Socrates 74
Soderstrom, Lukas 57, 173n18
solipsism 4, 8, 13, 18, 74, 85, 121, 122, 126
Spencer, Herbert 64, 73
stochastic approach 65, 118, 126
Stoicism 1, 11, 154
struggle 83, 104, 111
   cellular 57
   and competition 68, 73, 89
   and contest 88, 89, 173n17, 179n49
   for existence/survival 56, 57, 71, 73, 76, 85, 86, 89, 153
   heroic 97
   life-negating 87
   personal 86
   physical 88
   struggle-to-the-death 85, 89
subjectivity, autonomous 117
suffering 18, 30, 36, 48, 50, 83, 84, 129, 132, 137–8
   see also pain; struggle
   and abundance 51
   alleviating 138, 139, 153
   Dionysian 49
   indifference to 14
   metaphysical interpretation 72
   and pain 128
   as part of existence 37, 41, 44, 49
   psychological 42
   shared 135
   voluntary 28
superabundance 48
   see also abundance
   of the individual 100, 124
   of natural world 6
   in new Homerism 51–2
   personal 15, 23, 33, 48, 49, 51–2, 73

taste
   changed 108
   common 108
   and drives 67, 112, 119, 120
   general 109

individual 8, 80, 119
  moral 106, 119, 120
  new 109, 112
  refined 128–9
  shared 108
  single 122
teleology 65, 114, 132
Thiele, Leslie Paul 94, 97, 98, 99, 134, 167n47
  Politics of the Soul 96
thing-in-itself 45
Torrance, T. F. 21–2
Trinity doctrine 20, 22, 29, 168n50
truth 33, 59, 82
  access to 82
  and drives 111
  and error 112
  and goals 132–4
  knowledge of 109
  objective/scientific 56, 59
  provisional 60
  quest for 109
  value of 110
  will-to-truth 110

value standards 121
  higher 146
  singular 119, 120
Verkerk, Willow 132, 133
violence 14
voluntary suffering 28

Wagner, Richard 46, 47, 74, 100
wakefulness 105, 141–2
warrior-ethics 144, 145
will
  and function of art 83
  and knowledge 42, 111–12
  metaphysics of 35–6, 37–44, 83, 84
  psychological analysis 37, 47
  and purpose 114, 115
  Schopenhauer on 47–8
  to suffer 41
  to truth and to life 110
will to life 56, 89, 110, 129
will to power 54, 56, 64–6, 89, 95, 129, 172n7

www.ingramcontent.com/pod-product-compliance
Lightning Source LLC
Chambersburg PA
CBHW062226300426
44115CB00012BA/2236